Quotable

"... For each We have appointed a divine law and a traced out way. Had Allah willed He could have made you one community. But that He may try you by that which He hath given you (He hath made you as ye are). So vie one with another in good works. Unto Allah ye will all return, and He will then inform you of that wherein ye differ."

- *Quran 5:48*

"It is the duty of every cultured man or woman to read sympathetically the scriptures of the world. If we are to respect other's religions, as we would have them respect our own, a friendly study of the world's religions is a sacred duty."

- *Mahatma Gandhi. Indian Saint & Freedom Fighter (d. 1948).*

"The problem to be faced is: how to combine loyalty to one's own tradition with reverence for different traditions."

- *Abraham Joshua Heschel. Jewish Rabbi & Activist (d. 1972).*

Essays On Cultural Pluralism

The sacred religious symbols of the human family are pregnant with an in-exhaustable range of mystical interpretations. According to Scholem, the mystical symbol is a window into a "hidden and inexpressible reality".

Also by Jamal Khwaja

* Living The Quran In Our Times

* Authenticity and Islamic Liberalism

* Five Approaches to Philosophy

* Quest For Islam

* The Call Of Modernity And Islam

* The Vision Of An Unknown Indian Muslim

* Numerous articles and scholarly essays

To learn more about the author, visit

www.JamalKhwaja.com
Download free Digital Books, Lectures, Essays and more ...

Essays On Cultural Pluralism

A Philosophical Approach To Interfaith Spirituality In The Age Of Science

Jamal Khwaja
Formerly Professor of Philosophy
Aligarh Muslim University

ALHAMD PUBLISHERS, LLC

Los Angeles

Copyright © by Jamal Khwaja 2015

All rights reserved. Copyright under Berne Copyright Convention, Universal Copyright Convention, and Pan American Copyright Convention. No part of this book may be reproduced, stored in a retrieval system, or transmitted in any form or by any means, electronic or mechanical or otherwise, including photocopying and recording, without prior written permission of the publisher, except for the inclusion of brief quotations in a review.

For permission to reproduce selections from this book contact the Publisher.

Published and distributed worldwide by ALHAMD Publishers, LLC.
3131 Roberts Ave, Culver City, CA 90232, USA.
www.AlhamdPublishers.com

Printed and bound in the United States of America
Book and Jacket Design by Sandeep Sandhu and Raisa Shafiyyullah.
Author Photo by Kenny Zepeda

More information about the Author and his works can be found at www.JamalKhwaja.com
Look for FREE Downloads of Essays & Articles written by the Author.

ISBN: 978-1-935293-57-6 (Hard cover)
ISBN: 978-1-935293-52-1 (Soft cover)
ISBN: 978-1-935293-55-2 (Epub)
Publisher's SAN #: 857-0132

BISAC Subject Headings: Religion/Islam/Koran & Sacred Writings (REL041000),
and Religion/Philosophy (REL051000)

In the Name of God, Most Beneficent, Most Merciful.

Dedicated to the memory of:
Pandit Sundarlal, Raja Mahendra Pratap, Dr. Tara Chand, and all those who strive for interfaith harmony without fear or favor

Quotable

"Be not angry that you cannot make others as you wish them to be, since you cannot make yourself as you wish to be."
- *Thomas A. Kempis. Catholic Monk (d. 1471).*

"All ... religions show the same disparity between belief and practice, and each is safe till it tries to exclude the rest. Test each sect by its best or its worst, as you will, by its high-water mark of virtue or its low-water mark of vice. But falsehood begins when you measure the ebb of any other religion against the flood tide of your own. There is a noble and base side to every history."
- *Thomas Wentworth Higginson. American Abolitionist (d. 1911)*

"The test of courage comes when we are in the minority. The test of tolerance comes when we are in the majority."
- *Ralph W. Stockman*

TABLE OF CONTENTS

Author's Preface 11

Introduction 13

PART 1

Essay 1:
An Essay on the Bhagavad Gita 19

Notes To 'An Essay on The Bhagavad Gita':
(1) Epithets Used in the Gita for Lord Krishna and Arjun 61

(2) Resources for Understanding the Bhagavad Gita 63

PART 2: OTHER ESSAYS

Essay 2:
Religion & Spirituality in the Age of Science: Some Basic Aspects 67
Notes to Essay 2 90

Essay 3:
Unity in Variety in the Sphere of Religious Faith 95

Essay 4:
Religious Faith and Values 111

Essay 5:
History: Its Theory, Philosophy and Wisdom 119

(Continued)

Contents

Essay 6:
Towards a Humanist Interpretation of History and Politics 145

Essay 7:
Mughal-Sikh Relations in Medieval India 159

Essay 8:
The Concept and Role of Tolerance in Indian Culture 189
Notes to Essay 8 206

Essay 9:
Critique of Astrology 223

Essay 10:
Reincarnation and the Modern Mind 233

Afterword: 247

Appendix 1:
About the Author 251

Index 255

Author's Preface

This volume comprises ten essays out of which four were published in different places at different times, and one was presented at the Khuda Bakhsh Library, Patna. The rest are being published for the first time. The point for bringing them together in this volume is that each essay is an attempt to understand (with the utmost critical empathy) some seminal ideas and values of some Indian and Western sages. *An Essay on the Gita* was originally published but not disseminated by the Abul Kalam Azad Foundation; *History: Theory, Philosophy and Wisdom* first appeared in the journal, *Man and Development*, Chandigarh, June 1983, and *The Concept and Role of Tolerance in Indian Culture* in the proceedings of a seminar on *Tolerance in Indian Culture*, Indian Council for Philosophical Research, New Delhi, 1992. *Towards a Humanist Interpretation of History and Politics* was published in *The Economic and Political Weekly*. *Mughal-Sikh Relations in Medieval India* was presented at the Khuda Bakhsh Library, Patna. I acknowledge my gratitude to all the above agencies for publishing my work or providing me with a platform. I have made slight changes/improvements in some of the above essays as printed here.

Each essay covers a separate theme, yet reflects the same sincere effort to appreciate and critically evaluate the knowledge, wisdom and insights of an enduring scripture, or some intellectual or cultural tradition of the human family transcending all parochial barriers. It is my hope that readers will find the essays interesting and illuminating.

I would like to point that while the essays included in the collection, *The Call of Modernity and Islam*, deal with Islamic themes, the essays in this volume deal with Hinduism and Sikhism, the historical method and the interaction between religion, spirituality and science. I would have loved to add one essay on Christianity and one on Marxism, viewed as a secular religion in the functional sense, if I had more time at my disposal.

Jamal Khwaja
Aligarh, 2015

Note on suggested reading pattern for the work:

The explanatory notes at the end of some Essays are meant to develop the theme and the line of the argument in the text. Each note contains some important information or insight. Reading each note along with the text should considerably add to the pleasure and the profit of reading the Essay.

Using two bookmarks, one in each section, would make the process effortless. This arrangement aims to serve the requirements of readers who are hard pressed for time as well as readers who can devote more time for pondering highly complex issues.

INTRODUCTION

A sociological and critical historical survey of the human condition from primitive times to the present age shows that the human family has developed from very primitive and crude proto-human levels of consciousness or awareness to the present stage of development in every dimension of human life. The term 'modernity', as used in the context of this work, means the underlying basic beliefs, values, attitudes and world outlook that began to take shape and crystallize in Western Europe from the 15th century onwards and attained fairly stable and identifiable contours by the closing years of the 19th century. This set of beliefs, values and attitudes is, of course, still undergoing internal changes due to ever growing human knowledge of nature, clearer insights into the human condition and cumulative human experience based on trial and error. As of today modernity, means possessing an open critical mind that demands appropriate evidence or justification before accepting any truth-claim as true or false, unconditional respect for the human person, irrespective of race, region, religion, caste or gender, equality of status, human rights, and opportunity, free enquiry based on deductive reasoning and scientific investigation and verification, tolerance of disagreement, and the sharing and transfer of political power through peaceful means as pre-conditions of human welfare and universal peace.

Modernity in the sphere of religious faith also implies accepting and appreciating inter-faith spirituality. The pre-modern view was that only one faith led to salvation, or, in other words, only those who spoke one particular language of the spirit or practiced one particular set of sacred rituals could reach the highest level of felicity or salvation.

This approach or view may be called the belief in exclusive salvation. But cultural pluralism makes the substance of religious faith as well as the choice of symbols and rituals optional rather than mandatory for attaining success and salvation.

Cultural pluralism lays primary stress upon authenticity of faith and righteous conduct, rather than any particular creed or conceptual formulation as a factor of salvation. The inner transition of the individual from mandatory religious monism to permissive religious pluralism and even to neutral secular humanism is the crucial mark of modernity. Modernity, by itself, does not give any mandate to accept, or reject but only to respect all authentic beliefs, provided they do not violate a set of human rights.

The Islamic paradigm, which I have projected in my work, *Living the Quran in Our Times*, on the basis of semantic analysis of Quranic texts, does not clash with the concept of religious pluralism. Evidently, Islamic orthodoxy has followed a different interpretation of Quranic texts and projected a different paradigm of Islam. However, several great Muslim thinkers, scientists, sages, poets and mystics in the creative classical period of Islamic history (explicitly or implicitly) differed from the orthodox position. Unfortunately the dominant orthodox sections in medieval times completely sidelined these creative spirits, many of whom were even persecuted by those in power. Thanks to modern Western scholarship, at its best, those dubbed as heretics in medieval times are being admired and venerated today as great intellectuals and spiritual leaders cutting across different religions.

Religious sensibility today (in all religious groups) distinguishes the timeless primary verities and intrinsic values of their cherished religion or faith: faith in one supreme Creator, the supremacy of Divine justice or cosmic law of karma, ultimate supremacy of good over evil, the establishment of justice, and the values of truthfulness, compassion, self-knowledge, respect for life, rational altruism and so on: from the secondary temporal instrumental rules for realizing the above primary verities and values. Cultural pluralism affirms that this distinction and its consistent application to human society are far more important for both success and salvation than unreflective and unconditional adherence to instrumental rules found in different religious traditions. I have thoroughly analyzed and discussed these complex issues in my introductory keynote chapter in the *Quest for Islam*.

For the convenience of readers of my collected essays in two volumes *The Call of Modernity and Islam,* and *Essays on Cultural Pluralism*, this chapter has been reproduced, in full, in *The Call of Modernity*.

PART 1
AN ESSAY ON
THE BHAGAVAD GITA

The mystical, sacred Sanskrit monosyllable "Aum" is the signifier of the ultimate truth that "All is One". It is so laden with spiritual energy that whosoever gets to know this one syllable obtains all that he desires.

All auspicious actions begin with "Aum". The "Aum" symbol is therefore, placed at the beginning of most Hindu Texts and the "Aum" sound is chanted at the beginning of all religious rituals.

Quotable

Thus hath been opened thee
This Truth of Truths, the Mystery more hid
Than any secret mystery—Meditate!
And—as thou wilt—then act!

Nay! But once more
Take My last word, My utmost meaning have!
Precious thou art to Me; right well-beloved!
Listen! I tell thee for thy comfort this.

Give Me thy heart! Adore Me! Serve Me! Cling In faith and love and reverence to Me!
So shalt thou come to Me!
I promise true,
For thou art sweet to Me!

And let go those—Rites and writ duties! Fly to Me alone!
Make Me thy single refuge! I will free
Thy soul from all its sins! Be of good cheer!

- Bhagavad Gita
(Translated by Sir Edwin Arnold)

Essay 1

An Essay On The Bhagavad Gita

Introduction

When I look at world history it seems that the human family had to wade through rivers of blood and tears to find the road leading to universal peace and fellowship. Much greater international cooperation in global management and still greater inter-religious understanding are the twin rails on which humanity must further travel to reach the final destination.

Notwithstanding the continuing sway of racial and tribalistic prejudices in the conduct of politics and the misuse of religion for political gains perceptive and honest minds among all religious communities now see different religions as diverse "languages of the spirit", each valid and spiritually nourishing in its own way. This approach of religious pluralism is likely to spread among the masses and eventually displace the old tradition of religious exclusivism: the belief that there is only one road to salvation.

The plural approach to religion is common to Western liberal Humanism, Vedanta, and contemporary liberal Christianity. Religious pluralism also characterizes the pure *Quranic* Islam without the later gloss of Islamic theology and jurisprudence. *Sufi* poetry in Persian and Urdu greatly extols tolerance and universal love. However, it is the Bhagavad Gita, which teaches, in the most unambiguous and consistent manner, the doctrine of religious pluralism. This feature of the Gita fascinates me most and has moved me to write the present essay.

All irrespective of their professed religion should gather the pearls of wisdom embedded in the Gita.

My study of Indian philosophy is based entirely on the English writings of Indian and Western scholars. For the purpose of this essay on the Gita I have confined myself to Radhakrishnan's celebrated translation and commentary on the Gita. All quotations from the Gita are taken from the above work. Though I have greatly profited from several other works by eminent writers on the subject, my approach to the Gita is my own. I alone am responsible for any shortcomings or errors in my understanding and critical appreciation of the Bhagavad Gita. I crave the kind indulgence of those who are much better qualified than myself for this task.

The purpose of this essay is not to enter into the deeps and eddies of Gita scholarship but simply to explain the basic message and wisdom of the Gita in a modern critical idiom. Ours are times when religion is systematically being used; unconsciously by some, and deliberately by others, in the service of politics, rather than spirituality.

If this modest essay could motivate even a handful of fellow Muslims and others to turn to the Gita and also motivate all sincere truth-seekers to acquaint themselves with pure *Quranic* Islam and *Sufi* wisdom expressed in Persian and Urdu poetry I shall feel rewarded.

1. THE GITA AS SCRIPTURE

The Bhagavad Gita, a long thematic poem, and part of the great Indian epic, Mahabharata, since time immemorial, is the core scripture of Hinduism in the modern age. Millions hold the Gita sacred and normative quite independently of how they may view the great epic or the exact connection between the Gita and the Mahabharata.

According to tradition the Mahabharata was compiled by the legendary sage, Vyasa, who is also regarded as the author of the Gita.

The dates of Vyasa are variously estimated. Radhakrishnan assigns the original composition of the Gita to the 5th century BC. Alterations or additions, if any, took place later.

The poem is in the form of a dialogue between the ruler of the Pandava clan, Arjuna, and Sri Krishna, whom the Gita takes as the incarnation of the Hindu god, Vishnu. The occasion of the dialogue is the impending battle between the Pandavas and their kinsmen, the Kauravas. Arjuna is deeply reluctant to shed the blood of his near and dear ones, but Sri Krishna, the Divine Guru of the Prince, exhorts him to fight on the principle that the destruction of life in the defense of right is sanctioned by '*dharma*'. The Gita is a poetic exposition of Sri Krishna's religious philosophy and ethical teachings.

The Gita has 670 stanzas divided into eighteen chapters or sections of unequal length. The longest section comprises seventy-eight stanzas, while the shortest twenty. The Sanskrit meter is short and the language, in the opinion of Sanskrit scholars, is marked by superb elegance. Although each chapter has a primary theme the treatment of ideas and themes is not systematic. Different aspects of the same topic or subject are mentioned in widely scattered verses. This however is no defect in a poetic composition.

Being a philosophical poem rather than a philosophical treatise, the Gita does not seek to inquire or argue on behalf of any truth claim, philosophical or religious. The Gita accepts the Vedantic standpoint, some elements of the *Sankhya* doctrine and of the *Vaishnavite* tradition centered on the divinity of Sri Krishna, and expounds them all in a moving poetic form.

The Vedantic component of the Gita includes the ideas of the primacy and omnipresence of the one eternal Self-existent Spirit (*Brahman*) and its supremacy over mind and matter, the essential identity of man's higher self (*Atman*) and *Brahman*, the ceaseless cycle of birth and death, creation and destruction of the phenomenal world as the cosmic play (*leela*) of *Brahman*, the unfailing and unalterable operation of the law of just recompense (*karma*) in the cosmic process, the migration and rebirth of individual souls in accordance with the above law, the inherent evil and suffering of finite existence, the possibility and desirability of permanent release and salvation from the cycle of finite existence, the pre-eminent role of higher knowledge (Brahmavidya) and spiritual discipline (*yoga*) in achieving this end.

The strand of Sankya school of thought comprises the doctrines of '*Purush*' (Spirit) and '*Prakriti*' (Nature), and the three modes (*gunas*) of *Prakriti*: '*sattva*', '*rajas*' and '*tamas*'. The Gita, however, transcends the ontological Dualism and Pluralism of the *Sankhya*.

The component of popular *Vaishnavism* in the Gita comprises belief in a supreme personal God (*Ishwar or Bhagwan*) who, under certain conditions or circumstances, takes on human form and intervenes in history to make good prevail over evil, the divinity of Sri Krishna, the regular ritualistic worship of representative images and symbols of the Divine, personal devotion and supplication to God, as the loving and compassionate Cosmic Father, the belief that the virtuous enter heaven (*swarga*) temporarily as a reward for virtuous conduct and the desirability of complete and permanent salvation through devotion (*bhakti*) to God.

The 'anthrotheistic' belief that Sri Krishna was a divine incarnation, obviously, goes beyond the far more general doctrines of Monotheism, *Brahmanical Monoism* and *karma*. Many who might be in full or part agreement with the Monotheism or Monism in the Gita may feel rather disinclined to accept this 'anthrotheistic' stand in the Gita. In fact, there is no dearth of thoughtful Hindus themselves who cherish the ethical Theism in the Gita, but relegate its *Vaishnavite* components to the domain of myth or legend.

Different sections of the poem expound the above ideas and beliefs in a smooth and spontaneous transition, which however is not a logical progression. Several serious thinkers, Hindu as well as others, who admire and feel deeply moved by the Gita admit this feature of the work. Some attribute this to the poet's well-meaning desire to make the Gita appeal to persons with varied attitudes and personality needs. However it is quite plausible to hold that the Gita does not seek to please or appease different sects or groups, but it rather seeks to accommodate the different metaphysical perspectives in a super conceptual space or spiritual perspective.

In other words, we may say that the approach of the Gita is neither conceptually constrictive, nor eclectic, but rather permissive and irenic. The Gita stresses that what leads to spiritual growth and salvation is not any particular belief, symbol or ritual, but the sincerity of the devotee and right conduct for the sake of righteousness. This remarkable tolerance and conceptual permissiveness constitutes the unique charm and perennial relevance of the Gita.

2. THE METAPHYSICAL VISION OF THE GITA

In what follows my purpose is not any synoptic exposition of the entire thought of the Gita. Several eminent scholars and writers have already done this. But all great scriptures, like great poetry, are perennial rivers of the spirit serenely flowing down the ages. And every age, rather every intelligent and authentic soul, is required to bring his own conceptual vessel or cup to drink of the nectar. I shall, therefore, attempt to highlight what I hold as the nuclear core of the Gita's metaphysical vision together with my critical appreciation thereof. This core consists of three principal themes;

(a) The nature of ultimate Reality,

(b) The essential truth about the human situation, and

(c) *Vaishnavite Anthro-theism*, i.e. faith in the divinity of Sri Krishna.

I shall proceed in the same order.

(A) The Nature of the Universe

Following the Vedanta school the Gita teaches that the ultimate Reality behind the ever-changing plurality of the impermanent physical world is the one eternal Self-existent, changeless Cosmic Spirit (*Brahman*). *Brahman* is the infinite Source and Ground of all finite existents and concepts, of reason and understanding, of good and evil, of beauty and ugliness, of life and death, of creation and destruction, indeed of everything that exists in any form or that can be imagined as existing. However, *Brahman* itself can neither be perceived as an existent among other existents, nor conceived as a concept among other concepts. Any determinate concept applied to *Brahman* will break down or collapse in the very act of being applied to *Brahman*. But the simultaneous affirmation and negation of some concepts will partly illuminate the nature of *Brahman*. This is what we find in the Gita. Here are some instances:

(10:39)
"And further, whatsoever is the seed of all existences that am I, O Arjuna; nor is there anything, moving or unmoving that can exist without Me."

(10:41)
"Whatsoever being there is, endowed with glory and grace and vigor, know that to have sprung from a fragment of My splendor."

(9:4-6)
"By Me all this universe is pervaded through My unmanifested form. All beings abide in Me but I do not abide in them.
And (yet) the beings do not dwell in Me; Behold My divine mystery. My spirit, which is the source of all beings, sustains the beings but does not abide in them.
As the mighty air moving everywhere ever abides in the etheric space (akash), know thou that in the same manner all existences abide in Me."

(15:12-15)
"That splendor of the sun that illuminates this whole world, that which is in the moon, that which is in the fire, that splendor, know as Mine.
And entering the earth, I support all beings by My vital energy; and becoming the sapful soma (moon). I nourish all herbs (or plants).
Becoming the fire of life in the bodies of living creatures and mingling with the upward and downward breaths, I digest the four kinds of food.
And I am lodged in the hearts of all; from Me are memory and knowledge as well as their loss. I am indeed He who is to be known by all the Vedas. I indeed (am) the author of the Vedanta and I too the knower of the Vedas."

(7:12)
"And whatever states of being there may be, be they harmonious (sattvika), passionate (rajasa), slothful (tamasa) - know that they are all from Me alone. I am not in them, they are in Me."

(13:14-16)
"He appears to have the qualities of all the senses and yet is without (any of) the senses, unattached and yet supporting all, free from the gunas (dispositions of Prakriti) and yet enjoying them.
He is without and within all beings. He is unmoving as also moving. He is too subtle to be known. He is far away and yet is He near.
He is undivided (indivisible) and yet He seems to be divided among beings. He is to be known as supporting creatures, destroying them and creating them afresh."

(10:20)
"I, O Gudakesha (Arjuna), am the self seated in the hearts of all creatures. I am the beginning, the middle and the very end of beings."

(7:26)
"I know the beings that are past, that are present, O Arjuna, and that are to come, but Me no one knows."

(2:29)
"One looks upon Him as a marvel, another likewise speaks of Him as a marvel; another hears of Him as a marvel; and even after hearing, no one whatsoever has known Him."

(B) THE HUMAN SITUATION

The most basic feature of the cosmic processes is the recurring cycle of birth and death and ceaseless flux, the transition from 'being' into 'non-being', or ceaseless 'becoming'. Man is an integral part of this cycle of birth and death (*sansar*). The birth of man is, however, the temporary conjunction of *Atman* and a living body (*jiva*), while his death an equally temporary disjunction. The *Atman*, which is, essentially, a portion of *Brahman* gets repeatedly conjoined and disjoined with a living body. Says the Gita:

(8:17-20)
"Those who know that the day of Brahma is of the duration of a thousand ages and that the night (of Brahma) is a thousand ages long, they are the knowers of day and night.
At the coming of day all manifested things come forth from the unmanifested and at the coming of night they merge in that same, called the unmanifested.
This very same multitude of existences arising again and again merges helplessly at the coming of night, O Partha (Arjuna), and streams forth into being at the coming of day.
But beyond this unmanifested, there is yet another Unmanifested Eternal Being who does not perish even when all existences perish."

Now, according to the teachings of the *Upanishads* this process at the human level is something more than a mere biological phenomenon; it is regulated by the metaphysical or ethical law of just recompense (*karma*). This law states that every human action, good or bad, from the trivial to the serious, confers a corresponding merit or demerit upon the doer. The doer cannot escape just reward or punishment for his actions. If the '*karmic* audit' remains incomplete in one lifetime the (*jiva Atma*) is born afresh to clear the *karmic* account of reward and punishment. Pain and suffering burn out the evil consequences of previous wrongs, while inner joy and happiness are the reward of previous good deeds. Only when the *karmic* account becomes fully even does the *jiva Atma* qualify for deliverance from the cycle of birth and death. The actual release from the cycle is called '*mukti*'. The person who attains '*mukti*' never again gets entangled in the web of '*sansar*'. Suicide out of despair is quite different since it does not lead to '*mukti*' and the person who commits suicide is reborn in the vale of tears from which he had vainly attempted to escape. Here are some relevant verses on this theme:

(6:40-41)
"O Partha (Arjuna), neither in this life nor hereafter is there destruction for him; for never does any one who does good, dear friend, tread the path of woe.
Having attained to the world of the righteous and dwelt there for many years, the man who has fallen away from yoga is again born in the house of such as are pure and prosperous."

(6:43)
"There he regains the (mental) impressions (union with the divine) which he had developed in his previous life and with this (as the starting point) he strives again for perfection, O Joy of the Kurus (Arjuna)."

(9:21-22)
"Having enjoyed the spacious world of heaven, they enter (return to) the world of mortals, when their merit is exhausted; thus conforming to the doctrine enjoined in the three Vedas and desirous of enjoyments, they obtain the changeable (what is subject to birth and death).
But those who worship Me, meditating on Me alone, to them who ever persevere, I bring attainment of what they have not and security in what they have."

(8:14-16)
"He who constantly meditates on Me, thinking of none else, by him who is a yogin ever disciplined (or united with the Supreme), I am easily reached.
Having come to Me, these great souls do not get back to rebirth, the place of sorrow, impermanent, for they have reached the highest perfection. From the realm of Brahma downwards, all worlds are subject to return of rebirth, but on reaching Me, O Son of Kunti (Arjuna), there is no return to birth again."

Though the *Upanishads* allows the possibility that human '*jivas*' may be reborn as non-human ones, in accordance with the law of *karma* the Gita does not specifically mention 'retributive' regress as a means of educative punishment and subsequent growth of a '*jiva*' in the cycle of life and death (*sansar*).

The question whether 'cosmic auditing' is the act of God, the Creator, Law Giver and Ruler of the universe, or the inherent mode of working of the impersonal *Brahman* is not central to Hindu religious thought, including the Gita. What is central is faith in the law of *karma* as such. The 'faith axiom' of Hinduism, indeed of all religions of Indian origin, is '*karma*', not God, in the monotheistic sense. The monotheistic belief is optional, though it always has commanded a wide popular appeal. The Gita also favors this belief while the *Upanishads* veer to the concept of *Brahman*.

Following the Vedanta the Gita also teaches that the root cause of all human suffering and evil is ignorance (avidya) and uncontrolled desire (*ichha*). The mix of these two turns man into a rudderless boat tossed by the waves of a turbulent sea. The chief desires or passions are fear, anger, greed, and sexual lust. No spiritual development and inner illumination is possible without controlling the above passions.

Spiritual discipline has several dimensions,
    (a) Regulated food, sleep and sexual activity,

(b) Regular pursuit of spiritual knowledge (Brahmavidya),

(c) Regular meditation, and

(d) The detached performance of one's duties (*swadharma*) prescribed by the scripture.

Those who find the path of knowledge beyond their capacities could turn to the path of devotion (*bhakti*) to a personal God.

(C) ANTHROTHEISM IN THE GITA

Anthrotheism is the belief that God or Deity at times takes on the form of a human being in order to help men in their darkest hour in the perpetual struggle between good and evil. This view obviously goes beyond the Vedantic concepts of Divine immanence in all finite beings, human as well as non-human. The Gita holds Sri Krishna to be a Divine incarnation (*avatara*). I shall first give some relevant verses on the theme of Divine incarnation, and then pass on to those, which give an enchanting description of Arjuna's mystical experience of the Divinity of Sri Krishna.

> (4: 6-9)
> *"Though (I am) unborn, and My self (is) imperishable, though (I am) the Lord of all creatures, yet establishing Myself in My own nature, I come into (empiric) being through My power (maya). Whenever there is a decline of righteousness and rise of unrighteousness, O Bharata (Arjuna), then I send forth (create incarnate) Myself.*
> *For the protection of the good, for the destruction of the wicked and for the establishment of righteousness, I come into being from age to age.*
> *He who knows thus in its true nature My divine birth and works, is not born again, when he leaves this body but comes to Me, O Arjuna."*

Here is a selection of verses on Arjuna's mystical experience:

(11:7,8)
"Here today, behold the whole universe, moving and unmoving and whatever else thou desirest to see, O Gudakesha (Arjuna), all unified in My body.
But thou canst not behold Me with this (human) eye of yours; I will bestow on thee the supernatural eye. Behold My divine power."

(11:12-21)
"If the light of a thousand suns were to blaze forth all at once in the sky, that might resemble the splendor of the exalted Being.

There the Pandava (Arjuna) beheld the whole universe, with its manifold divisions, gathered together in one, in the body of the God of gods. Then he, the winner of Wealth, (Arjuna) struck with amazement, his hair standing on end, bowed down his head to the Lord, with hands folded (in salutation) said:

"In Thy body, O God, I see all the gods and the varied hosts of being as well, Brahma, the lord seated on the lotus throne and all the sages and heavenly nagas.
I behold Thee, infinite in form on all sides, with numberless arms, bellies, faces and eyes, but I see not Thy end, or Thy middle or Thy beginning, O Lord of the universe, O Form Universal.
I behold Thee with Thy crown, mace and discus, glowing everywhere as a mass of light, hard to discern (dazzling) on all sides with the radiance of the flaming fire and sun, incomparable.
Thou art the imperishable, the Supreme to be realized. Thou art the ultimate resting-place of the universe; Thou art the undying guardian of the eternal law. Thou art the Primal Person, I think.
I behold Thee as one without beginning, middle or end, of infinite power, of numberless arms, with the moon and the sun as Thine eyes, with Thy face a flaming fire, whose radiance burns up the universe.
This space between heaven and earth is pervaded by Thee alone, also all the quarters (directions of the sky). O exalted One, when this wondrous terrible form of Thine is seen, the three worlds tremble.
Yonder hosts of gods enter thee and some, in fear, extol thee, with folded

hands. And bands of great seers and perfected ones cry, "hail" and adore Thee with hymns of abounding praise."

(11:40)
"Hail to The in front, (hail) to Thee behind and hail to Thee on every side, O All; boundless in power and immeasurable in might, thou dost penetrate all and therefore Thou art all."

(11:44)
"Therefore, bowing down and prostrating my body before Thee, Adorable Lord, I seek Thy grace. Thou, O God, shouldst bear with me as a father to his son, as a friend to his friend, as a lover to his beloved."

The *yogic* peak experience not only gives inner certitude and peace but also liberates the *yogi* from bondage to the cycle of birth and death, and makes him long for the final merger with *Brahman*. This is the state of spiritual deliverance (*mukti*). The *yogi* who lives and works in this condition is called '*jivanmukta*'. The '*Atman*' residing in the '*jivanmukta*' gets merged with *Brahman* at a time chosen by Him. This is the ultimate destination and also the destiny of all finite existence, but the '*jivanmukta*' embraces his destiny with clarity, courage and grace.

Thus, according to the Gita the cosmic mystery and the inmost secret of the origin, nature and destiny of man in the universe was made known to Arjuna, not through reasoning but through the mystical experience vouchsafed to him through Sri Krishna's Divine grace as an incarnation of Vishnu. The Gita tells how Arjuna clearly saw with his mind's eye that Sri Krishna was not only his boyhood friend but also the "Infinite Primal Person" (*Ishwar/Bhagwan*). This specific secret truth was revealed or manifested to Arjuna much later in the course of his liberating dialogue though he had already come to accept the more general Vedantic view that the *Atman* and *Brahman* are identical in essence and that, in the final analysis, *Brahman* alone is the one and ultimate Reality (*Sat*).

After Arjuna's liberating experience all doubts, uncertainties and inner perplexities were removed and he tasted supreme bliss and peace. The Gita, thus, represents the convergence of three streams of thought, namely, the idealistic Monism of the *Upanishads*, pure ethical Theism in general, and the Anthro-theistic *Vaishnavite* faith whose epicenter was Mathura in North India. However, the Gita does not explain or explicate the various concepts involved, namely, God Vishnu, Vishnu's incarnation (*avatara*), and the relationship between the incarnation and *Ishwara*. Numerous terms are used without a clear and consistent connotation, and this baffles all efforts, at the conceptual level, to arrive at clear ideas relating to the themes concerned. This however is not a negative criticism or devaluation of the ontological significance or value of the great dialogue in the Gita.

Concluding Remarks On The Metaphysical Vision of The Gita

How shall we judge Gita's truth claims relating to *Brahman, Atman*, Sri Krishna as a Divine incarnation, *karma*, etc.? Statements containing such highly abstract terms as '*Brahman*', '*Atman*', '*Purush*', 'Spirit', 'Universal Self', 'incarnation' and so on are highly complex in their logical structure and ambivalent in their function. Such statements both illuminate and mislead the listener or reader. Consider the following truth claims: "*The universe is the manifestation or creation of Brahman*", "*Brahman is the Self or Spirit of all beings*", "*Brahman is the seed of all existence*", "*Brahman sustains all things but does not abide in them*", "*He is far away and yet near*", "*Sri Krishna is the incarnation (avatara) of Lord Vishnu*".

We shall completely miss the significance or the function of the above statements if we take them as a descriptive or scientific truth claims and then proceed to ask for their verification. The above truth claims are metaphysical perspectives on the universe, and represent the human quest for relating himself to the cosmic process. Such statements are more evocative then descriptive, more poetic than scientific, and more directive than informative. Their basic function is not to give information about the universe, as an object, but to transform human attitudes and responses, as a subject, condemned to relate himself, in some way or other, to a mysterious universe.

The cosmos is marked by puzzling and baffling polarities of life and death, purpose and chance, pleasure and pain, good and evil, beauty and ugliness, the benevolence and malevolence of nature, and so on. There is the music of the nightingale, the language of the flowers, the colors of the sunset, the majesty of the mountains, the song of the brook, the silence of the forests, but there is also the redness of the tooth and claw in nature, the enormity of waste and destruction in the struggle for existence, the dead ends and reversals in the evolutionary process, the fury of the flood and storm, the havoc of the epidemic, the scourge of the locust, the viciousness of the bacteria, the aberrations in the womb, the pathos and indignity of incurable insanity, the tragedy of the accident on rail or road, the agony of the victim of rape, the strangulation of equity, the miscarriage of justice, the tragic waste of talent, the recurring arrests and retreats of value in history, and so on.

Humans feel impelled to discover some meaning or purpose, some significance or pattern in the cosmic process in order to form a stable, consistent and fully satisfying way of responding to the mystery of the cosmic process marked by the above polarities. A metaphysical perspective on the universe is a way of viewing and responding to the cosmic mystery. Every specific perspective illuminates the cosmic situation and simultaneously misleads us. It highlights or reveals some significant aspect of the cosmic situation, but tends to ignore or conceal some other side or aspect of a complex totality, and thereby leaves us perplexed and devoid of inner peace.

Every metaphysical perspective, in other words, attempts to fit all the known pieces of the cosmic jigsaw puzzle, as it were, into a coherent conceptual picture. But as soon as a picture begins to take shape some facet of our experience strikes a jarring note, as it were, and refuses to fit into the pattern.

Doubts and problems also arise in the domain of science but the onward march of mathematics and factual knowledge resolves them. Technology makes even faster progress through the method of trial and error. This self-corrective growth is absent in the domain of philosophy and religion. Thus in these fields, unlike science and technology, we continue to grapple with the same problems and perplexities faced by the ancients. In other words, though the area of objective certainty has expanded enormously existential perplexity lingers on in the human breast. This creates and sustains spiritual or conceptual space in which faith, whether religious or philosophical, tries to set at rest our inner perplexities or uncertainties about the nature and destiny of man in the universe.

Let us now try to see how some of the truth claims in the Gita illuminate and also mislead us, even as all metaphysical perspectives must, by the very nature of human language.

We see or experience portions of the gigantic universe but we do not come across any agency at work in the past or living present. Since, however, we experience and come across sufficient regularity, structure and order in the universe we feel inclined to attribute them to some powerful but unseen agent or creator. This inclination on our part is rooted in our experience that whenever and wherever regular patterns of events exist there is some doer, who designs and produces the said patterns. In other words, our experience that there is no watch without a watchmaker, or no machine without a designer or manufacturer, inclines us to apply the same logic to the universe as such. This is the justification for saying that God is the Supreme Unseen Creator of all that exists.

Further reflection, however, easily leads us to realize that there is a basic difference between the creative activity of finite agents, whether human or non-human, and the inferred creative activity of God, the Supreme Creator or *Brahman*, regarded as the unknowable Self-existent external Being. The difference lies in the fact that finite creators work upon material already given and existing independently of their creative activity. But it is obvious that we cannot apply this analogy to God's creative activity. The prior existence of matter in any shape or form, independently of God, would obviously compromise and contradict God's absolute supremacy and primacy.

In other words, the analogical discourse in regard to Divine creation is based on a pseudo-analogy, which is extremely misleading. To say that creation by God means absolute creation, or creation of matter out of nothing at all amounts to lifting ordinary words from a context we all understand and transferring them to a context we do not understand at all. Consequently, using the words 'creation out of nothing' produces an illusion that the said expression has a palpable meaning or sense like the expression 'creation out of earth or clay'. But in the strict sense, the expression in question leads only to what may be called 'cognitive vacuity', if not, 'nonsense', as some logical positivists said during the heyday of Logical Positivism and the revolt against all Metaphysics.

Difficulties of the sort mentioned above have, therefore, led Vedantic expositors and others to say that the universe has not been created by God, but that it is the manifestation or outer reflection of the supreme Self-existent eternal Being (*Brahman*). Now the word 'manifestation' is an extremely open ended term. We do understand what it means or refers to in various human contexts, say where a person manifests his anger or love or where something hitherto obscure or doubtful becomes clear or evident. But we can hardly claim to understand what or which situation is referred to by saying that the cosmos is the manifestation of *Brahman*. So, using the word 'manifestation' in place of 'creation' does not really resolve our perplexity.

The *Upanishads*, in an attempt to clarify the nature of the relation between *Brahman* and the cosmos, also give the analogy of a spider spinning its web out of its own body. But this analogy is also a pseudo-analogy. It is obvious that what goes into the original formation, sustenance, and activity of the spider exists independently of it.

Let us offer some comments upon another Vedantic variation on the theme of *Brahman*. The Gita contains several references to this variation, namely, that *Brahman* is the Self or Soul of the universe. It is clear that this analogy is suggested or that we feel inclined to accept this view on the basis or our sense of an enduring personal identity in the flux of fleeting sensations, perceptions, images and numerous other mental acts. In addition we firmly believe or rather have a clear and immediate awareness that I am a person comprising an integrated body distinct from other objects or persons. We can hardly claim to have a similar direct awareness of the self of other human beings. However, everyday contact with fellow humans makes it impossible to doubt that they are persons just like us, that their bodies react to stimuli just like ours, and that they think, feel and behave in more or less similar ways.

Now the point is that we just do not perceive the cosmos in the way we perceive our own body or are aware of our own self or personal identity. Nor do we, or can we deal with the universe as we deal with other human beings. When, therefore, we say that *Brahman* is the Self of the cosmos we again lift words from a known human context and apply them in a context totally different from the human. Indeed, the cosmos is far too differentiated, diffuse and spread over space and time to resemble an organic unity like a human being, animal or plant. The cosmos comprises diverse structures and functions endlessly cooperating, competing, struggling, destroying, building, propagating and dying, so that the cosmos could hardly be said to be an integrated mega-organism. Nevertheless, in some respects the universe bears a better comparison with a self-creative, self-renewing and living organism than with a fabricated giant machine or a lifeless mega-structure. Consequently, there is a point in saying that *Brahman* or God is the indwelling Self-creative Power or Force, and the perceptible world, its expression.

The concept of *Brahman* and its correlate, 'Atman', becomes emotionally satisfying and ethically fruitful, perhaps to the highest degree, when the individual identifies his 'Atman' with *Brahman* without equating the two and without excluding other beings from this identity. This means the awareness of the person's identity with *Brahman*, in essence, but not in existence. This self-view or perspective elevates human status to the highest ontological and creative level without producing any trace of 'hubris' or vicious destructive egoism. Perhaps, this self-image or view of Philosophical Anthropology is the most felicitous way to reinforce or promote moral excellence, compassion and spiritual growth.

Difficulties also arise when we say or imply that this or that was God's purpose in the creation of the universe. We know the meaning of this concept only in the human context of desiring something, which we do not possess. Purpose, thus, necessarily implies some deficiency in being; having or achieving, in short, a condition of imperfection of some sort. But if *Brahman* or God is deemed to be perfect, there remains no point in attributing any purpose, whatsoever, to the Supreme Being.

Let us now turn to the belief in *karma*, which is a central part of Gita's teachings. The theory of *karma* holds that the individual soul (*jiva*) is repeatedly reborn until it gets completely cleansed of all traces of evil through merited suffering in proportion to its guilt in previous births. The belief in *karma* can be divided into two parts or layers,

> (a) The general enunciation of the metaphysical law of just recompense, namely, as the soul sows, so shall it reap in the present birth or future birth/births, and

> (b) The more specific belief that the individual soul (*jiva*) has no fixed material frame (*prakriti*) for its locus in the chain of births and deaths, so that the *jiva* may even migrate from one species to another, depending upon the degree of its cumulative guilt and the requirement of cosmic justice.

The belief in *karma* is a metaphysical perspective on the cosmic process, and not a hypothesis, which could be verified or falsified. Numerous persons who seem to be good and virtuous are made to suffer, while others who seem to be bad and vicious prosper in the world. The belief appears to make this enigma explicable up to a point.

With regard to the first part of the belief in question one may well ask whether looking upon the phenomenon of birth and the subsequent career of an individual as the enforced serving out of a sentence of punishment for guilt incurred in a previous life or lives will promote a positive celebration of life, or whether it will tend to promote a negative sense of life weariness. Leaving aside this issue for the present it may be said that the first part of the said belief deters man from evil doing, even though it does not fully explain the distribution and quantum of pain and suffering among humans or animals.

The second part of the belief in *karma* presents a much greater difficulty. Instead, it becomes almost unintelligible if taken in the literal sense. This part implies that there are no boundaries or genetic identities between different species of living beings, and that the soul in or of an elephant could migrate in its next birth into the body of a fly, or the soul in or of a human being may take on the body of, say, a frog or mosquito. This version of the belief does not make any sense since it obliterates all distinctions of structure, complexity and quality among living beings. Though the Gita itself does not refer to this version of the belief in *karma*, this view is widely held. However, one may interpret this version of the theory of *karma* as a mythical pointer to the belief in the essential oneness of life. This would mean that all living beings, from the meanest microbe of fly to a majestic elephant, have a common sap of life flowing in their arteries entitling them to due respect as living beings. This would mean that one may not irreverently destroy the meanest living being, though one would be justified in eliminating mosquitoes that infect and tics that torment. However, other metaphysical beliefs or perspectives could also lead to this existential reverence for life and mystical sense of its oneness. In the final analysis, therefore, the belief in *karma* and rebirth is a matter of cultural conditioning of the believer rather than of systematic reflection or reasoning as to the origin and justification of pain and suffering in the universe.

An Essay on the Bhagavad Gita

The same remarks apply to the belief in the Divinity of Sri Krishna. The enchanting description of Arjuna's mystical experience, as given in the Gita, does not analyze or clarify the structure of this belief. This is quite understandable since the Gita is a poetic testament of faith, not a philosophical treatise. One is, in consequence, left wondering what is the exact connotation of 'Divine incarnation' (*avatara*). Moreover, one is left wondering about the exact identity of the Being which incarnates itself: whether it is the supreme Personal God (*Ishwara*) or some member of the Pantheon? Or is it that *Ishwara* is the same as Shiva or Vishnu? Again, how is one to relate the principal members of the Pantheon with the '*Atman*' of the *Upanishads*? The broad view of Divine immanence, in varying degrees, in all finite beings, is affirmed by the *Upanishads*. But the Gita affirms that this Divine immanence reached its peak in the person of Sri Krishna. This claim is, obviously, a dogma or article of faith produced by cultural conditioning or indoctrination rather than a philosophical interpretation formed through pure reflection on or contemplation of the mystery of the universe.

The Gita seems to imply that the inner peace and bliss consequent upon the mystical experience of Arjuna is sufficient by itself and obviates the need of any further query or probe into methodological or epistemological issues. The Gita also seems to imply that the liberated *yogi* penetrates into the secrets of the why and how of the unity and plurality of the universe, its eventual re-absorption or reunification with the Eternal Source (*Brahman*), and also the why and how of the strife and destructiveness, along with the unity and harmony found in the cosmic process. But this is very far from being the case.

Only while the *yogi* is in the exalted state of spiritual illumination can he claim to have overcome the opaqueness, absurdity and contingency found in both nature and history. But as soon as the *yogi* returns to the normal level of conceptual awareness, as indeed he must, can he sustain this claim? Can he deny that no thorns are to be found in the rose of his normal awareness and day-to-day experience? He himself may not be troubled by any sense of disharmony after having once gone though his liberating mystical experience and his inner peace may be perfectly genuine. But what if someone else points out the disharmony and contradictions, the absurdity and opaqueness, the unjust pain and suffering, the waste and convolutions of nature and of history, the tragedy and evil in society, the injustice and wickedness in personal relations that meet the eye of the sensitive observer of the cosmic scene? Can the *yogi* pull out the thorns of others? Can he make the other see, through reasoning or spirituality, the beauty, goodness, justice and transparency of the cosmic process as he claims to have seen it in his exalted condition?

It seems the *yogi* could partially convince others that there was more to reality then what appears on the surface. But I submit, in all humility, that he would not be able to remove the elements of absurdity and contingency as perceived by others. At best, the *yogi* could prompt and even persuade honest and perplexed seekers of truth to prefer the path of mystical experience to conceptual inquiry or scientific investigation. But the *yogi* cannot resolve the riddles or answer the queries of the inquiring mind or create transparency in the place of opaqueness. Nor can he give competent concrete guidance to others in various worldly matters, though *yoga* may well result in mental peace, courage and hope, and thereby activate man's potential creative powers.

The upshot of the above linguistic analysis of truth claims relating to *Brahman, Atman,* Divine attributes, belief in *karma* and the Divine status of Sri Krishna is that no statement which uses ordinary words drawn from the human context in the non-human or transcendental sphere could be said to avoid the distortion of reality or Being. The Gita itself repeatedly points out the utter inadequacy of all human efforts in this regard. The moment we predicate any attribute or state of *Brahman* we are called upon to negate it. However, the conscious use of analogical affirmation and its dialectical negation is the only way in which human communication is possible on the mass scale.

Despite the above-mentioned poetic distortion or even cognitive vacuity necessarily resulting from analogical discourse on transcendental themes the human existential response to the mystery of the cosmos will and must go on. Man's yearning to seek a 'holistic' significance of the cosmos is irrepressible. Indeed, this yearning or aspiration is as valuable and precious as the human aspiration for goodness, beauty and love.

The quest for scientific truth must not be permitted to make us insensitive or indifferent to the quest for holistic significance of the cosmos. This search is an integral dimension of the human quest for truth. The themes of the Gita touch a level of reality that is not amenable to the methodology of science based on observation and experiment. This method cannot be applied even to morality and art. So, why should one's scientific conscience be hurt if the truth claim, say, relating to the essential identity of *Atman* and *Brahman* cannot be scientifically established. Spirituality could, well, have its own logic and methodology.

The scientific attitude and temper have come to stay and rightly, so, in the human family. Technology is the daughter of science and the blessings of technology are, indeed, immense. They extend to the human pursuit of moral, social and cultural values, apart from purely material or physical. Traditional religious opinion, perhaps, does not fully appreciate this role of technology in promoting spiritual and moral values. On the other hand, rationalist and scientific opinion does not seem to appreciate that if scientific truth be allowed to become the sole model or paradigm of truth, and if the quest for certainty (in the scientific sense) be allowed to stifle all other quests which do not yield objective certainty neither art, nor morality could flower in human society. Pure scientism will reduce the many colored rainbow of human response to the cosmic process to one single and exclusive strand of scientific knowledge and procedure and, thus, turn humans into one-dimensional creatures of the laboratory. The quest for multi-dimensional growth and excellence will no longer be possible.

The quest for spirituality is the quest for transmuting the base metal of the human state into pure gold (if possible) through discovering the philosopher's stone (if any). This quest carried on through honest prayerful striving, in the spirit of humility and tolerance, is, to my mind, the most sublime of all human quests for value.

The most remarkable thing about the Gita is that though it has its own metaphysics and mystique it does not make their acceptance a necessary condition of human felicity or salvation. The necessary condition, according to the Gita, is the quest for ultimate truth and the performance of duty for its own sake. In today's idiom, the Gita gives primacy to authentic being and ethical action rather than to any specific philosophical or religious faith, even though it does affirm that authentic being and ethical action will blossom best in the ambience of *Brahman* and *bhakti*.

3. Values And The Good Life According To The Gita

It is almost impossible to define the word 'value' in a manner which would satisfy every inquiring mind. But, broadly speaking, we could say that any state of affairs (be it an inner state of thinking, feeling or willing, or any objective situation) is a value for the person desirous of creating, preserving or promoting the said states of affairs. Values, in this sense, can range from the bare physical to the moral and the spiritual plane. The Gita is concerned with the inner states of human thinking, feeling and willing. These inner states comprise judgments, feelings, volitions, attitudes, motives, and depth responses in the widest sense.

The Gita holds that these inner states of the mind are the source-springs or seeds of human conduct, which flows from them as the fruit flows from the root. Higher knowledge (*Brahmavidya*) and living at the spiritual (*saatvic*) level purifies the soil or ground, which supports and sustains the habitual external behavior of the individual. In addition to the above the doer must also know or understand the exact nature of basic spiritual and moral values. When all the above three conditions are satisfied the *yogi* develops the power to discriminate right from wrong conduct. He also begins to do what is right and avoid what is wrong as an inner demand of his purified and illumined inner state, rather than as an act of obedience to any external authority or out of fear or hope of gain. This is, obviously, the ideal. In actual practice imperfections (in varying degrees) linger on in every mortal until he finally qualifies for '*mukti*'.

The Gita mentions a large number of spiritual and moral values. Since, however, the Gita is a poem and not an ethical treatise, the value terms are not analyzed or explained. Moreover, they find mention in widely scattered verses. A far greater difficulty is met with in giving a one to one translation of the original Sanskrit value terms.

In Radhakrishnan's English translation of the Gita, some values have been positively designated by a single abstract noun in the English language, while others have been negatively designated, as freedom from some 'dis-value', while still others have been designated by a descriptive phrase. The learned translator had to do this in order to convey the exact meaning of the Sanskrit terms. Resort to this method becomes inevitable due to the unique vocabulary and idiom of each language.

It is beyond the scope of the present essay to analyze or explain the spiritual and moral values stressed in the Gita. It is the task of the spiritual teacher (*guru*) or the ethical thinker to illuminate the highly complex nature or structure of values. I shall limit myself to the lesser task of giving a more or less complete catalogue of the values mentioned in the Gita. Since, however, I am using Radhakrishnan's English translation of the original Sanskrit value terms I am clubbing them in three separate lists according to their linguistic form in the English translation, rather than according to their conceptual relationship. The three linguistic forms, as already indicated, are;

(a) Single abstract noun,

(b) Compound negative expression and

(c) Descriptive phrase.

The values in the first category of 'single abstract noun' are as follows:

- Serenity, detachment, contentment (12:17-20)
    - Compassion, patience, determination, self-control, universal kindness, purity (12:13-16)

    - Fearlessness, charity, sacrifice, austerity, uprightness, truth, non-steadiness, vigor, forgiveness, fortitude (16:1,2,3)

    - Liberation, wisdom (4:23)

    - Humility, integrity, steadfastness, self-effacement, (13:7,8)

    - Understanding, knowledge, calmness (10:4,5)

The values in the second category of "compound negative expression" are as follows:

- Freedom from egoism, freedom from joy and anger, freedom from fear and agitation, freedom from expectation (12:13-16)

- Freedom from covetousness, freedom from malice and excessive pride (16:1,2,3)

- Freedom from jealousy (4:22)

- Freedom from bewilderment (10:4,5)

The values in the third category of 'descriptive phrase' are as follows:

- Indifference to dualities (12:17-20)

- Even mindedness in pain and pleasure, skillfulness in action, unconcern (12:13-16)

- Steadfastness in knowledge and concentration, study of scriptures, aversion to fault-finding, (16:1,2,3)

- Rejoicing in doing good to all creatures (5:25)

- Being without affection on any side, not loathing as one obtains good or evil, remaining the same amidst the pleasant and unpleasant things, firmness of mind, regarding both blame and praise as one, being the same in honor and dishonor, being the same to friend and foe, serving God with unfailing devotion (14:24, 25)

- Service of the teacher, indifference to objects of sense, perception of the evil of birth, death, old age, sickness and pain (13:7,8)

- Absence of clinging to son, wife, home and the like, constant equal mindedness to all desirable and undesirable happenings, resort to solitary places, dislike for a crowd of people, constancy in the knowledge of the spirit, insight into the end of knowledge of Truth (13:9,10,11)

- Equal mindedness among friends, companions, and foes, among those who are neutral and impartial, among those who are hateful and related, among saints and sinners (6:9)

The highest cardinal virtue, according to my understanding of the Gita's value system, may be said to be "the detached, serene, unswerving adherence, at all times and in all matters, to the inner voice of the *'Atman'*."

The *yogi* whose conduct is shaped by the above values will do what is right and avoid what is wrong. However, a proper insight into the ethos of the Gita (proper conceptual understanding of what exactly the said values mean and what pattern of conduct 'the inner states of being' lead to) is provided by the guru, through spiritual guidance, precept and example.

The Gita lays primary stress upon the inner transformation of character through knowledge and spiritual discipline and less on supplying ready-made rules governing right behavior. The accent is on the spiritual autonomy of the illuminated and purified soul. This approach to morality is favored by the doctrine that the *Atman* is a finite limb of *Brahman*.

Says the Gita:
(18:63)

> "Thus has wisdom more secret than all secrets, been declared to thee by Me. Reflect on it fully and do as thou choosest."

4. Psychological Insight And Wisdom In The Gita

The Gita provides us with several remarkable psychological insights and pearls of wisdom. Modern investigations and findings confirm the practical wisdom of the Gita. In what follows I shall attempt to bring out some of its salient features.

1. The Gita mentions that there are three basic personality or temperamental types, which shape and color the thoughts, words and deeds of every individual. These types are the '*sattvic*', the '*rajasic*' and the '*tamasic*'. The *sattvic* person naturally inclines to truth and compassion, the *rajasic* to power and glory, and the *tamasic* to physical pleasures and sloth. Individuals are rarely of a pure type. Most belong to mixed types and possess different qualities (*gunas*) in ever-different proportions. However, individuals can be classified on the basis of their dominant quality.

The *sattvic* type is the highest and the *tamasic* the lowest. All thoughts, words and deeds of a person could be graded on this scale. Everything a person thinks, says or does, be it his behavior as a house holder, giving gifts, performing religious rites, acquiring knowledge, governing a state, fighting a war, punishing a wrong doer, all could be done in the *sattvic/rajasic/tamasic* manner. The Gita implies that every action occupies a position on this scale from the pure *sattvic* to the pure *tamasic*.

The Gita exhorts the individual to rise to the *sattvic* level in every sphere of human activity. All, irrespective of caste, color, creed or gender can reach this level where the individual performs the duties of his station or situation *(swadharma)* without attachment to their fruits. Modern personality psychology calls such a person a 'spiritually autonomous, self-directing and integrated person'. Says the Gita;

(14:5)
"The three modes (gunas) goodness (satwa), passion (rajas), and dullness (tamas) born of nature (prakriti) bind down in the body, O Mighty-armed (Arjuna), the imperishable dweller in the body."

(18:26-28)
"The doer who is free from attachment, who has no speech of egotism, full of resolution and zeal and who is unmoved by success or failure - he is said to be of the nature of "goodness".
"The doer who is swayed by passion, who eagerly seeks the fruit of his works, who is greedy, of violent nature, impure, who is moved by joy and sorrow-he is said to be of 'passionate nature'."
"The doer who is unbalanced, vulgar, obstinate, deceitful, malicious, indolent, despondent and procrastinating, he is said to be of the nature of "dullness".

(18:41)
"Of Brahmans, of Kshatriyas and Vaishyas as also of Shudras, O Conqueror of the foe (Arjuna), the activities are distinguished, in accordance with the qualities born of their nature."

(9:32)
"For those who take refuge in Me, O Partha (Arjuna) though they are

lowly born, women, Vaishyas, as well as Shudras, they also attain to the highest goal."

(17:7)
"An action which is obligatory, which is performed without attachment, without love or hate by one un-desirous of fruit, that is said to be of "goodness"
"But that action which is done in great strain by one who seeks to gratify his desires or is impelled by self-sense, is said to be of the nature of passion."
"The action which is undertaken through ignorance, without regard to consequences or to loss and injury and without regard to one's human capacity, that is said to be of the nature of "dullness".
"Even the food, which is dear to all, is of three kinds. So are the sacrifices, austerities and gifts. Hear thou the distinction of these."

(17:11-12)
"That sacrifice which is offered, according to the scriptural law, by those who expect no reward and firmly believe that it is their duty to offer the sacrifices, is "good".
"But that which is offered in expectation of reward or for the sake of display, know, O best of the Bharatas (Arjuna) that sacrifice to be "passionate"."

(6:5-7)
"Let a man lift himself by himself, let him not degrade himself for the Self alone is the friend of the self and the Self alone is the enemy of the self."
"For him who has conquered his (lower) self by the (higher) Self his Self is a friend but for him who has not possessed his (higher) Self, his very Self will act in enmity, like an enemy".
"When one has conquered one's self (lower) and has attained to the calm of self-mastery, his Supreme Self abides ever contented, he is at peace in cold and heat, in pleasure and pain, in honor and dishonor."

2. There is another psychological insight in the Gita, namely, the destructive role of negative thoughts and emotions and the key role of thought-control in the good life.

Says the Gita:

(2:62-63)
"When a man dwells in his mind on the objects of sense, attachment to them is produced. From attachment springs desire and from desire comes anger."
"From anger arises bewilderment, from bewilderment loss of memory, the destruction of intelligence and from the destruction of intelligence he perishes."

(3:43)
"Thus knowing Him who is beyond the intelligence, steadying the (lower) self by the Self, smite, O mighty-armed (Arjuna), the enemy in the form of desire, so hard to get at."

(16:21)
"The gateway of this hell leading to the ruin of the soul is threefold, lust, anger and greed. Therefore, these three, one should abandon."

3. The Gita teaches that the faith of an individual is a very personal matter and that it should be respected and not disturbed by others. Those at a higher level of knowledge of Reality (*Brahmavidya*) should give loving help and guidance to others in raising their level through proper striving but must never unsettle the honest beliefs or convictions of others. Help and advice must flow from a heart full of compassionate love rather than stern disapproval and rejection of others. Says the Gita:

(17:3)
"The faith of every individual, O Bharat (Arjuna), is in accordance with his nature. Man is of the nature of his faith: What his faith is, that, verily, he is."

(3:26)
"Let him (jnanin) not unsettle the minds of the ignorant who are attached to action. The enlightened man doing all works in a spirit of yoga, should set others to act (as well)."

(3:29)
"Those who are misled by the modes of nature get attached to the works produced by them. But let no one who knows the whole unsettle the minds of the ignorant who know only a part."

4. Another pearl of timeless wisdom found in the Gita is that the individual should overcome any inner doubts, which may linger in his mind, consciously or otherwise, pertaining to the human situation. While extolling the individual's freedom of choice and of conscience the Gita, at the same time, stresses the importance of a firm commitment, which is essential for the good life. In other word, the Gita stresses what modern existentialist thinkers call 'authentic' commitment. Says the Gita:

(4:40)
"But the man who is ignorant, who has no faith, who is of a doubting nature, perishes. For the doubting soul, there is neither this world nor the world beyond nor any happiness."

(4:42)
"Therefore, having cut asunder with the sword of wisdom this doubt in thy heart that is born of ignorance, resort to yoga and stand up, O Bharata (Arjuna)"

5. The fifth insight is that though the letter of scripture is important, the spirit is even more so. The *yogi*, at the highest level, therefore, should concern himself more with the realization of basic objectives and values taught in the scripture rather than with obeying rules and regulations in the literal sense. Changed circumstances may even require the modification of or rather going beyond such rules, which are instrumental in character. This is a remarkably courageous exhortation and has few parallels in the spiritual history of man. Says the Gita:

(2:42-44)
"The undiscerning who rejoice in the letter of the Veda, who contend that there is nothing else, whose nature is desire and who are intent on

heaven, proclaim these flowery words that result in rebirth as the fruit of actions and (lay down) various specialized rites for the attainment of enjoyment and power."
"The intelligence which is to be trained, of those who are devoted, to enjoyment and power and whose minds are carried away by these words (of the Veda) is not well established in the Self (or concentration)."

(2:46)
"As is the use of a pond in a place flooded with water everywhere, so is that of all the Vedas for the Brahmin who understands."

(2:53)
"When thy intelligence, which is bewildered by the Vedic texts, shall stand unshaken and stable in spirit (samadhi), then shall thou attain to insight (yoga)."

6. The sixth basic insight of the Gita is the paramount importance of action in the broad sense. Human life remains essentially futile and meaningless without proper action or purposive striving. The Gita says:

(3:8)
"Do thou thy allotted work, for action is better than inaction; even the maintenance of thy physical life cannot be effected without action."

(3:12)
"Fostered by sacrifice the gods will give you the enjoyments you desire. He who enjoys these gifts without giving to them in return is verily a thief."

7. The seventh insight or piece of wisdom is that action done out of the right motive (namely, performance of duty without attachment to fruits) is more important for salvation then having the right theory of reality. However, at other places the path of knowledge is held to be superior to all other paths. It may, therefore, be said that Gita holds that though the path of knowledge (*gyanayoga*) is supreme it could be substituted by the path of devotion to God (*bhaktiyoga*). Similarly, the path of total renunciation of works could be substituted by the path of detached performance of duty (*niskama karma*). In the final analysis, the Gita seems to imply that it is immaterial whether the *yogi* follows the path of knowledge or the path of devotion, provided he performs his duties without attachment to their fruits.

Here are some relevant verses:

(5: 4-5)
"The ignorant speak of renunciation (Sankhya) and practice of works (yoga) as different, not the wise. He who applies himself well to one, gets the fruits of both."
"The status, which is obtained by men of renunciation is reached by men of action also. He who sees that the ways of renunciation and of action are one, he sees (truly)."

(6: 1-2)
"He who does the work which he ought to do without seeking its fruit, he is the sanyasin, he is the yogin, not he who does not light the sacred fire, and performs no rites."
"What they call renunciation, that know to be disciplined activity, O Pandava (Arjuna), for no one becomes a yogin who has not renounced his (selfish purpose)."

(3:19)
"Therefore, without attachment, perform always the work that has to be done, for man attains to the highest by doing work without attachment."

(18:10-11)
"The wise man, who renounces, whose doubts are dispelled, whose nature is of goodness, has no aversion to disagreeable action and no attachment to agreeable action."
"It is indeed impossible for any embodied being to abstain from work altogether. But he who gives up the fruit of action, he is said to be the Relinquisher."

(18:8-9)
"He who gives up a duty because it is painful or from fear of physical

suffering, performs only the relinquishment of the "passionate" kind and does not gain the reward of relinquishment.
"But he who performs a prescribed duty as a thing that ought to be done, renouncing all attachment and also the fruit - his relinquishment is regarded as one of "goodness""

(7:47)
"To action alone hast thou a right and never at all to its fruits; let not the fruits of action be thy motive; neither let there be in thee any attachment to inaction."

(9:27)
"Whatever thou doest, whatever thou eatest, whatever thou offerest, whatever thou givest away, whatever austerities thou dost practice - do that, O Son of Kunti (Arjuna), as an offering to Me."

8. Finally, the Gita disapproves of asceticism and recommends moderation in eating, sleeping and the satisfaction of other bodily needs as the best means of spiritual growth as well as all round personality development. Modern psychology, once again, has reached the same conclusion. Says the Gita:

(17:5-6)
"Those men, vain and conceited and impelled by the force of lust and passion, who perform violent austerities, which are not ordained by the scriptures."
"Being foolish oppress the group of elements in their body and Me also dwelling in the body. Know these to be demoniac in their resolves."

(2:64)
"But a man of disciplined mind, who moves among the objects of sense, with the senses under control and free from attachment and aversion, he attains purity of spirit."

(6:16-17)
"Verily, yoga is not for him who eats too much or abstains too much from eating. It is not for him, O Arjuna, who sleeps too much or keeps awake too much."

"For the man who is temperate in food and recreation, who is restrained in his actions, whose sleep and waking are regulated, there ensues discipline (yoga) which destroys all sorrow."

CONCLUDING REMARKS ON PSYCHOLOGICAL INSIGHT AND WISDOM IN THE GITA

The detached performance of duty without any emotional or sentimental involvement of the doer will certainly lead to altruistic and harmonious human relationships. But it seems the ethic of detached living would liberate humans not merely from the evils of egoism, passion and lust, but also from the blessings of friendly warmth of the heart, romantic altruistic love at its best, merriment and wit; in short, not merely from the sufferings and tears of life, but also from the joys and poetry of life.

Imagine a world of saints who (under the Gita's inspiration) are engaged all the time in preparing for merger into *Brahman*. What will happen in such a world to the will to enjoy, to compete in sport, to know the secrets of nature and to control it, to restructure society nearer to the heart's desire, to create beauty, to alleviate suffering, to make life comfortable and congenial for optimum all round creativity? It seems, in other words, that fulfilling the letter of the Gita in man's quest for salvation would lead to a sort of life-negation and would discourage the active involvement of the individual in the mixed joys and sorrows, achievements and failures, cooperation and competition which are the inseparable ingredients of human living.

The above fear seems justified up to a point. However, it will lose its sting if we look at the gospel of detached action in the light of the traditional Hindu concepts of *'ashrama'*, namely, that the normal span of human life is hundred years divided into four stages (*ashramas*) each of twenty-five years duration. The first two stages namely, '*brahmacharya*' and '*grahasta*' could well be regarded as periods of life affirmation, the third, *'vanaprasta'*, as a twilight period of preparation for entry into '*sanayasa*': the fourth and final stage of life-negation. One could, then, hold that the Gita teaches courageous and optimistic all round life-affirmation in the first half of life, and its gradual tapering in the second. Even the last stage of life could be viewed as life affirmation at the level of transcendence rather than as life-negation. This point needs further clarification.

One may say that the Gita holds different values and their corresponding duties as appropriate for the different stages of life. All these different values and duties can be subsumed under one master-value or 'master-duty', appropriate for each stage of life. This master-duty is the '*ashramadharma*'. We may look at the '*ashramadharma*' not as a single atomic duty but as a 'spectrum of duties' appropriate to the individual's stage of life. This spectrum would change at different stages of life, so that each stage will have a specific structure of duties, together with an accent on some of them, rather than any monolithic or exclusive duty.

Likewise, we may not understand '*varna*' as hereditary caste but rather as the inner constitution or personality type of each individual irrespective of the family of his birth. On this view total renunciation may become the master duty of some people in the last stage of life. However, even '*sanayasa*' need not be a total 'flight from life'. It could be viewed as transcendental living with a constructive social purpose. Perhaps, this is the implication of the following verse of the Gita:

(4:18)
"He who in action sees inaction and action in inaction, he is wise among men, he is a yogin and he has accomplished all his work."

We may well conclude that the Gita says that the dominant concern of the good life, in the first half, must be morally regulated all round creative development of the individual as a specific personality type. In the second half the accent should shift to progressive contemplation and transcendence. Each stage of life entails a characteristic spectrum of duties. The figure of Arjuna, 'the archer', represents self-assertion and purposive action in the first half of life; while the figure of Sri

Krishna, 'the charioteer' represents wisdom in the second half. These two activities complement each other in the flowering of the good life. What is required is a proper blending of the two in optimum proportions during the different stages of life. Vigorous action, symbolized by the shooting of the arrow, must be guided by wisdom and morality symbolized by the 'charioteer' in control of the movement and direction of the vehicle. This interpretation makes the classical Hindu doctrine of *'varnashrama'* practically synonymous with the modern Western values of 'Self-Realization' and 'authentic being'.

Says the last verse of the Gita:

(18:78)
"Wherever there is Krishna, the lord of yoga, and Partha (Arjuna), the archer, I think, there will surely be fortune, victory, welfare and morality."

5. CONCEPTUAL PERMISSIVENESS AND TOLERANCE IN THE GITA

Conceptual permissiveness within a religious tradition means that the acknowledged custodians of the tradition allow fellow-believers a measure of freedom to redefine the basic concepts and values of the religion without attracting the charge or guilt of being disloyal or inimical to the tradition. Conceptual permissiveness is, thus, the willing acceptance of plural interpretations within the tradition, while 'conceptual strictness' imposes a rigidly uniform commitment.

The Gita stands for conceptual permissiveness. It says that God can be worshiped in different ways, and that all lead the sincere worshipers to the Supreme. The plural approach fosters tolerance and cultural inclusiveness, while the stress on uniformity to proselytism and exclusiveness. The Gita prescribes that willing adherence to one's own duty (*swadharma*) is the best means of spiritual growth. The stress of the Gita is on spiritual discipline and detached action, not on any particular metaphysics or theology. Says the Gita:

(4:11)
"As men approach Me so do I accept them: men on all sides follow My path, O Partha (Arjuna)."

(7:21-23)
"Whatever form any devotee with faith wishes to worship, I make that faith of his steady."
"Endowed with that faith, he seeks the worship of such a one and from him he obtains his desires, the benefits being decreed by Me alone."
"But temporary is the fruit gained by these men of small minds. The worshipers of the gods go to the gods but My devotees come to Me."

(9:23-24)
"Even those who are devotees of other gods, worship them with faith, they also sacrifice to Me alone, O Son of Kunti (Arjuna), though not according to the true law."
"For I am the enjoyer and lord of all sacrifices. But these men do not know Me in My true nature and so they fall."

(9:26)
"Whosoever offers to Me with devotion a leaf, a flower, a fruit, or water, that offering of love, of the pure of heart I accept."

(9:29)
"I am alike to all beings. None is hateful or dear to Me. But those who worship Me with devotion they are in Me and I also in them."
The Gita does hold Sri Krishna as a Divine incarnation. But the Gita does not reject other beliefs. Says the Gita:

(12:2-5)
"Those who fix their minds on Me, worship Me, ever harmonized and possessed of supreme faith - them do I consider most perfect in yoga."
"But those who worship the Imperishable, the Undefinable, the Unmanifested, the Omnipresent, the Unthinkable, the Unchanging and the Immobile, the Constant."
"By restraining all the senses, being even-minded in all conditions, rejoicing in the welfare of all creatures, they come to Me indeed (just

like all the others)."
"The difficulty of those whose thoughts are set on the Unmanifested is greater, for the goal of the Unmanifested is hard to reach by the embodied beings."

The above verses seem to imply that the monistic or non-theistic approach to ultimate Reality is also permissible, though its difficulties are stated to be much greater for ordinary mortals. The only view, which the Gita categorically repudiates is Nihilism: the rejection of all values and of the doctrine of *karma*, and the consequent unbridled amoral pursuit of impulse or passion. The following verses make this explicitly clear:

(16:7-8)
"The demoniac do not know about the way of action or the way of renunciation. Neither purity, nor good conduct, nor truth is found in them."
"They say that the world is unreal, without a basis, without a Lord, not brought about in regular causal sequence, caused by desire, in short."

(16:10-12)
"Giving themselves up to insatiable desire, full of hypocrisy, excessive pride and arrogance, holding wrong views through delusion, they act with impure resolves."
"Obsessed with innumerable cares which would end only with (their) death, looking upon the gratification of desires as their highest aim, assured that this is all."
"Bound by hundreds of ties of desire, given over to lust and anger, they strive to amass hoards of wealth, by unjust means, for the gratification of their desires."

(16:18-20)
"Given over to self-conceit, force and pride and also to lust and anger, these malicious people despise Me dwelling in the bodies of themselves and others."
"These cruel haters, worst of men, I hurl constantly these evil-doers only into the wombs of demons in this cycle of births and deaths."

"Fallen into the wombs of demons, these deluded beings from birth to birth, do not attain to Me, O Son of Kunti (Arjuna), but go down to the lowest state."

Now, though Mahavira and Buddha denied *Brahman* and the sanctity and infallibility of the Vedas, they both accepted basic moral and spiritual values and the principle of *karma*. It is, therefore, reasonable to hold that the followers of Mahavira and Buddha, or for that matter, the followers of any other religious tradition (provided they eschew the moral evils or vices mentioned above) do not come under the purview of the above verses of the Gita.

In other words, the approach of the Gita is so catholic that notwithstanding its own commitment to *Vaishnavite Anthro-theism* (faith in the divinity of Sri Krishna), it seems to permit the conceptual elimination of even God/*Brahman* from one's value system for agnostics and others.

Possibly, this is the explanation of how and why both Jainism and Buddhism, after an extended period of conflict with *Brahmanical* orthodoxy, and even a measure of persecution by the custodians of the Vedic tradition, eventually came to be regarded as unorthodox schools or sects of Hinduism in the larger sense.

Blessed are the good and simple and authentic believers in a caring Personal God. Blessed are they who can plumb the depths of their being and can hear 'the music of the spheres' and see 'the light of a thousand suns blaze forth all at once', and act dutifully without attachment to fruits. Blessed too are they whose journey in inner space brings them to *'Brahman without attributes'*, and fortifies the *'Atman'*. But what about those whose honest and sustained quest for truth meets with a bewildered inner silence and the darkness of an unending night of the soul, and yet they remain sensitive to truth, goodness and beauty, and go on responding to the call of duty for its own sake? This is the crucial question facing and dividing humanity today.

"They too are blessed", seems to be how Gita implicitly answers the crucial question. And this, to my mind, is tolerance at its best and the perennial wisdom of the Bhagavad Gita.

Notes To Essay 1
An Essay On The Bhagavad Gita:
(1) Names Used for Shri Krishna and Arjuna in the Bhagavad Gita

Throughout the Bhagavad Gita conversation, Lord Krishna and his disciple Arjuna are referred to by numerous epithets, such as *Keshava* (Krishna) or *Partha* (Arjuna). A list of these names is given below. Each one of these '*names*' underscores, the philosophical point being made in that particular verse. These names also enhance the beauty and lyrical quality of the Sanskrit poem.

(A) List of Names used for Shri Krishna

Achyuta: Changeless One; Matchless One; Unfallen.
Anantarupa: One of inexhaustible form.
Aprameya: Illimitable One.
Apratimaprabhava: Lord of power incomparable.
Arisudanna: Destroyer of foes.
Bhagavan: Blessed Lord.
Deva: Lord.
Devesha: Lord of gods.
Govinda: Protector of cows. Chief herdsman.
Hari: Stealer of hearts.
Hrishikesha: Lord of the senses. Bristling-haired.
Isham Idyam: Adorable One.
Jagannivasa: Cosmic Guardian (Shelter of the world).
Janardana: Granter of men's prayers.
Kamalapattraksha: Lotus eyed.
Keshava, Keshinisudana: Slayer of the demon Keshi; Destroyer of evil.
Madhava: God of fortune.
Madhusudana: Slayer of demon Madhu; Slayer of ignorance.
Mahataman: Sovereign Soul.

Prabhu: Lord or master.
Prajapati: Divine Father of countless offspring.
Purushottama: Supreme Spirit.
Sahasrabaho: Thousand armed.
Varshneya: Scion of the Vrishni clan.
Vasudeva: Lord of the world; the Lord as Creator/Preserver/Destroyer.
Vishnu: The All-Pervading Preserver.
Vishwamurte: Universe-bodied.
Yadava: Descendent of Yadu.
Yogeshvara: Lord of Yoga.

(B) List of Names used for Arjuna

Anagha: The sinless one.
Bharata: Descendent of King Bharata.
Bharatashreshtha: Best of the Bharatas.
Bharatarishabha: Bull of the Bharatas, that is, the best or most excellent of the descendents of the Bharata dynasty.
Bharatasattama: Foremost of the Bharatas.
Dehabhritan Vara: Supreme among the embodied.
Devadatta: Arjuna's Conch Shell.
Dhananjaya: Winner of wealth.
Gudakesha: Conqueror of sleep; Thick haired.
Kaunteya: Son of Kunti.
Kiritin: Diademed One.
Kurunandana: The pride or choice son of the Kuru dynasty.
Kurupravira: Great hero of the Kurus.
Kurusattama: Flower (best) of the Kurus.
Kurushreshtha: Best of the Kuru Princes.
Mahabaho: Mighty armed.
Pandava: Descendent of Pandu.
Parantapa: Scorcher of foes.
Partha: Son of Pritha.
Purusharishabba: Flower among men (Bull or chief among men).
Purushavyaghra: Tiger among men.
Savyasachin: One who wields the bow with either hand.

Notes to Essay 1

(2) Resources For Understanding The Bhagavad Gita

1. **The Bhagavad Gita** translated into English by Eknath Easwaran; 2nd edition (May 17, 2007); ISBN-13: 978-1586380199; 296 pages.

2. **Bhagavad-Gita: The Song of God**, translated into English by Swami Prabhavananda and Christopher Isherwood; July 2, 2002; ISBN-13: 978-0451528445; 144 pages.

3. **God Talks with Arjuna: The Bhagavad Gita translated (with commentary) into English** by Paramahansa Yogananda; (August 1, 2001) ; ISBN-13: 978-0876120316; 1224 pages.

4. **The Bhagavad Gita According to Gandhi** by Mahatma Gandhi (Paperback - May 19, 2009); ISBN-13: 978-1556438004; 245 pages.

5. **The Bhagavad Gita** by Lars Martin Fosse (Paperback - April 15, 2007); Bilingual edition - Original Sanskrit and translation; ISBN-13: 978-0971646674; 224 pages.

6. **The Bhagavad Gita** (Harvard University Press) by Franklin Edgerton; ISBN-13: 978-0674069251; 224 pages; Essays at the back explain a great deal about the Gita's subtle philosophy and its place in Hindu tradition.

7. **The Hindu Religious Tradition (The Religious Tradition of Man)** by Thomas J. Hopkins; ISBN-13: 978-0822100225; 168 pages. A general introduction to Hinduism.

8. **Upanisads** (Oxford World's Classics) by Patrick Olivelle; November 19, 1998; ISBN-13: 978-0192835765; 512 pages.

9. **The Oxford History of India by** V. A. Smith (Author), Percival Spear (Editor); ISBN-13: 978-0195612974; 964 pages.

10. **Mahabharata** by William Buck; ISBN-13: 978-0520227040; 440 pages.

Part 2

Other Essays On Cultural Pluralism

Quotable

"My Lord ! Enrich me with Knowledge…"
- *Quran: 20:114*

"And they will further say: "Had we but listened or used our intelligence, we should not (now) be among the Companions of the Blazing Fire!"
- *Quran: 67:10*

"The middle path is the way to wisdom."
- *Mevlana Rumi. Renowned Sufi mystic and poet (d. 1273).*

Essay 2

Religion and Spirituality in the Age of Science: Some Basic Aspects

1. Modes of Interpretation of Human Experience:

Every human baby from the moment of birth begins to feel and behave at some level or other. Its feelings, to begin with, are extremely nebulous and undifferentiated. The baby feels she is a helpless creature in a totally dark and unknown situation, yet, at intervals, she feels assured, secure and nourished by some caring 'other'. This unknown other is the mother as the epicenter of family protection and love. The family, however, is itself a part of a wider social unit that lives in a geographical space as well as an 'inner cultural space'. This inner world or space is filled with a mental picture of the world all around and a general idea of right and wrong. The general mental picture of the world and of what is right or wrong is expressed in sacred symbols, rites and approved patterns of behaviour. This inner world of the family enters into the innermost being of the growing child who may well be regarded as a microcosm reflecting the social macrocosm. Neither the outer geographical world nor the inner is a matter of choice but something given to every individual at birth. However, the inner world is subject to slow change in the course of time.

The given 'inner world' is the traditional group cultural response to some 'inherent and inalienable features' woven into the warp and woof of human life. These inseparable features are the birth, growth, decay and death, of living beings. The ceaseless struggle for survival, the flux of creation and destruction, the regular sequence of events, the power of reason to grasp their inter-connections jointly through imagination and observation, the variety and power of human emotions, the sexual instinct, the mutual attraction of the sexes, the experience of triumph and tragedy, the sense of morality and beauty (distinct from concrete judgments that something is moral or beautiful) and, finally, a persistent sense of wonder and mystery about the 'riddle of the universe'.

An abiding depth concern with the above mystery or riddle is an integral part of being fully human. Man cannot live by bread alone. Nor can he live by morality, legality, or science alone without any concern to solve or, at least, to relate himself in a stable and satisfying manner to the mysterious universe. This is done through an 'existential interpretation of the human situation'. Such interpretations have been supplied by myth, religion, philosophy and spirituality at different stages of human development.

Just as the child assimilates the natural language spoken in his milieu, he also assimilates the 'spiritual language' or the 'style of existential interpretation' of the milieu. Again, just as there is a plurality of natural languages there is a plurality of 'spiritual languages'. Every such language comprises myths, rites, rituals, to enable the individual to relate himself to the great mystery of the cosmos and thereby find inner strength and peace. No language of the spirit can claim that it alone renders transparent the essentially inscrutable mystery or riddle of the cosmos. In fact, every language of the spirit is instinct with 'paradox and faith', rather than clarity and proof. However, to those who have been born into and speak a particular 'language of the spirit' their mother tongue sounds sweetest of all.

The great myths of the human family are centered on superhuman beings, gods and goddesses or spirits embodied in the elemental forces of nature. These superhuman beings were either benign or malignant. Weak and helpless as was man, he could, supposedly, either cajole or overcome them through penance or magic. Such myths were the primitive archetypal response to the cosmic mystery. Myths were also morality tales that were meant to give moral guidance and direction to society. They, thus, reflected the conceptual level and basic attitudes that prevailed at the time. Myths appealed and helped not only ordinary humans but also ruling chiefs or kings, or the tribal elders who sincerely venerated the spiritual leaders and priests who were the traditional custodians and guardians of secret knowledge.

The great prophets of the Semitic tradition, the great seers and sages of the Aryan tradition in Iran and India, and the savants in Greece in later times, and the great sages of China, all in different styles and idioms, outgrew the stage of myth and ushered in a new style of response or existential interpretation of the human situation. This was the over powering conviction that the supernatural or superhuman world was the product of fancy and fear rather than a disclosure of the real truth. They all proclaimed that there was only one all powerful supreme Creator or Principle and He alone is the Source of all help and guidance. This was the core of Monotheism and it gradually became the common denominator of several theistic variants in the scattered human family.

Mythical elements from the infancy of the human species, however, have lingered on in its psyche. Myths still fascinate millions of humans because of their sheer dramatic power as well as the fact that myths originally satisfied some powerful inner impulses, attitudes and depth fancies of primitive man. Ethical Monotheism, on the other hand, sprang from a, relatively, much higher cerebral vision. Indeed, the official or orthodox version of Monotheism insists that God 'revealed' Himself to His chosen prophets, not that the aspiring seekers discovered God. As a matter of fact, the fascination for myth is so deeply embedded that all versions of ethical Monotheism generate their own 'folk versions'. This is the case with all historical religions.

The ideas and values of the human family, however, have continued to develop, thanks to an inner logic of ideas and of human creativity. The idea that one supreme God was the Creator and Sustainer of all that exists logically generated the idea that God had also created a set of laws and everything or event was bound to behave or act according to divinely ordained laws. In other words, the idea of a just and all powerful God, probably, helped in generating the idea of cosmic laws, as pointed out by the eminent British thinker, Whitehead, in *Science and the Modern World*.

This new dimension in the evolving idea of God led Arab Muslim scientists after the advent of Islam to lay primary stress upon systematic observation and experimentation to discover the divinely ordained laws of nature. The medieval Arab intellectuals in their creative phase were the pioneers of the inductive or scientific method that much later blossomed in Western Europe into the scientific revolution of the modern age.

The scientific method of enquiry and the resultant technological growth has given man awesome control over nature, but has also blinded him to the limitations and dangers of making the scientific method the only valid paradigm of seeking knowledge. A large number of highly intelligent, informed and intellectually honest creative minds in the Western world have become indifferent to any truth-claim that is, avowedly, not verifiable in the narrow scientific sense. This approach indirectly devalues the crucial significance and centrality of truth-claims in the spheres of religion, ethics, aesthetics and spirituality. Truth-claims in the above spheres are removed from the category of objective truth and dumped into the 'lower' category of subjective belief or opinion. This approach is a blessing and a curse as well. It gives a deathblow to intolerance and fanaticism, but it also inhibits reflective enquiry in matters relating to domains other than natural science and technology.

Man, however, has desires or yearnings other than the satisfaction of his physical or material needs. He also seeks moral goodness or virtue, beauty, fullness of truth and spiritual bliss. Pure science without philosophy, art and spirituality is like a banquet where only one single item or dish is served. Science reveals the empirical structure of the universe, but not its depth meaning, if there be any meaning at all. Even if it be the case that any significance the individual attaches to the universe, as an object of reflection, is, ultimately, his own projection, this issue remains important all the same. Biology can tell us about the nature of life and death up to a point. But it tells us nothing as to how to relate ourselves to life and death. The same remarks apply to the phenomenon of sex or sexual love.

2. Existential Interpretations of the Human Situation

Natural science concerns itself only with the empirical how and why of the regular sequence of observed events. But it does not concern itself at all with the depth significance of the various undeniable features of the cosmic process in its totality. The way in which one interprets the 'ontic dimensions' of the human situation, as mentioned above, deeply influences the human mindset or attitudinal orientation of the individual. On the other hand, the original personality bent of the individual deeply influences the way in which he or she interprets the above features. In other words, there is a mutuality of cause and effect or a dialectical relationship between personality orientation and existential interpretation. Different existential interpretations lead to different ways of relating oneself to the universe, or different basic life styles and their value or validity. Thus, for example, if one interprets the uniformity of nature as a mere accident which may well not have occurred one's scientific enquiry and investigation would tend to be concerned with practical or utilitarian research, while the scientist who finds design in the uniformity of nature is more likely to have purely theoretical concerns.

Similar remarks can be made about the pursuit of morality. All societies follow some moral code or the other. The codes may differ, but the basic sense of morality or the urge to follow the customary code is more or less permanent. We may very well hold that the human sense of morality is merely an accidental trait of the species, or we may view this trait as an expression of the Divine spark embedded in humankind. However, human motivation to pursue moral and spiritual values, probably, becomes far deeper and more compelling in the latter case. All spiritually oriented interpretations of this universal feature of the human species imply that the quest for value is not 'a cry in cosmic wilderness', but a profound insight into the inscrutable mystery of the universe. Belief in a Personal Creator God is only one form of this basic existential interpretation. But this interpretation acquires a unique advantage over all other interpretations. This is the practice of the I-Thou dialogue or spiritual prayer of religion, as distinct from non-creedal pure meditation or contemplation. And spiritual prayer is, perhaps, the most potent form of motivational reinforcement for humans.

3. Existential Interpretations and Poetic Metaphors

An existential interpretation resembles a poetic expression. Poetic metaphors do not give verifiable descriptions, but express feelings and emotions or describe images evoked by some object or situation or experience. The purpose of a poetic metaphor or poetry in general is self-expression, while that of an existential interpretation is to provide a convincing justification for life orientation to the universe as a whole, or to some significant aspect of it: death, conscience, sexual love etc. One may, for instance, interpret death as the final release from the tyranny or tragedy of life, or as the blind axe that destroys the tree of life, or as a change of abode or of bodily apparel, or as a destination of life, or as a welcome union with the Infinite. These interpretations give a poetic flavor, no doubt. The primary aim, however, is not to give pleasure, but to give meaning and direction to life. Likewise, the interpretation that life is a rocky battleground differs from the interpretation that life is a blooming garden, not merely in terms of the imagery but also in terms of its directive function. The first interpretation suggests the ethic of power and action; the second the ethic of beauty and of contemplation. Similarly, different interpretations of 'eros' will imply different codes of sexual conduct even when there may be agreement on all the relevant facts of life. Similarly, to interpret conscience as the voice of God within man or as the Divine spark makes for a different quality of man's inner life as well as his relationship to society than to interpret conscience as the 'internalized censor'. These existential interpretations enable man to conduct his life in a consistently meaningful manner. In one word, the primary function is the 'nurturing and grooming of the spirit' rather than the providing of 'aesthetic delight', although when the interpretation really grips the individual his entire being is suffused with a sense of profound joy, perhaps, more intense than aesthetic pleasure itself.

An existential interpretation is not a substitute for scientific explanation, just as a poetic metaphor is not a substitute for a scientific description or theory. But an existential interpretation, by virtue of its essential directive function, may well promote or impede scientific enquiry, or in some cases, even of a particular scientific hypothesis. For example, the interpretation that man is the vicegerent of God Who has granted man power and dominion over the rest of creation, including the sun and the moon, the wind and the ocean, tends to promote scientific enquiry, while the interpretation that man is only a self-glorifying worm born out of a cosmic accident, tend to inhibit the arduous and sustained labour which science demands. Indeed, as already mentioned, according to Whitehead, the theistic interpretation of the universe facilitated the belief in the ultimate rationality and orderliness of nature, as the creation of a perfect Creator. In any case, an existential interpretation always acts as an ethical motivator.

Existential interpretations of the universe must take into account the full range of the different features of the universe without suppressing any feature that may not harmonize with the favoured interpretation. This task presupposes a base of reliable factual knowledge as data. For instance, one must be aware of not only the beauty of nature, but also the extent of the aggression, pain and suffering inbuilt in the order of nature as such. For example, the interpretation that every particular event (in the literal sense) serves a cosmic purpose, or the interpretation that God loves and cherishes (in the literal sense) every single creature He creates does not grip or convince us in the face of such facts of life as the food chain or the enormous waste in the processes of nature. The existential interpretation, therefore, must not be based on selective data only.

Speculative philosophers and theologians, however, tend to ignore facts that do not fit into their conceptual picture by revising the ordinary meanings or uses of words and expressions of a particular natural language. They project new or extraordinary meanings to the words of the language in question. They say, for instance, that God's love for His creatures is not the same as maternal love, or that what appears as tragic or evil is an instrumental good in a larger context. In other words, philosophers and theologians redefine, qualify, and prune the ordinary or usual meanings of words and expressions we use. The theologian does so in a spirit of defensive reverence to the tradition, while the philosopher freely assess whether or not he 'resonates' to the religious interpretation in question. This activity, however, does not involve deductive or inductive reasoning but existential elucidation: illumination of one's hidden depth attitudes and inmost interpretative responses. The existential interpretation made by the philosopher is, thus, functionally similar to, but genetically different from religious faith. However, the philosopher's interpretation does partake of 'faith' in some sense and he cannot claim that it can be proved.

An existential interpretation of some kind or other is unavoidable. We can only opt for this or that interpretation but we cannot opt to do away with interpretation as such. We may claim to avoid all contact with metaphysics or religion, which we may view as the hallmarks of a pre-scientific mentality. Yet the fact is that we cannot live as integrated human beings without some kind of worldview or total perspective on the cosmos. And this total perspective, be it religious or philosophical, is at bottom always an existential interpretation of the 'ontic dimensions' of human experience: cosmic law and order, the mysteries of birth, growth and death, the beauty as well as the fury of nature, good and evil, joy and tragedy.

4. Religion, Spirituality and Inner Integration

As previously stated, every religion offers a basic view of, or perspective on, the universe and prescribes a basic value system exemplified in social institutions. Religion gives a sense of group solidarity, support and a sense of direction to the individual in his life journey. Yet, most individuals face some doubts or spiritual perplexities about the purpose of human life or the existence of a loving Creator who permits so much suffering and pain in the universe. Theologians (who may well have passed through similar inner perplexities themselves) try to explain the mystery without questioning the basic framework of their own religion. Philosophers resort to free enquiry and may also help the perplexed. But there are others who still remain dissatisfied and perplexed by the conceptual revisions offered by philosophers. Among this group some turn to poetry or music or some other creative engagement that gives them sense of purpose and direction to their life. Some other highly sensitive souls in this group are dawn to the lore of mystical experience and Divine grace. They honestly believe and fervently hope that intense prayer, meditation and self-purification will attract the gift of Divine grace and blessings that will flood their inner being with inner 'peace that passeth all understanding'. They are the mystics and they are found in all religious traditions without exception.

Studies in comparative mysticism and the direct testimony of the great mystics of different religions confirm that the basic structure of the mystical experience is the same in all cases. However the symbols and the concrete content of the mystical experience relate to the antecedent beliefs or cherished traditions of the mystic concerned. The experience dissolves the old conceptual perplexities of the individual. The mystic, thereafter, loses his previous concern with reason because no perplexity remains in his mind. He also loses all interest (if he, at all, previously had in the past) in acquiring any supernatural powers to benefit himself, or others. (Ironically, others believe he does have such powers).

The religious experience produces a deep inner peace and an unshakeable spontaneous assurance that the cosmic process and history are not blind changes, but a journey leading to a blessed destination. The mystic becomes existentially certain that good shall ultimately prevail over evil even though one may not be able to foresee and control the intervening stages of this tortuous consummation.

Every individual has to make sense of these features in some way or other. Even to hold that these features are just due to blind chance and nothing more is a way of making sense out of brute facts. And this amounts to making an 'existential response', as I understand the term. I have dealt with this issue in depth in my earlier work, *Quest for Islam*, first published in 1977.

Every religion comprises a world view and a system of morals. A true believer is one who stands spontaneously committed to the world view and the correlated value system and acts accordingly without any intellectual disputation. However, the believer, inevitably, interprets these beliefs and values in the traditional conceptual framework of one's milieu and also one's own level of understanding and information. Every religious tradition has a common vocabulary or idiom, but words, such as God, creation, revelation, incarnation, rebirth, heaven, hell (that do not have any fixed and clear meaning) remain in circulation in cultural space as if they had fixed meanings; just as currency notes in any independent economy have fixed denominations. Since this is not the case, controversy and disagreement are unavoidable even within one's own religion and between different religions.

Many souls, however, cannot avoid an inner perplexity over some doctrine or moral rule of their cherished faith. They seek and often get inner peace through reflecting, clarifying or qualifying their beliefs, but sometimes they do not succeed. The agonizing perplexity of some highly sensitive truth seekers sometimes ends in a unique psycho-physical experience of quite shattering proportions. They report back that some mysterious light engulfed them and they lost the sense of being an isolated ego, and an ecstatic joy and inner peace and sense of oneness with the cosmos overwhelmed them. They all say that this experience cannot be explained to others who have not had a similar experience. These are the mystics and seers who are found in all religions down the ages. They, however, give more or less similar reports of their experience, though this is punctuated by different symbols and images.

The experience leaves the mystics deeply and fully convinced that the cosmos was not a mere accident 'full of sound and fury signifying nothing', but a gigantic process, somehow, related to the human quest for truth, goodness and beauty. In other words, the experience inwardly and fully convinced them that the human quest for value and the pain and suffering and struggle were not accidental or isolated events in a chaotic meaningless desert of brute existence, but that very cry of the human heart for the cause of truth, goodness, beauty and justice is a link in a great chain of human aspiration and quest for value.

This quest has its ultimate source in a trans-empirical Being/Power, whose nature and modes of operation and whose plans or purposes are beyond human understanding. However, despite all appearances to the contrary, one may well cherish an inner faith (without violating any axiom or logical reasoning) that good shall prevail over evil, though one may be unable to foresee when and how this will happen. The mystical experience is open to all humans, but some highly sensitive souls are more prone to have it.

5. INTERNAL SIMILARITY AND DIFFERENCES IN MYSTICAL EXPERIENCES

The concrete content of the mystical experience is always in terms of the mystic's own language of the spirit and the cherished symbols and myths of his cultural environment. Every religion has several versions. The differentia of the mystical version lies in its inwardness, and its power and intensity of faith that blossoms into spontaneous action. The mystic lives and acts not because of any fear of external authority, or lure of reward in this world or hereafter, but as one following the inner dictates of a purified self impregnated by Divine presence in the depths of his soul.

A 19th century English writer has said that Mysticism takes three distinct forms, though they may overlap or not, as the case may be: *Theosophy, Theopathy* and *Theurgy*. I shall follow this division in what follows.

The Theosophical Form of Mysticism: As already mentioned, the essential core of every religion is a worldview and a correlated value system. The founding father of the tradition does not intellectually and systematically formulate them; he is inwardly led to them after a long existential search to unravel the mystery of the human situation in the cosmos. The founding father goes through a super-mystical experience, which results in a spiritual rebirth, as it were. An overpowering conviction develops in him that he has glimpsed into the supreme mystery of the universe. He encapsulates the overpowering conviction born of his experience into a key statement or creed. In the course of time this creed flowers into a developing conceptual and value system or Theology.

The process is creative, to begin with. But with the passage of time it becomes repetitive. Human creativity does not stop, but the creativity and inner vitality of racial or ethnic groups waxes and wanes. The barbarians of yesterday take over from the elite of today in the flow of history. Moreover, knowledge grows, new questions, issues and challenges arise and new fields of enquiry emerge, new thought patterns, new interpretations, new methods of production, new social and political ideals create new perplexities and new solutions. Traditional theologians partially succeed but eventually fail to cope with the complexities of an ever-growing thought system and challenges coming from different schools of thought or the emergence of new social, political and economic forces.

Some highly creative souls are gifted both with a powerful poetic imagination as well as a sharp logical mind. When such a complex and versatile person is visited by dreams or some paranormal psycho-physical experience in the waking sate he takes it as direct or confirmation of the theological truth-claim or creed that had defied his pure theological disputation and reasoning without the use of imagination, metaphor or myth. The combination or intersection of the way of the theologian and the way of the mystic gives birth to Theosophy. Thus, Theosophy is Theology impregnated by Mysticism.

Theosophy teaches techniques of reaching states of altered consciousness or awareness, prophetic dreams, paranormal communion with human and extra-human beings, living or dead, intensive meditation, and similar other occult practices that are supposed to open new doors of perception that are not accessible to the theologian, philosopher or scientist. The practitioners of Theosophy are least concerned if their truth-claims are not susceptible of validation through empirical investigation or intellectual enquiry. However, they stress the need for active guidance from an accomplished spiritual guide.

The Theopathic Form of Mysticism: Theopathy is the sustained and intensive culture of the spiritual, moral and emotional sides of the individual soul. The ordinary believer habitually strives to follow the prescribed moral code and is motivated by both fear of punishment and hope of reward. The mystic makes an all-consuming love for God the sole motive of all his actions. He seeks to live in the constant presence of God, the Supreme beloved. He feels he would be unworthy of nearness to the Creator unless he thoroughly cleans his soul in order to remove and purify evil elements that lie unknown and undetected by himself or others. The Theopathic mystic may or may not be concerned with Theosophy or Theology. His focus is always on self-awareness to its depths, the culture of inner attitudes and impulses, the taming of the ego, the conquest of pride and anger, growth of altruistic love, universal compassion, contentment, patience and above all truthfulness to the highest degree. Unless he sincerely labours to cultivate the above virtues, he deems himself quite unworthy of nearness to God. To reach this stage rather than to understand the nature of the Creator is the burning concern and aspiration of the Theopathic mystic. Prophet Muhammad ﷺ is, indeed, the fount of Theopathic mysticism in Islam.

The Theurgical Form of Mysticism: The central plank of Theurgical Mysticism is the belief that the all powerful and loving Creator is always actively concerned to help His creatures if they petition the Creator for Divine intervention in the natural course of events. Theurgy gives special importance to the efficacy of prayers by mystics and saints on behalf of their clients. In other words, Theurgy believes in miracles through Divine help.

Theurgy has always been much more popular than either Theosophy or Theopathy. The common man is hardly bothered with the mystery of Divine attributes, love for God, duty for the sake of duty, the idea of dying before death, and so on. He wants God, the All Loving and powerful Father, ever to give sweets and wipe the tears of the believers.

To my mind, the true or proper vocation of the mystic is not to aspire to perfect knowledge of God (*gnosis*), but rather the aspiration to love and serve God's creation as best as he can, without seeking any supernatural power to benefit himself or others. Ironically, the common folk venerate mystics just because they believe that mystics do have such power.

6. MYSTICISM AND ISLAM

The Theopathic form of mysticism was intensively and extensively practised in early Islam. Hazrat Ali (d. 661), the close companion of Prophet Muhammad ﷺ and the first of the line of imaams (spiritual leaders in *Shia* Islam), Hasan Basri (d. 728) and Imaam Jafar Sadiq (d. 765) are the father figures of Islamic mysticism (*Sufism*). They were followed by Shibli (d. 846), Dhun Nun Misri (d. 859), Al-Bistami (d. 875), Al-Nuri (d. 908), Junayd (d. 910). They were all outstanding mystics but had to undergo considerable suffering as suspected heretics. Mansur Hallaj (d. 922) and Suhrawardi Al-Maqtul (d. 1191) were actually put to death on the charge of heresy. Al-Ghazzali (d. 1111) was the greatest reconciler and creative bridge builder between Philosophy, Theology and Mysticism. Ibn Arabi (d. 1240) was the greatest ever-creative systematic theosophical mystic and Jalaluddin Rumi (d. 1273) the greatest philosopher poet and theosophist in the Islamic world.

The *Sufi* anecdote in Persian poetry is the most powerful medium for conveying the thought and practice of the *Sufi* saints and for exhorting Muslims and others to walk on the path of righteousness and universal harmony. The anecdote is in the form of a dialogue or story. What is important is not the historicity of the story but its message or insight.

The *Sufi* anecdotes seem to lack the normative status of the authentic reports about the sayings or doings of the Prophet ﷺ or of the *shariah*. However, several eminent *Sufis*, such as Jalaluddin Rumi (d. 1273), Fariduddin Attar (d. 1229), Shaikh Saadi (d. 1291) and Jami (d. 1492) have been highly venerated normative figures in the Islamic world. Yet, neither philosophy nor mysticism could ever attain to the dominant status of Islamic Jurisprudence. In other words, the power of the theologian and the jurist prevailed over the power of the mystic and the thinker in historical Islam, despite the tremendous popular veneration of the *Sufi* saints because of their presumed supernatural powers and mystical closeness to God. I mention a few anecdotes of striking beauty and power in the notes.[1]

It would be necessary to reconstruct the different versions of the *Sufi* thought and value systems to render them optimally fruitful for the modern age. Just to give one instance, the classical *Sufi* concept of, say, humility, self-abnegation, voluntary poverty, trust in God, withdrawal etc will not hold water today in the literal sense. A well-balanced spiritual life needs life affirmation and disinterested 'valuegenic' or purely ethically motivated action, not withdrawal and seclusion. Likewise, trust in God need not exclude the 'tying of the camel' or the prudent ordering and planning of time or money. The need for voluntary poverty has to be understood in the context of the present technological age.

The fact of the matter is that 'the good life' demands a multi-dimensional integrated approach rather than exclusive concern with some selected intrinsic value or virtue. In the final analysis, therefore, almost all the *Sufi* interpretations of the basic spiritual values would have to be reconstructed in order to make them relevant to the modern age of science and technology. The core or essence of Theopathic *Sufism* will, however, continue to shine by its own light, and this core is the stress on inwardness, on sensitivity to the wiles of the ego, the fear of the inner Satan rather than of external evil mongers, the general need for the culture of the raw emotions and instincts, the stress upon the inner quality of obligatory prayers rather than their mere regular external performance, the stress on work ethic (*akl e halaal*) and social responsibility rather than mere performance of rituals, and finally, the inner realization that the love of God is best reflected in unconditional human love for God's creatures, without presuming that there is only one exclusive language of or path to salvation.

7. THE IMPACT OF SCIENCE ON RELIGION

Fabricating and using material tools, cherishing some sort of world-picture, practicing some code of morality and creating art, have been integral features of human life and culture from the most primitive times to the present. The fabrication and use of tools for self-protection and sustenance through agriculture and some relief from the inclemency of the climate became possible only when man acquired a set of more or less correct factual beliefs or knowledge of nature. Anthropology and cultural history make it clear that natural science, which is the indispensable foundation of all technological progress, developed much more slowly and haltingly than art, morality, mythology, theology or philosophy. This is why the graph of human cultural development, generally speaking, reveals that while the human family made tremendous strides in achieving excellence in art, literature, religion, philosophy and spirituality, its level of control over nature and its fund of scientific knowledge (in the modern developed sense) remained, relatively, meager.

A momentous change took place in Western Europe with the advent of what may best be called the 'scientific revolution' of the 18th century. The scientific revolution brought about a radical change in the role of science in human life as a whole. The essence of this revolution lies in the crystallization of the scientific method of enquiry and investigation: accurate sense observation, quantitative experimentation to discover the regular connection and sequence of events, formulation of hypotheses or empirical laws whose consequences can be deduced in theory and verified in practice. This gradually led to a conceptual unification of the entire range of human sense experience and a method of transforming what is given into what is desired. In other words, the focus of human concern shifted from contemplation and logical reflection upon the real to its manipulation and control for satisfying human needs. The seeds of this pragmatic approach had been sown in the creative phase of Arab experimental science in the medieval period much before the advent of Renaissance and Reformation in Western Europe. However several centuries elapsed before the full flowering of the scientific method took place in Western Europe.

The tremendous success in the application of the scientific method has changed the model or paradigm of knowledge. The ancient and medieval paradigm was derived from either deductive logic or revealed articles of faith; sense perception was secondary. The new paradigm was based on the postulate that belief turns into knowledge only when the belief can be verified according to the standard procedures of science. Those truth claims that could not be so established began to be looked upon as opinions or views, or as feelings and attitudes rather than as instances of knowledge. Such beliefs that the soul survives the body after death, or that there is a Creator, or even simple ethical or aesthetic judgments that cannot be proved in the scientific sense stood devalued in relation to the verifiable propositions of natural science and the logically demonstrable propositions of pure Mathematics. In short, knowing how things happen at the material or physical level became more prestigious and important than why they happen or what purpose they serve. This meant that the study of natural phenomena and their interconnections was all that was important for study and research, while all other issues of art, ethics, religion, philosophy and history should be left in the domain of personal and private concern of the individual. What became crucially important was the knowledge of actual causal connections (which knowledge is essential for controlling nature) rather than trying to settle the question whether the actual causal connection is due to Divine providence or is just a brute fact.

The above approach implied that experimental science was a body of useful knowledge while philosophy and theology were useless. Man could well control nature through surrender to natural law instead of endlessly arguing and debating (in vain) if the said laws have been created by a Supreme Creator. That the laws operate is undeniable, all else is pure speculation and beyond proof. Therefore, controversy is futile. In addition to the above factor the practical success of science and technology also had a great impact on the modern mind. In Western Europe science and technology began to conquer disease, hunger, poverty, illiteracy, superstition, intolerance, gender inequality, and such other long established evils. The ancient and medieval view was that God had created poverty and wealth just as He had created mountains and valleys, or male and female and other pairs of attributes or qualities. But the new sciences of Economics, Sociology, Anthropology, Eugenics and Genetics etc. helped open out new ways of looking at the human situation; that man could himself sit at the wheel and steer the engine of progress in desired directions, instead of passively submitting to a hypothetical Divine providence.

The progress of physical sciences led to vastly improved, quicker and more productive methods of mass production, quicker transportation and communication; the progress of the biological and chemical sciences led to the ever-growing conquest of disease and better agriculture. Facilities of travel enabled social scientists to study at close range and with great accuracy the thought, religious and cultural patterns of scattered and distant societies and to cultivate the rare virtue of intellectual empathy for plural cultures. The disciplines of Comparative religion and philology emerged. Perhaps, the greatest cultural emergent of all times was the scientific concept of biological and geological evolution. The combined and cumulative effect of all these factors led to a crisis of belief in the best-informed and enlightened souls in Western Europe. Some thoughtful and brave individuals became straight atheists or disbelievers in religion and spirituality; some turned anti-Christian but not anti-religious as such; some turned into positivistic

Humanists, some turned to Mysticism while still others attempted to redefine the essence of religious experience and faith. Perhaps, the most significant and lasting results of the persistent turmoil in the inner world of several highly sensitive and virtuous souls of Western Europe was the birth of the idea of humanistic tolerance and the idea of redefining the proper jurisdiction of religion. This led to the idea of the principled separation of church and state.

8. The Idea of Religion in the Medieval and modern Periods

The separation of the functions of religion and of the state became fully de jure in the new world when the sprawling British colony in North America broke away from the mother country and emerged as the very first sovereign secular democratic United States of America after the Revolution in 1776. The separation of religion from the state and from political activity does not mean the rejection of religion or spirituality. The new idea was that the essence of religion lies in existential awe and surrender to the cosmic mystery, and that religious piety lies in following the cherished basic spiritual and moral values rather than a set of some fixed and closed code of laws mandated by some Authority. The founding fathers of the American constitution never for a moment imaged themselves as atheists or non-Christians; they affirmed only that no religion should claim to be the sole established or official religion of the state as such. They were quite emphatic that their stand was not the rejection of religion but only the rejection of the medieval idea of the union of state and religion.

The above idea of religion has been called 'religious liberalism' and the idea, in the course of time, has captured the imagination of the greater part of the human family. However, several Muslim quarters do not appreciate this logic and persist in what has been termed 'religious fundamentalism'. In the final analysis, the choice between fundamentalism and liberalism in the sphere of religion cannot be settled in a conclusive manner; the choice is a matter of the total worldview or existential perspective of the individual. This, again, requires tolerance or the agreement to differ. However, this much should be conceded by all sides to the dispute that the separation of politics from religion should not be confused with separation of politics from morality. Secular politics does not necessarily imply amoral or immoral politics in the pursuit of naked power. Moreover, though religions differ in theology they, to a remarkable extent, agree on fundamental moral values. In fact, many honest religious skeptics and even atheists function morally and responsibly, while self-styled religious believers function like thieves and thugs. A broad democratic agreement is, thus, quite possible in the sphere of public morality and governance, though almost impossible in the case of religion. This insight into the human situation is the basic justification for the separation of the church and the state. And it is certainly not the rejection of religion or spirituality as such.

Secularism, as a political concept, holds that the state should not advocate or oppose any particular religion. However, it does oppose the 'fundamentalist' version of religion, no matter what the religion may be. The term 'religious fundamentalism' in modern parlance means treating a particular religion as a total code or blueprint of right conduct for every sphere of life. This approach bears the seeds of endemic tensions in plural societies, while 'religious liberalism' promotes tolerance, intellectual honesty, authentic spirituality and responsible autonomy to the individual and society.

9. THE VISION OF THE FOUNDING FATHERS OF THE INDIAN CONSTITUTION:

The founding fathers of the Indian constitution were inspired by the idea of secular democracy. Secularism, as a political concept, has a definite and clear-cut connotation. However, Muslims stand at the crossroads of religious liberalism and religious fundamentalism. This was always the case, but the stakes are much greater today due to the complexities of the modern age. Muslims must not commit the fallacy of reducing Islam to one favoured model (that, supposedly, meets all the requirement of the modern age) and then just dismiss the idea of secular democracy as unnecessary or redundant for 'true' Muslims. Exactly the same remarks apply to those Hindu quarters that decry Nehru's alleged penchant for imitating the West.

Religious fundamentalism appeals, primarily, to those Muslims or Hindus who see clearly the limitations and failures of the West, but miss its achievements and positive values. The fundamentalists are under the delusion that when they capture power a golden age will commence. Little do they realize that power corrupts not only secular politicians but others as well. In the final analysis, despite all its limitations and defects (writ large on the contemporary Indian scene) liberal democracy is the best antidote against corrupt rulers. Democracy alone provides for their peaceful removal and for promoting the long-term welfare of the masses.

The term, 'Islamic Liberalism', as I use it in my writings covers both Theology and Mysticism in the entire career of Islam, provided they stress universal compassion and unconditional love in their value system. In this broad sense, Ibn Sina (d. 1037), Jalaluddin Rumi (d. 1273), Fariduddin Attar (d. 1229), Hafiz (d. 1390), Ghalib (d. 1869), Sir Syed (d. 1898), Shibli (d. 1914), Amir Ali (d. 1928), Iqbal (d. 1938), Azad (d. 1958) are all Islamic liberals of varying degrees and shades. The quintessential eternal Islam needs continual redefinition and restatement, ever receptive to the continuing growth of human knowledge and insight. The idea of a fixed or closed version of 'Islamic Liberalism' strikes me as self-contradictory.

CONCLUDING REMARKS

In today's global world the only credible form of religion or spirituality is the theory and practice of 'Spirit-centred Humanism'. Spiritualized morality is non-controversial, unlike theological morality. Different organized religions and sects may practice and enjoy different forms and patterns of worship, devotion and meditation, cherish their own distinctive symbols, visit their chosen holy shrines and calendars, or even adhere to their personal laws (so far as this does not violate 'genuine' public interest), but they may not repudiate or violate the essential oneness of the human family and the inalienable responsibility and accountability of every individual to work for the welfare of all creation as a manifestation of the Supreme Being. This is, precisely, the underlying basic message of the *Quran*. This message has a timeless appeal and validity as an intrinsic value and as the fixed coordinate of any derivative or instrumental rules that the Prophet ﷺ or other normative authorities may have prescribed at any stage of its long career. Exactly the same remarks apply to the Gita's core concept of 'disinterested righteous action' (*nishkama saatvic karma*), Gautama Buddha's core concept of 'continual inner awareness' (*vipasna*), and the historical Jesus' stress on 'living in the presence of God'. These core ideas are found in the highest versions of all religions.

The great *Sufi* saints and Indian seers and sages of the past were quite ignorant of modern science and technology and their information was much less than the level of common knowledge today, but their minds and hearts were founts of love and wisdom. To spread humanistic love, to promote the welfare of the entire human family without any distinction of 'we' and 'they', to exhort all (irrespective of their religion or sect) to feel and respond to the presence of the Supreme Spirit in their own soul rather than to convert others to formal Islam or any other religion was their principal mission of life. It is another matter that (due to some social and political factors) common people, especially the weaker and under-privileged segments of society, freely embraced formal Islam. The fact that the Sikh scriptures abound in *Sufi* texts, and followers of all religions deeply revere saints like Kabir and Sai Baba of Shridi is eloquent testimony to this truth and the genius of the Indian people.

About two hundred years ago Ram Mohan Roy and his distinguished associates founded the Brahmo Samaj movement in Bengal and redefined modern Hindu religion and spirituality for India as a whole. A galaxy of intellectual and spiritual luminaries arose in modern

India. Gandhi, Tagore, Rajagopalachari, Nehru *et al* are the finest fruits of the Bengal Renaissance. The Muslims were left behind due to various reasons, but Sir Syed, eventually, rose to the occasion and bravely tried to redefine Islam and Islamic piety for the modern age. But his dreams have been fulfilled only partially. One can hardly say that Iqbal and Azad have had the same impact on Indian Islam as Gandhi, Tagore and Nehru have had on Modern Hinduism. However, I am not pessimistic about the future.

Notes To Essay 2
Religion and Spirituality in the Age of Science: Some Basic Aspects

1. Prophet Moses and the Shepherd: Moses once came across a young shepherd who, while his flock was grazing, was deeply engrossed in expressing his devotion to God as if God had physical attributes. Annoyed by the ignorant impudence of the lad Moses admonished him to desist from such blasphemy. On learning of his unwitting sin the lad uttered a cry of remorse and fled into the jungle, leaving behind his flock. Immediately afterwards God revealed to Moses that he was wrong in chiding the shepherd who was engaged in true communion with God. The Creator also admonished Moses that his own conception of the Divine Being might not be adequate to the glory of God. **(Rumi)**

The implication is that one should never equate one's conception of God with God Himself. Nor should one become an unwitting prey to spiritual conceit. There is always the danger of worshipping one's subjective conception of God without realizing that one thus commits idolatry.

2. Hazrat Ali and His Foe: While a battle was on Ali felled an armed opponent and was about to slay him. Just at that point the foe spat on Ali's face. Ali withdrew and spared his antagonist's life on the ground that this act of the enemy had aroused in him personal hatred and anger and a desire for revenge. Ali offered to fight after his anger cooled down. Awe struck and dumb founded, the enemy fell down at Ali's feet and begged pardon and desired to convert to Islam. **(Rumi)**

The point of the anecdote is that God can be reached through different paths, provided the seeker is sincere.

3. One day Gabriel came to learn that God was specially pleased at a worshipper's devotions and prayers, but did not disclose the identity of the worshipper. Gabriel was curious to know him and searched every nook and corner where a good Muslim could be found in the act of prayer. But he found no one. He then beseeched the Lord to remove his perplexity. God directed him to go to a particular spot. There Gabriel found an idol worshipper praying. Shocked, the angel thought he had misunderstood God's directions. He again prayed to God Who confirmed that the idol worshipper was, indeed, the right person, despite some wrong notions of the idol worshipper. **(Fariduddin Attar)**

The point of the anecdote is that God can be reached through different paths, provided the seeker is sincere.

4. Rabia Basri's Strange Behaviour: The lady saint, Rabia (d. 801), was once seen walking on the street with a bowl of water in one hand and a plate of burning coals in the other. When asked for an explanation of her strange behaviour, she said she was going to quench the fires of hell with the bowl of water, and to put paradise on fire with the burning coals. The reason why she wanted to do was that people may do good and shun evil without desire for reward or fear of punishment. **(Aflaki)**

The point of the anecdote is that love of God is all that ought to matter for the true believer rather than belief in heaven or hell.

5. Prophet Abraham and His Guest: Prophet Abrahamﷺ would not take any food unless there was some guest. Once no guest appeared for a number of days and Abraham went out in search. He met an old man in the valley and politely invited him to a meal at his house. The stranger had heard of Abraham's hospitality and readily accepted. When food was served the guest started to eat without first invoking God's name. The host chided the guest. Thereupon the visitor said that he was a fire worshipper and had never been taught to mention God's name before starting to eat. Abraham got even more angry and abused the old man and was about to turn him out. Immediately afterwards an angel informed Abraham that God was severely displeased at this unkindness to the fire worshipper. Did Abraham not realize that God had granted the fire worshipper long life and sustenance despite his false beliefs? **(Saadi)**

The point of the anecdote is that one should show solicitude and respect to all humans irrespective of their religion.

6. The Ardent Pilgrim: A good Muslim started upon a journey by foot to the *Kaaba*. In the exuberance of religious feeling he started offering prostrations to God after every third or fourth step. He reasoned that this method would enhance his status. Soon he heard an angel's voice declaring that he had fallen into Satan's trap. Satan had deluded the pilgrim that this way he was giving something to God. The angel said that God would have been more pleased if the pilgrim had done a good turn to his fellow men instead of doing excessive prostrations.
(Saadi)

7. Here are three short selections from the poetry of Rumi and Saadi:

(a) *Tell me Muslims, what should be done?*

I don't know how to identify myself

I am neither Christian, nor Jewish

Neither pagan, nor Muslim.

I don't hail from the East or the West.

I am neither from land, nor sea

I am not a creature of this world ...
(Rumi)

(b) All children of Adam are limbs of one single body since they have been created from the same essence. When one limb is in pain the entire body suffers. One not sensitive to the suffering of others is not fit to be regarded as human.
(Saadi)

Notes to Essay 2

(c) To worship God is, essentially, to serve humanity rather than to carry the rosary and the prayer carpet or to wear patched clothes.
(Saadi)

Essay 3

Unity In Variety In The Sphere Of Religious Faith

An impartial study of different religions shows the underlying unity in the diversity of religions. All religions are attempts to satisfy the human sense of wonder and awe at the inscrutable mystery of the universe. This common function produces the unity while the diverse conditions in which different religions arise and grow produce the diversity. However the differences in belief, on a deeper analysis, turn out to be merely different ways of performing the same function in the basic economy of human life. In other words, different beliefs turn out to be different versions or species of a more basic generic belief. For instance, the belief that God reveals His will to a human messenger or prophet and the belief that God incarnates Himself in human form are two different versions or species of the more fundamental conviction that God intervenes in history to guide man on the right path. Neither of the two beliefs is fully intelligible or transparent to the human mind and both are full of mystery. Likewise, the basic Aryan belief in repeated rebirths in this world and the basic Semitic belief in one single eschatological rebirth are twin species of the more fundamental conviction that as a man soweth, so shall he reap in one form or the other. Both beliefs posit the continuity of life, either in the 'linear' or the 'cyclical' sense, and both motivate man to the same end.

In like manner, the Semitic concept of salvation as everlasting felicity in heaven and the Hindu concept of *'moksh'* as also the Buddhist concept of *'nirvana'* for all their structural or conceptual difference perform the same function: the promotion of moral rectitude. The principle of unity and variety also applies to the value systems of different religions. The moral codes vary in several matters but the basic values are the same.

A large proportion of sincere Muslim believers have a very confused idea of polytheism or '*shirk*'. They suppose, for instance, that all Hindus are polytheists and that all Christians (despite being 'people of the book') are also polytheists. But this is not at all the self-image of an authentic Christian believer. He is very clear that he believes in one Supreme Being or God. The same remarks apply to Hindu believers. They certainly do not equate idols with the Supreme Being or *Brahman* or *Bhagwan*. The idol worshipper (rightly or wrongly) believes the idol is a 'locus' of the Supreme or some aspect of the Supreme, not the Supreme Being as such. The formal monotheist hardly suspects numerous believers in One God also equate their own subjective conception of God with the Supreme Being as He is in Himself beyond all human comprehension. Conceptual fanaticism, as pointed out by the great *Sufi* poet, Jalaluddin Rumi, and others, is a subtle form of idolatry that escapes detection.

Qualitative differences do exist between different religions and different versions of the same religion. However, every version sounds true to the believer concerned. And this sentiment must be respected and viewed with sympathy, even when one continues to cherish one's own. Every great religious tradition has plural versions, and their higher versions are found to be remarkably close to each other. Sectarian enthusiasm generally prompts polemical believers to contrast the higher version of their own religion with the lower version or versions of other religions. This results in an unfair and misleading comparison. It is also essential to avoid the evil of spiritual pride that quite, unknowingly, tempts believers to think they are the exclusive custodians of truth. Granting equal status to other religious traditions, perhaps, tends to lower one's unique importance in the scheme of things.

Every world religion may be said to be a spiritual seed that has grown and blossomed in a particular soil. The unity of the different religions is due to the essential similarity in the seeds of different religions, while diversity due to differences in the soil. The spiritual seed of all religions is, ultimately, rooted in 'existential wonder', the supreme Divine gift to man. All world religions are, in the final analysis, human responses to the cosmic mystery. In other words, all religions are different languages of the human spirit seeking to express man's experience of wonder and mystery, when he contemplates himself and the universe. Just as every language has its own grammar and vocabulary, so does every religion have its own characteristic and recurring metaphors and modes of interpreting the mystery. The concrete interpretation may differ not only in details but sometimes even in a more basic sense. Yet, as pointed out above, even these basic differences are rooted in a still more fundamental similarity or unity of interpretation and function. Hence as long as religious interpretation reinforces or deepens man's quest for value the label of the religion is unimportant. To give an analogy, if lovers feel deeply fulfilled through Sanskrit poetry there is no point in prescribing German or Arabic for this purpose. If, however, a particular religion does not provide complete inner satisfaction but generates doubt in the individual and if the doubt persists in spite of all possible efforts to resolve it, then the basic function of religion is not served. In such a case the individual should no longer try to cling to the interpretation in question. The criterion of religious truth is existential. Religion must inspire man joyfully to accept the burden of life. It is better to be an authentic Hindu, Jain or Sikh believer with an integrated personality and possessing the deep inner peace that 'passeth all understanding' than to be a Christian or Muslim, who merely verbalizes a creed without any commitment.

The approach that all non-Muslims are either disbelievers (*Kaafirun*) or polytheists (*mushrikeen*) with the exception of the 'people of the Book' is incompatible with numerous *Quranic* verses quoted in previous pages, to the effect, that God has sent His messengers to all peoples in all ages. The *Quran* specifically points out that only a few of them have been named. There must have been Indian, African and Chinese prophets. Some Islamic quarters hold that even if Ram, Krishna and others were prophets the Hindus cannot be included among the 'people of the book'. This sounds rather arbitrary in the light of the fact that the ancient Indian tradition accepts the Vedas as revealed (*sruti*) while other religious books or laws as comments or opinions (*smriti*) on the revealed truths. Moreover, there are striking parallels and similarities in expressions used in the *Quran* and the *Upanishads*, no less than between the *Quran* and the Old Testament. Indeed many attributes of God are identical in the *Upanishads* and the *Quran*. Thus Muslims are spiritually akin not merely to the Jews and Christians but all religions are spiritually akin. No discrimination is warranted between religions of Semitic, Indian and Chinese origin.

An abiding depth concern with the mystery of existence is an integral part of being human. Man cannot live without air, water and food, but he does not live by them alone. Nor can he live by morality, legality or science alone. Man yearns to find or give some central over-arching significance to the cosmos. The quest for grasping 'cosmic significance' is the essence of religion and spirituality.

Just as there is a plurality of natural languages there exist plural patterns of cosmic significance. They may be called diverse languages of the spirit among the human family. The child effortlessly assimilates the spiritual language spoken in his milieu as naturally as he assimilates the mother tongue, body gestures, and moral and aesthetic norms. All spiritual languages serve the same purpose of giving solace, peace, courage, stability in the midst of the stresses and storms of life and all promote the inner growth and purification of the individual. All languages of the spirit, therefore, merit the highest respect and they must be allowed to grow in the atmosphere of freedom. This is the sum and substance of Humanism.

Every language of the spirit comprises myths, rites and rituals. Nevertheless the Mystery of existence remains. Theology also fails to remove some perplexities. The mystics claim that their perplexities have been fully resolved. But it is significant that every mystic speaks in his own traditional language of the spirit and uses the concepts, categories and symbols current in his own tradition. Moreover, no mystical experience renders any mystic infallible in his reasoning or judgments, or protects him against disease and suffering, or confers on him any extraordinary powers to achieve normal human goals without reliance on normal causality. Folklore certainly invests mystics with such powers, but the mystics themselves persistently deny this popular myth.

There is a natural tendency to think that one's own language of the spirit for describing the great mystery of existence bears a more accurate likeness to the reality. Moreover to concede that all languages serve the same function to the same extent decreases one's group pride and sense of uniqueness in history. One tends to overlook the glaring fact that every language of the spirit partakes of paradox and faith rather than clarity and coercive proof as found in logic and science. However the plain fact is that the admission of alternative languages of the spirit does not diminish the actual beauty and power, range and wealth of any particular language as such, just as the beauty of Shakespeare's works does not detract from the literary excellence of any other poet. If there is hardly any reason why the entire human family should speak only one natural language, say English or Sanskrit, why should it be terribly important or desirable that the entire human family speaks only one language of the spirit, be it Buddhism, Christianity or Islam? Indeed, true religious piety and loyalty to one's own religious tradition lies more in being authentic and sincere to one's own cherished faith, and in righteous action, rather than in converting others. I would like to submit that doing away with diversity reflects a concern for power rather than for piety.

Even the concern that the entire human family should come round to making spirituality the dominant concern of their lives is, I submit, a subtle form of seeking power. It is true that spirituality fortifies man in the midst of temptation, tragedy and failure, but it is not strictly necessary for morality and the pursuit of value in general. The plain fact is that many intelligent and noble souls are unable to accept any religious or spiritual convictions but still lead morally virtuous lives. Spirituality, like human love, cannot be willed by the person himself or forced through logic. It is born, not from the womb of reason but in the fullness of human response to an inscrutable mystery, or, perhaps, Divine grace. Humanism is the only philosophical perspective that accommodates every kind of existential interpretation and shade of belief from agnosticism, atheism and Positivism to faith in a personal God or Spirit (*Brahman*). However, Humanism will also fall short of universal acceptance if it degenerates into an extreme form of Scientific Positivism that were to brush aside or denigrate the human response of wonder and awe when confronting the mystery of existence.

HINDU RELIGIOUS LIBERALISM

Ancient Indian spirituality, best reflected in the Bhagavad Gita, adumbrates the above approach to religion. This approach permits plural perspectives based on the concept of individual choice of Deity (*isht Devata*). This freedom or permissiveness extends even to honest agnosticism or atheism provided the individual does not abandon morality. Denying God is permissible; but not the denial of morality and the brazen embrace of Nihilism. Unfortunately the Hindu thought and value system suffered a grievous degradation due to the institution of hereditary caste. Creedal tolerance became tainted by the monstrous vice of a rigid fragmented caste society in total disregard of the oneness of the entire human family. The humanistic verses of the *Quran* and the *Sufi* approach to Islam are also remarkable for their spirit of pluralism and humanistic tolerance, though the traditional Islamic concept of tolerance suffers from creedal narrowness. The significant point is that the *Quran* (when it is read afresh without the gloss of traditional interpretations) and the Gita (when it is read without the gloss of *smriti* literature of the Hindu tradition) converge on a broad Spirit-centered Humanism.

The ancient Indian tradition of 'conceptual permissiveness' has given birth to a wide spectrum of beliefs and values, all under the banner of 'Hinduism'. The most celebrated strand in the Hindu spectrum is Vedanta. The central thesis of the Vedantic view is the organic view of all existence and the belief that the cosmos is the 'external body' of the supreme impersonal Spirit (*Brahman*). It is, however, quite permissible and even recommended to view *Brahman* as '*Ishwar*' in the sense of 'God as the Sovereign Person'. The central thesis of the

Semitic religions is that the eternal self-existent Supreme Being is a personal Creator God (*Rabbul Alameen*).

Vedanta leads to the belief that the impersonal Supreme Spirit is immanent in the cosmos, while the Semitic perspective leads to the belief that the one God has created the cosmos. However, the Indian perspective does not exclude or reject the relative validity of the Semitic theistic perspective for those who might find devotion to a personal God necessary for attaining inner peace and integrity. The Indian perspective leads the believer, logically and psychologically, to seek union with the Supreme Being through release from finite existence (*mukti/nirvana*); the Semitic perspective leads the believer to a total surrender to a personal God and implicit obedience to His commands. The Vedantic style of piety implies progressive inner purification and self-illumination. This gives the believer insight into the difference between right and wrong and also moves him to righteous conduct without the idea of an external Lawgiver. The Semitic perspective promotes morality in the form of adherence to Divine commands communicated in the Book. Thus Indian spirituality promotes autonomous ethics; the Semitic promotes authoritarian ethics. But at the higher *Sufi* level the Semitic ethos coincides with the ancient Indian.

The mystical tradition in all Semitic religions emphasizes that the believer should advance from the fear based obedience to external law (*shariah*) to the next higher stage of love based morality (*tariqah*) and eventually to the third and highest stage of the total purification and transformation of human personality into the Divine Being as far as humanly possible (*haqiqat*). This spiritual journey of the soul is the fruit of mystical love (*ishq e haqiqi*).

Hindu spirituality, especially after Shankaracharya's revival of Brahmanism in the post-Buddhist era from the 8th century onwards made room for love (*bhakti*) for a personal God without breaking away from Monism. On the other hand, *Sufi* saints and poets in India and elsewhere throughout the medieval period encouraged Philosophical Monism (*wahdat ul wajud*) without breaking away from Monotheism. The long dialogue between Monism and Monotheism, in other words, between belief in *Brahman* and belief in *Allah/Ishwara* led to a more inclusive perspective that harmonizes and heals a rather unnecessary controversy.

Plato, Shankar and Rumi all proclaimed that truth had several layers or levels and that the believer could choose the level that best suited his stage of development. Both the Indian and the *Sufi* tradition allow conceptual permissiveness and plural conceptions of one Reality by whatever name it may be called.

Spirit-Centered Humanism

Humanism as an attitude is being woven slowly but steadily into the fabric of human society. The process, marked by advances, retreats and plateaus is maddeningly complex and tortuous. Democracy works in a rather slow and circuitous manner to propel society in the direction of global Humanism. Globalism is both beneficial and harmful. The contemporary challenge is to ensure that the blessings outweigh the curses of globalism. The main obstacle to the smooth implementation of very soundly prepared international plans or schemes is due to the simple fact that different nations are at different stages of development, and their needs and priorities can never be identical. What suits one hampers the other. If the Western world suffers from industrial saturation and longs for the calm of a sleepy Indian village, the third world suffers from under-nourishment and under-activity. As a consequence the West lays stress on ecology, the East on industry. However, the control of environmental pollution is the basic need of the entire human family.

Nations will have to give and take, not dictate. The only brotherhood that can save the world is the brotherhood of man, not any lesser one, be it the brotherhood of race, religion, region or a nation state. But even Humanism alone will not do if man forgets that 'there are more things in heaven and earth than are dreamt of in Horatio's philosophy'. Pure scientific Humanism itself becomes controversial and divisive if it ignores the dimension of a higher spirituality. The aggressive atheistic Humanism of the Communist ideology has already failed. The days of aggressive religious fundamentalism are numbered, though not immediately near. It seems a lot of blood and tears will flow before the sincerely committed believers (who have been liberated from the unconscious yoke of political manipulators and power seekers) come to see the hidden but fatal flaw inherent in the 'fundamentalist' approach to religion.

Whether man is nothing but a highly developed earthworm, or a micro-ray of Divine Light is, perhaps, a question that has no conclusive answer. One can only search for one's own inner response and answer to this cosmic mystery in profound humility and loving tolerance and respect for all others, no matter how different their answers may be from one's own. All organized historical religions will have to come to terms with this ethos and approach. This requires that the body of the different believers and their spiritual leaders display a high order of intellectual honesty, humility and the moral courage to resist the pressures of conformity. This task is not easy. Yet it is not beyond what has actually happened several times in the long story of the slow march of the human family to a higher level of social and cultural progress.

If we really accept that matters of faith (religious beliefs or secular convictions) can never be conclusively proved every enquirer should be granted the right to arrive at his or her own 'resting point of faith', no matter where and when the seeker 'arrives'. It amounts to 'spiritual conceit' to equate one's own 'resting point of faith' or 'perspective upon Reality' with Reality as such. The Islamic view of God is not God as such; it is how Reality appears to the believer or how the believer perceives Reality. Exactly the same remarks apply to the Christian, Hindu or other views. Faced with such diverse resting points or conclusions of highly intelligent, informed and creative minds I, for my part, am left with only one option—to drill into my own existential depths till I reach the bubbling spring of inner conviction or hear the voice of authentic conviction that fills me with inner *'peace that passeth understanding'*. This option implies that I should welcome others to do just the same and that I should, unconditionally, respect their choice whatever it might be.

ISLAM IN THE FUTURE: A PROJECTION OF AN ISLAMIC SELF-IMAGE IN THE DISTANT FUTURE

The pristine Islam of the Prophet ﷺ flowed from his super-mystical or prophetic experience. The first Muslims responded to his call due to the powerful impact of his moral excellence, charismatic personality and the miracle of the Arabic *Quran*. No body of Theology, or Mysticism in the sense of secret teachings and practices (Theosophy) or magical formulas and techniques to satisfy human needs and wants (Theurgy) existed apart from the *Quran* as such, or the verbal teachings and the living example of the Prophet ﷺ. The Muslims were quite content with simple pietism and more or less unquestioning obedience to the Messenger of God. However, the Prophet ﷺ taught and practiced not merely rituals and external acts of piety, such as obligatory prayers, fasting, eschewing gambling and intoxicants, etc. but clearly stressed the paramount importance of purifying the soul and striving for higher levels of spirituality. This meant constant living in the presence of the Creator and cultivating moral and spiritual qualities through remembrance of Divine Names and inner openness to Divine blessings and grace. This striving constitutes the core content of Theopathy.

However, some vital 'seeds' or elements of an underlying 'Theopathy' were certainly present in the *Quran* and the mystical experiences and practices of the Prophet ﷺ. It is the common belief among all sects and sub-sects of Islam that Ali (one of persons closest and dearest to the Prophet ﷺ) was specially gifted and also concerned with this 'theopathic' dimension of the *Quran* and the teaching and practices of the Prophet ﷺ. It was, therefore, inevitable, that a full-fledged 'theopathic' Islamic mysticism (*Sufism*) would emerge and evolve in the course of time. The distinguishing feature of this type of mysticism lies in its almost total focus on the purely ethical and spiritual human quest for 'mystical nearness' and union with the Divine Creator and surrender to Divine Will rather than super knowledge of reality, or obtaining power or profit.

Cultural forms, like biological forms, develop from the simple to the complex. The parent body of the faithful gets diversified into different sects who give plural interpretations of the original scripture. This also is inevitable since all language, as such, is vitiated by an inherent ambiguity or possibility of plural interpretations. Since different segments of the believers have different material interests they naturally tend to interpret scripture in the way that suits them best. This is a natural human response to an inbuilt feature of all language and it also gets reflected in the way gender difference leads to different interpretations of the same text. This is not to deny the sincerity or question the motives of the persons whose perceptions differ. In the course of time smaller sub-groups arise and create new symbols or rituals as marks of their identity. Cultural differentiation, thus, occurs through a complex and subtle fusion of interests and ideas or ideals of the parent Church in the sociological sense.

'Theurgic' *Sufism*, which, traditionally, has had the greatest hold upon popular imagination both among Muslims and others, is the weakest candidate for acceptance in the modern scientific age. Its rejection, however, does not imply the rejection of Theopathy or Theosophy or of religious faith in general. Theosophical *Sufism* (which reaches its highest level of genius) in the writings of Ibn Arabi will, probably, continue to fascinate those who do not care much for the scientific ethos of exact quantification and verifiability as the paradigm of knowledge and truth. But theosophical mysticism will hardly have much of an appeal to those who are temperamentally cautious and are deeply conscious of the risk of subjective fantasies, pitfalls of imagination and the misleading potential of metaphorical language. The most distinguished analytical minds today do not reject Metaphysics or Theosophy as plain nonsense, as the ultra-positivist thinkers once did in the first half of the 20th century. But they certainly reject the classical view of the nature and function of metaphysical or theosophical truth-claims.

According to this line of thought, metaphysical systems do not describe the ultimate nature of Reality (as the metaphysician himself mistakenly presumes); they are just possible alternative ways of organizing human experience by unconsciously but skillfully changing the ordinary meaning or use of the words of a natural language. The modified use or meaning of words enables the metaphysician to remove some felt intellectual perplexity or contradiction in the beliefs of the common believer or the common man in general. This gives logical and emotional satisfaction to the metaphysician or theosophist who wants to share it with others. But the truth-claims he makes are neither self-evidently true nor deducible from any such a premise or premises.

When one claims that one's mystical experiences are direct glimpses into ltimate Reality, or that metaphysical truths give higher forms of knowledge than deductive logic or natural science one indirectly recommends that others too should take to the spiritual discipline or practices that brought about the elevated state of the mystic, or accept the definitions and meanings of words as stipulated by the metaphysician himself. This stand is not logically compelling, though it is far more plausible than belief in 'Theurgy'. However, those whose dominant life concern is ethical righteousness and who also stand committed to the scientific ethos of the modern age will not be much drawn to Theosophy, while they will certainly reject Theurgy. To my mind, therefore, 'Theopathic' *Sufism* alone is acceptable in the modern age. This, however, applies only to the spirit rather than the letter of *Sufism*.

The thought and value systems of Theopathic *Sufism* in history, like all thought and value systems in general, were deeply influenced and shaped by the total situation, social, political and economic, prevailing in their times (the macro-factors) as well as the temperament and personality orientation of the individual *Sufis* (the micro-factors). The great Theopathic *Sufis* of the classical age during the Abbasid period in Baghdad and elsewhere were almost exclusively focused on the culture of the emotions and the purification of the soul and did not have or care for any mass following. Nor did they found any hospices, which sprang up much later, specially, after the gradual decline of political power and spiritual creativity of the Muslims of Arab and Persian descent. Many perceptive scholars both Muslim and others (including Iqbal, the great poet thinker of the modern age) have rightly pointed out that *Sufis* gradually degenerated into escapists and practitioners of Theurgy. Not only this, the seminaries founded by the great *Sufis* came under hereditary management regardless of the spiritual or moral level of the successors or family members of the venerated saint. This was bound to result in the drying up of the springs of creative spirituality and intellectual vigor. Ideas and institutions need freedom of thought and enquiry and able leaders as stewards and custodian regardless of their lineage.

The thought and value system of Theopathic *Sufism*, therefore, must be reconstructed to render it optimally fruitful for the modern age. Just to give one instance, the classical *Sufi* concept of, say, humility, self-abnegation, voluntary poverty, trust in God, withdrawal etc will not hold water today in the literal sense. A well balanced spiritual life needs life affirmation and disinterested 'valuegenic' action, not withdrawal and seclusion. Likewise, trust in God need not exclude the 'tying of the camel' or the prudent ordering and planning of time or money. The need for voluntary poverty has to be understood in the context of the present technological age. The fact of the matter is that 'the good life' demands a multi-dimensional integrated approach rather than exclusive concern with some selected intrinsic value or virtue. In the final analysis, therefore, almost all the *Sufi* interpretations of the basic spiritual values would have to be reconstructed in order to make them relevant for the modern age of science and technology. The core or essence of Theopathic *Sufism* will, however, continue to shine by its own light, and this core is the stress on inwardness, on sensitivity to the wiles of the ego, the fear of the inner Satan rather than of external evil mongers, the general need for the culture of the raw emotions and instincts, the stress upon the inner quality of obligatory prayers rather than their mere regular external performance, the stress on work ethic (*akl e Halaal*) and social responsibility rather than mere performance of rituals.

To my mind, the quintessence of *Sufism* in today's global society is the genuine acceptance and practice of 'Spirit-centered Humanism'. Spiritualized morality is non-controversial, unlike positive law or even theological morality. Different organized religions and sects may engage themselves in piety and prayer and worship and devotion and meditation and pilgrimage and the vision of heaven or hell or even adhere to their personal laws (so far as this does not violate 'genuine' public interest), but they may not repudiate or violate the essential oneness of the human family and the inalienable responsibility and accountability of every individual to work for the welfare of all creation as a manifestation of the Supreme Being beyond human comprehension. This is, precisely, the underlying basic message of the *Quran*. This message has a timeless appeal and validity as an intrinsic value and as the fixed coordinate of any derivative or instrumental rules that the Prophet ﷺ may have prescribed or that may have entered the traditional Islamic value system or legal system at any stage of its long career. Exactly the same remarks apply to the Gita's core concept of 'disinterested righteous action' (*nishkaama saatvic karma*), Gautama Buddha's core concept of 'continual inner awareness' (*vipasna*) and the historical Jesus' stress on 'living in the presence of God'. These core ideas are also found in the highest version of Judaism, Sikhism and Chinese wisdom.

The great *Sufi* saints of the past were quite ignorant of modern science and technology and their information was much less than the level of common knowledge today, but their minds and hearts were founts of love and wisdom. To spread humanistic love, to promote the welfare of the entire human family without any distinction of 'we' and 'they', to exhort all (irrespective of their religion or sect) to feel and respond to the presence of the Supreme Spirit in their own soul rather than to convert others to formal Islam was their principal mission of life. It is another matter and due to some social and political factors that a large number of common people, specially, the weaker and under-privileged segments of society, freely embraced formal Islam. The great *Chishti Sufi* saints were Spirit-centered humanists. What can be a greater acknowledgment of their role as well as of the genius of the Indian people than the fact that the Sikh scriptures abound in *Sufi* texts? The reverence numerous Indians of all shades of belief show for the Sai Baba of Shridi is also an eloquent testimony.

In the last one hundred and fifty years the *Sufi* saint who, to my mind, has creatively reconstructed from within the *Sufi* tradition is Waris Ali Shah (d. 1905) of Deva, near Lucknow. His life and views have started to attract wider attention in and outside India, and deservedly so. In some respects he has made a radical departure from the classical *Sufi* tradition. He very sparingly, if at all, accepted any formal disciple, he strongly disapproved of praying to God on behalf of the numerous persons (of different religions) for granting their petitions concerning worldly matters, he refused to appoint any spiritual successor after his death, he made no distinction between Muslim and non-Muslim when he blessed them and never aimed to convert anybody to Islam, but merely exhorted his admirers and audience to try to live in the Divine presence and act righteously. To my mind, he can become the rallying point and role model for genuinely spiritually oriented modern scientific minds, irrespective of their religion or nationality.

A German scholar, Claudia Liebenskind, has done a sympathetic but penetrating study of Baba Waris in her work, *Piety on Its Knees: Three Sufi Traditions in South Asia in Modern Times, 1998*. An American psychotherapist and *Sufi* scholar, David Heinemann, also has written a remarkable work, *Sufi Therapy of the Heart*, 2003, dealing with a trans-religious or non-sectarian version of *Sufism*. The renowned scholar, (late) Annemarie Schimmel, has done remarkably sympathetic, incisive and insightful work on *Sufism*, in her *The Mystical Dimension of Islam*, and in several other very valuable studies including her *Gifford Lectures*. The British scholar of the history of Semitic religions, Karen Armstrong, is an inspiring bridge builder. Her lucid and candid writings, to my mind, are the happy portents of the coming world renaissance of inter-faith spirituality. It may be given any label or name depending upon the milieu in which one was born and grew up. What matters, in the final analysis, is the flowering of spirituality, righteous action and the gift of love.

A remarkably fresh and enlightened modern incarnation of authentic ancient Hindu spirituality (without any hidden political agenda) has already emerged in India, Europe and America. The Ramkrishna Mission and the various other Hindu or Vedanta Cultural Centers in the West are guiding and helping millions (without any idea of converting them to Hinduism) to tap the treasures that lie deep within the human soul now faced with the danger of turning into a money making machine. These are truly catholic and inclusive spiritual missions based on the vision of the luminaries of 'Spirit-centered Humanism'. *The Lake Shrine Center* established by Yogananda at Los Angeles is a symbol of a new dawn of spirituality that regards different world religions as co-pilgrims rather than as adversaries.

Modern Muslims should welcome the growing influence and progress of the inter-faith movement initiated by liberal Christians and Vedantic Hindus in the West. The fact of the matter is that Prophet Muhammad ﷺ and also the pure *Quranic* teachings, free from the gloss of medieval interpretations, have the same vision. The Prophet ﷺ desired to establish a spiritual commonwealth of Muslims, Jews and Christians when he initiated the Covenant of Medina. However, the *realpolitik* of the time led to a different destination. My projection of the self-image of Islam in the future is that Muslims will focus on the spirit of the *Quran* and the sublime character of Prophet Muhammad ﷺ, and in the course of time become active promoters of the movement of interfaith co-operation and harmony, rather than merely stress the need for 'adjusting' the *shariah* to situational needs.

Essay 4

Religious Faith and Values: Eighteen Theses on Religion

1. Religious beliefs, as basic convictions about man and the universe and the right way of life, are not rationally ascertained prior to their acceptance, but are straightaway inherited from one's milieu, even as the child learns a natural language. The basic convictions, metaphysical and ethical, constitute the religious life world, or language of the spirit into which the child is born and evolves into an adult through learning the concrete patterns of human response to the essentially inscrutable mystery of his own being and of the universe.

2. The exposure to alien life worlds or the inner growth of the individual may make him question his inherited religious convictions. He may then be led to justify them, wholly or in part, or he may reject them, secretly or openly, or turn skeptical, in some measure or the other, as the case may be. However neither their justification nor their rejection can deemed to be the fruit of pure reasoning without any antecedent bias, favorable or unfavorable, towards his inherited life world or system of concepts and values. The will to believe, or the will to reject, both of which are rooted in extra-logical situational factors, play a significant role in shaping the final outcome of the individual's quest for inner certainty, once his 'conceptual innocence' or anchorage of faith in his inherited life world has been lost, due to whatever reason.

3. Contemporary man may best regain his inner certainty by seeking, in a spirit of humility, honesty and sympathy, the elements in his own tradition that evoke his authentic commitment. He may then search his heart whether this commitment authentically prompts him to identify himself with his inherited religion, despite the elements of disvalue he finds in the tradition. If so, he may justifiably proceed to prune the avowedly negative elements from the traditional thought and value systems as restructured by him. He could honestly claim his redefined version to be one among the several versions constituting the total spectrum of the religious tradition. Such an approach definitely involves orthogenetic criticism, reinterpretation and persuasive definitions, but it does not involve hypocrisy or disloyalty to the tradition.

4. The reconstruction or redefinition of religious convictions, to make them more acceptable to the mature and rationally oriented believers and to prove or weed away crude mythical elements (unnoticed by uncritical credulous believers), represents the creative growth of a cherished tradition. This growth is different from mere rationalization, which is basically defensive, rather than exploratory. Genuine reconstruction of a tradition is rooted in conceptual clarity and moral courage which jointly lead to an integrated life world in which the believer really lives and acts; defensive rationalization is rooted in conceptual confusions and fear of change which jointly lead to accepting of more or less bad reasons for continuing to cling to the faith of one's forefathers; a faith which is verbalized with great vigor, but not lived with any inner consistency or rigor.

5. A religious faith, no matter how internally coherent and emotionally satisfying it might become as a result of the systematic reconstruction of its basic concepts and values, will always fall short of objective certainty which characterizes logical, mathematical or scientific truth. Religious beliefs are condemned to be existential convictions: the truths of being rather than the truths of logic or of perception. This, however, does not rule out the possibility of a logic of non-coercive criteria for evaluating existential convictions which should not be confused with pure whims or fancies.

6. The lack of logical or scientific objectivity should not be deemed to lower the cognitive status of existential convictions or

their assimilation to mere attitudes, feelings or emotional responses whose validity, or otherwise, is not worth bothering about by the truly cultured, critical and scientific intellect. The status of existential convictions ought to be linked with their crucial role in the complete humanization of man—the activation and flowering of the dimensions of human response, other than the purely logical or scientific, namely, of morality, art, and spirituality.

7. If one's honest and loving search for elements of permanent value in his own tradition leaves him so profoundly dissatisfied that he despairs of pruning it for enhancing its vitality and relevance to the contemporary human situation he would be quite justified in abandoning it and seeking spiritual anchorage elsewhere as an seeker of truth. The process of spiritual rehabilitation may take considerable time and be preceded by inner anguish and conflict. But a long dark night of the soul is, perhaps, the necessary prelude to the peace that passeth understanding. The true pilgrim on the journey of the spirit should not grudge the pangs of spiritual rebirth.

8. It is an untenable view that mystical experience supplies to the fully awakened soul a direct and infallible vision of reality, free from all refraction, distortion or fragmentation that are inseparable features of ordinary human perception and thought. It is much likely that mystical experience also suffers from limitations due to the contextual and interpretative elements inseparable from all experience, as such. Even if one were to concede, for argument's sake, that mystical experience is not human experience, in the ordinary contextual sense, but a Divine revelation to uncommonly sensitized souls, the mystic himself and all others need must interpret the mystical experience in order to know what it is all about and to make it relevant to the normal concerns and conduct of individual and social life. The act of relating the mystical experience (relatively rare and of short duration) with ordinary everyday experience inevitably would be done in the framework of the concepts and categories of the milieu.

9. Mystical experience is only one strand in the total spectrum of man's awareness and responses: the moral, the aesthetic, the logical and perceptual. A further difficulty arises from the *prima facie* resemblance between the mystical state and the altered states of consciousness induced by some drugs, electric stimulation of some nerve centers and other practices. Therefore, neither the uncritical attribution or assimilation to pathological states is justifiable, unless we first take into account the concrete impact of mystical experience upon the life history of the person concerned.

10. Granted that there are modes of awareness and Prophet than those normally available to humans, all concrete truth-claims, no matter how derived, must be subjected to a proper and adequate test of validation before being accepted as truth. If and when certain types of mystical experience occur in the human family, and such experience conflict with other normal veridical experiences, it would not be a proper method to denigrate or reject either the mystical or the normal in hasty one-sided manner. The conflict should be resolved by developing an epistemology, which takes into account the entire range of different types of experience. This caution is not intellectual pride, but rather humility and honesty in the face of the complexity and mystery of the universe.

11. The ultimate value and validity of mystical experience must be deemed to lie in its actual role in enriching the quality of human life and promoting moral and spiritual values in the individual and society. Mystical experience cannot be deemed to give to the mystic any super-authority, as it were, to annul or abrogate, or even modify, the clear and categorical verdicts of man's authentic conscience, the nexus of deductive logic or mathematical reasoning, or the verifiable truth-claims of science within the realm of human experience.

12. All religions stand for cultivating the attitude of wonder at the contemplation of the universe and of surrender to a mysterious Power, felt as sacred or holy, even though religions may differ in their respective theologies, symbols and rituals. This plurality does not negate the basic oneness of man's religious consciousness: his basic state of mind and of feeling, termed 'piety' or 'religious devotion'. Genuine spiritual sensitivity to the sense of 'the Holy Mystery', immanent in and transcending the world of matter, does not stand in the way of imaginatively enjoying diverse symbols and rites of other traditions, even as one appreciates works of art in different styles or in different media, while keeping one's own special style or medium of aesthetic expression. Even the denial of a personal God does not necessarily amount to the denial of religious experience (conceptualized in a non-theistic frame of reference) or the denial of moral and spiritual values in their broad non-sectarian sense.

13. Religious plurality does not produce any conflict, individual or social, so long as religion is treated as a means of spiritual growth rather than of political or economic power. Separating religion from politics, however does not amount to permitting the separation of morality from politics. In other words, the concept of secular politics does not logically imply amoral politics.

The religious attitude, by itself is not a panacea for human ills, or atheism the root cause of the strife and violence ever present in man's history. Strife and violence spring from man's struggle for survival in a harsh world, and his hunger, almost irrepressible, to reach out for the largest slice of the cake without caring for the other. The solution to the human predicament lies, not in moralizing or spirituality alone, but in our giving effective help towards the establishment of social justice in the human family as a whole.

14. Value oriented action or ethical conduct does not logically presuppose any particular theology or ontology over and above the true commitment to spiritual and moral values. A self-directing and mature person can habitually act ethically and responsibly, without fear of punishment or hope of reward. Nevertheless, most men, at some time or the other, do stand in need of faith in God or some metaphysical reality, as the invincible support and unfailing guarantor of the ultimate triumph of truth and justice in order to retain their moral courage and integrity of being in the face of the trials, temptations and tragedies of life.

15. The simple goodness of heart, spontaneous respect, kindliness and solicitude for all living creatures, as members of a large cosmic family, the habitual will to do the right and the just, for their own sake, the active aspiration to give one's best to society, at large, seeking fulfillment through personal love and loyalty, and the struggle for social justice, the ceaseless search for truth and beauty, and finally, the joyful acceptance of suffering, decay and death, as the other side of life itself. These are the basic values that ought to be deemed the indispensable categorical imperatives for contemporary man. How or through what means; religious/theological, or extra-religious, extra theological; the individual comes to internalize and to live out the above values should be optional for each individual. Others, be they themselves religious or non-religious, need not worry about the route each individual takes to do so.

16. The contemporary human situation is marked, specially, by the scientific temper and easy inter-cultural communication. The scientific temper has led to the verifiable and quantitative statements of science becoming the paradigm of all knowledge. Easy inter-cultural communication has made the world into a plural cultural society, as it were. Scientism and cultural pluralism have conspired to turn contemporary man into a 'doubting animal' who has lost forever his anchorage of faith in his inherited life world. This, however, does not mean an irretrievable breakdown of genuine faith. A mature authentic faith, rooted in man's response to the mystery of the universe, a faith purified from the crude mix of magic, myth and unexamined assumptions, a faith fully aware of the complexities of the human situation, a faith not, in the least, afraid aid of ceaseless enquiry and creativity of values – such a faith is still an open possibility.

17. The conflict, if any, between human reasoning and Divine revelation disappears when we review them as processes in history. The conflict between Humanism and Theism, or between man-centered religions and God-centered religions dissolves when we view God and man, not as totally alien to each other, but in an inscrutable relationship of the whole and the part, adumbrated in, but never captured, in the various analogies of the ocean and the drop, the sun and its rays, the sap and the plant, the self and the stream of consciousness, or in the distinction, if any, between *Brahman* and *Atman*.

18. The cardinal value for contemporary man is the quest for authentic being. Any religion or philosophy that denies or obstructs, directly or indirectly, man's extremely slow and tortuous progress towards this ideal is misleading and false.

Essay 5

History – Its Theory, Philosophy and Wisdom

Wisdom has been traditionally linked, in almost all cultures, with philosophy and old age. What is the link between old age and wisdom? Well, the older a person grows, the greater the span and matrix of his concrete experience is likely to be. History, as the story of the sum total of human experience of nature and interaction with fellow humans could and should have been regarded as the main source of wisdom, or, at least, as the prolegomena to the study of philosophy.

However, the vast majority of Eastern and Western philosophers have neglected history as the pathway to wisdom, and have tended to confine themselves to reflection on essences, speculation, or logical deduction from self-evident premises as the proper way of acquiring wisdom. Thus Socrates (d. 399 BC), Plato (d. 347-348 BC), Aristotle (d. 322 BC), Aquinas (d. 1275), Descartes (d. 1650), Leibnitz (d. 1716), Kant (d. 1804), were not enamored of the study of history. Ancient Indian sages were even less concerned with the dimension of time in their pursuit of the eternal verities of life. It goes to the credit of classical Muslim culture, that it gave the greatest importance to the study of history. It is, however, Hegel (d. 1831) and, after him, Marx (d. 1883), Dilthey (d. 1911), Troeltsch (d. 1923) and Collingwood (d. 1943), who recognized the crucial importance of the historical approach to the proper understanding of reality.

In this essay I wish to analyze the concept of history and show how history helps us to pursue wisdom, which is the avowed goal of the philosopher.

WHAT IS HISTORY?

What is history? History is a systematic and accurate, descriptive and explanatory study of the significant features of man's total recorded past, in every sphere of human activity or experience. History describes the past, which, however, cannot be perceived but only remembered or inferred from present experience. Thus, even though the descriptive propositions of history belong to factual discourse, as in the case of science, the facts of history are not straightforward facts given to us, like scientific data. These are constructed or inferred descriptions, on the basis of evidence deemed to be reliable by historiographers. Even such a simple historical fact, that Gandhiji was assassinated on January 30, 1948, cannot be perceived or verified in the scientific sense. The so-called facts of history are construed out of pieces of testimony, which come to us through a chain of reporters, going back to the direct experience of some person or persons. The same remarks apply to the difference between scientific and historical explanations. A scientific explanation reduces constant conjunctions or regular sequences of events to particular instances of a general law of nature. A natural law is not a logical necessity or purposive Divine command (from the standpoint of the scientist), but a descriptive generalization. A natural law is always verifiable in theory, directly or indirectly, though it may not be so in practice, at a given moment of time, due to our technological limitations. An historical explanation both resembles and differs from a scientific explanation

CULTURAL IMPONDERABLES OF HISTORY

An historical explanation partly resembles a natural explanation, in the sense that it makes use of empirical generalization. When, for instance, the historian explains the success of the British in India, in terms of their superiority in technological and administrative organization and the political disunity of the Indian people, he makes use of the empirical generalization, that superiority in such matters leads to political success. But a historical generalization is also something more: it is an insight into the workings of the human mind, the attitudes, motivations, morale of individuals and groups involved. And it is precisely here that a historical explanation transcends natural causation, and introduces cultural imponderables (which cannot be quantified or mathematically correlated) into its explanatory framework. In other words, history is something much more than chronology though the latter is integral to history.

The historian does not write history unless he connects and explains his carefully reconstructed facts out of the reliable historical data. Again, he cannot explain, unless he accepts some general beliefs as an explanatory base. This base is rooted in the worldview of the historian. The worldview is never a self-evident truth or a logical deduction or a verifiable hypothesis. Generally speaking, the worldview of the historian is seldom chosen, but is culturally conditioned, to begin with. The critical and mature historian may, however, transcend his tradition. Often, those who outgrow or reject their traditional worldview come into the grip of some other tradition, instead of winning and preserving their own independent spiritual autonomy. Such persons escape from one conceptual straightjacket, only to enter into another, instead of opting for an 'open' conceptualization of the human situation and the mystery of the universe.

It does not follow from the above analysis of historical explanation that history is condemned to be subjective and incorrigibly unreliable. There is a clear-cut sense, in which history may be subjectively or objectivity written, even after conceding that it can never be objective in the scientific sense of the term. What is important is not the insistence upon subjectivity or objectivity of history, but to decide whether there are some criteria to distinguish good history from bad. If so, reliable history may be said to be objective, while unreliable history subjective without equating historical objectivity with the scientific. The reason why some find themselves perplexed by this issue, is that they think under the spell or fascination of a single paradigm or model of objectivity, i.e., the scientific. They, thus, fail to see that the term 'objective' may well have other meanings or uses in other contexts.

Historical Objectivity

What are the features or distinguishing criteria of historical objectivity? The main features are: absence of bias or antipathy; a sympathetic but critical approach; awareness and utilization of all available records; critical assessment of the motives and personality orientation of the testifier or historian, on the basis of known factual truths or valid insights into human behavior; and help from archeological evidence. Good history must also reflect a judicious selection from the enormous range of factual material, in order to focus the attention of the reader upon specific issues. Selection also becomes necessary for reducing the cost of publication and also making the material reader friendly, especially for young readers.

No harm accrues from such selection, provided the motive is not to suppress truth at higher levels of research or fuller levels of comprehension, but merely to simplify it out of concern, not for any narrow group, but for human welfare as such. Thirdly, good history must enter into the spirit of the age or society, just as a good dramatist enters into the spirit of his characters, without passing value judgments. Finally, the work of the good historian must serve as a mirror to one's contemporary situation, in so far as there are genuine significant similarities between the past and the present.

In spite of all efforts to be objective, in the above sense, historians will continue to differ in their evaluation of historical personalities, their reconstructions of historical facts and their explanations. Like philosophical controversies, historical disagreements can never be settled once and for all. However, the issues of historical debate may become moribund or even dead, due to changed circumstances. Moreover, agreement about future objectives, and the will to achieve them help in creating the mood and inclination to agree to differ about the past without any bitterness. Again, numerous observers, with very varying backgrounds, often do come to agreed conclusions about the past, provided they are gifted with historical empathy. The reason is that critical reflection upon basic concepts and values and awareness of their growth in history lead to a more comprehensive and balanced understanding of how their different versions are shaped by situational factors. This promotes a deeper insight into their essence or basic function in human life, as well as the inner 'feel' of the movement and continuity of history.

This sense of movement in historical space makes man forward-looking and dynamic. Knowledge of the past liberates man from bondage to it, as distinct from a critical appreciation of the values already created in the past. Awareness of stages, that developed, one from the other, in the past makes man aware of the tremendous potentialities of the present, ever spilling over into the future. The active concern for the future prevails over the historical disagreement about the past.

EMPIRICAL ENQUIRY

History is an 'open' empirical enquiry into the total past, and should not be reduced to sociology or any form of sociological mechanics of socio-economic forces, viewed as determinants of the historical process, without any effective role played by the individual. As already indicated, every philosophical interpretation of the universe is an existential interpretation, which is not objectively verifiable, but which may be deemed to be valid or invalid on the basis of stated criteria. The systematic philosopher should spell out these criteria. The interpretation, which denies any effective role to the individual, is as invalid as the one, which ignores the role of the objective or situational factors, which mould the subject's choice of action. Indeed, if the historical process involves decision-making by persons (as it certainly does), and if decisions involve value judgments (as they certainly do), historical dynamics just cannot be reduced, without any remainder, to purely sociological dynamics of social forces hitting and pushing, as it were, human billiard balls, who have no choice of action.

Likewise, if the individual makes his decision in a concrete situation (which is not of his own choosing, but the cumulative deposit of past events or choices, which cannot be undone or wished away from the stage of reality), his decisions cannot be said to be totally free from situational constraints or compulsions modifying his decision, even in unwanted directions, or making his choice forced or 'tainted', as it were. This, however, does not amount to the elimination of the individual's role. Indeed, individuals possessing outstanding imagination, courage, determination and dedication to ideals have, in fact, given a decisive turn to the course of events throughout the ages. To believe that events would have run the same course, even without the contribution of such outstanding persons, would be unwarranted speculation.

Individual and Circumstance

Of course, it is quite reasonable to hold that the decisive turn could have been given by a similar contribution from some individual possessing similar qualities other than the individual who, in fact, steered events at the time under review. But this substitution of roles presupposes, not merely the abstract logical possibility but rather the actual existence, at the time and place concerned, of another such highly endowed individual or individuals. The actual existence of more than one highly talented or outstanding individual is, however, a contingent fact and certainly not a necessary event in the logical sense, such that it must always be the case. I doubt, if the course of events in 1917, and immediately thereafter, would have been, what it actually was, in the absence of the vision and techniques provided by Lenin. Going much further back, could the history of Arabia and the medieval world been, what it actually was, without the character and achievements of the Prophet ﷺ of Islam? The controversy, whether the individual or circumstance plays the dominant role in history, is, therefore, totally uncalled for and futile.

Questions of Philosophy

Can there be any philosophy of history apart from historiography? Could a super-historian formulate some laws of history, as a scientist discovers laws of nature? Are there any stages in the historical process as a whole, or any pattern in the birth, growth, decline and death of human societies, as in the case of individuals? Is there any meaning or over-arching purpose of history, as distinct from the undeniable operation of purpose in history? If this super-purpose be deemed to be the purpose of an omnipotent Creator God, does God habitually regulate history, or sometimes intervene or never at all, giving a long rope, as it were, to men, until the final day of judgment in the post-historical or eschatological future? Can we discover any direction in human affairs, quite apart from the metaphysical or theological question of Divine purpose? The discussion of the above questions may be said to constitute the philosophy of history, apart from historiography.

The study of universal history does bring out some basic similarities in the recorded story of different societies. On this basis, a philosophical or interpretative, as distinct from a purely empirical or investigative historian, could formulate general laws governing the course of history. The reliability and scope of such laws would depend upon the accuracy and comprehensiveness of the preceding historical investigation. Since historical data are not data in the literal sense, but a historical reconstruction out of present clues, at different spatio-temporal distances from the subject or object of history, any antecedent error in the processing of historical data doubly vitiates the subsequent historical laws arrived at on their basis.

Inadequacy of Historical Data

Moreover, historical laws are not at one but two removes from the raw data of human experience, and the facts of history are reconstructed from an enormous quantum and range of man's experience. Consequently, the historian cannot rule out that some crucially relevant facts may have been left out of the recorded survey. In short, any discrepancy (whether because of errors of commission or of omission) between the reconstructed historical past or the historical image of the past and the actual or real past vitiates historical generalizations and verification of putative sociological laws. The extremely high frequency of such errors of commission or omission, in the works of the universal or philosophical historians, makes the critical investigative historian highly suspicious of the validity of the approach of a Spengler, Toynbee or Sorokin, who seek to deduce laws from the study of universal history. Highly competent specialists in different areas of history have pointed out several factual inaccuracies or unwarranted assumptions in the processing of the historical data, on which Spengler or Toynbee have based their philosophy of history.

Subject to these limitations, it is both possible and useful to frame broad historical laws to help us foresee and effectively intervene in the course of events. Thus, for instance, Toynbee's laws of situational challenge and response, Spengler or Sorokin's typology of cultures, Spengler's rather misleading and pessimistic law of the cycle of societal birth, growth, decline and death, or Toynbee's revised and more accurate concept of societies, which may be creative, active, moribund or dead (with the proviso that a society may conceivably creatively renew its living tradition and thus avoid cultural stagnation and death), are pertinent sociological laws.

Marx's Fallacy

The most striking instance of a historical or sociological law, modeled after natural laws is, however, Marx's concept of historical stages of a society in terms of its mode of production of wealth. According to Marx, the mode of production and the relations of production and distribution generate the entire cultural and ideological super-structure (comprising the philosophy, religion, ethics, law, and art) of human society, which is inevitably moving towards the communist stage. There is an element of vital truth in the above penetrating insight, but this approach commits the fallacy of reductionism, since it reduces, without any remainder, the movement of history to a rigid and almost predictable movement of a machine.

The history of capitalist societies after Marx, however, makes it pretty evident that the dialectics of history is amenable to human creative striving, instead of being rigidly determined by sociological laws modeled after mechanics. According to Marx, capitalism is bound to accentuate the polarity between the wealthy and the poor, reducing the masses to near starvation and a state of revolutionary desperation, leading to the violent overthrow of the entire system under the revolutionary leadership of the organized workers. But, as we know, the actual course of history has not at all obliged the undoubted genius of Marx. Rather, paradoxically, his vision and genius have helped Western societies to develop their concept of political democracy into economic democracy, equality in voting rights into equality of opportunity, and a police state into a welfare state. Social therapy has thus corrected, or is in the active process of correcting, the imbalances or contradictions first pointed, out by Marx.

Fallacy of Sociological Determinism

Meanwhile new and unsuspected imbalances and evils have sneaked into the socialist system, which Marxist thinkers supposed to be proof against the temptations and corruptions inherent in a profit seeking highly competitive society. Such developments or changes in the historical process, especially the recent changes in Chinese society, point out the mechanistic fallacy of reducing the essential openness of history to sociological determinism. We would commit the same fallacy in a different garb, if we reduced the openness of history to say, theological or geographical or any other form of determinism. No goal or end is pre-determined or inevitable. Historical change is the outcome of complex causes, including striving by individuals and groups.

Man's potential freedom to choose goals and his actual striving to realize them always keeps history an open process with plural possibilities. Each historical outcome is the product of man's variable responses to an invariable or unchangeable past. No theological or speculative projection of an inevitable *'telos'* or end, no dialectical prediction of a final synthesis, no anthropological generalization, in short, no conceptual formula can extinguish the essential contingency, opaqueness and tragic brittleness of the human story. In other words, history can never be reduced to sociology or philosophy, though these disciplines are essential for mature historical understanding.

DIVINE PURPOSE OF HISTORY

Let us now turn to the question of an over-arching purpose of history, apart from the purposes of individuals and groups, whose interactions constitute the concrete course of events. The word 'purpose', as ordinarily used, implies a mind or person, who is aware of values and goals and understands the connection between ends and means or cause and effect. Thus the expressions 'purpose of history' or 'purpose of the cosmos' imply the concept of a Super Mind, in some sense or the other, which the philosopher or theologian seeks to unravel. The philosophical historian is only concerned with the question whether or not the course of history, as distinct from the course of nature, is characterized by features which prove, or at least suggest any over-arching Divine purpose? If we claim that the answer is 'yes', we must be able to understand and identify the said super-purpose and also to point out the ways and means actually found in history for realizing the above purpose.

It is precisely at this point that all our attempts to identify the super-purpose of God and His ways and means of realizing it breakdown. We think we have grasped the purpose only to find that some event or set of events in history defy the putative purpose and remain inexplicable brute facts, suggesting some other purpose or rather none at all, in the course of history. It is like finding a succession of numbers, which appear to conform to a mathematical formula long enough to make us believe we have correctly identified it, only to discover, moments later, that the next actual number or numbers fail to conform to the predicted number in the series. To give another illustration, when we think we have identified both the super-purpose and the method of its realization, the supposed purpose or the means or both give us the dodge, and, like Falstaff, escape through the keyhole.

No Super-Purpose of History

The validity of the teleological argument for God's existence is a philosophical and not a historical issue. But even if we antecedently accept on faith or on philosophical theological grounds that God exists, the question, whether or not the course of history is guided by God, and, if so, in what way and to what extent, cannot be given any conclusive answer on the basis of empirical history. The complexity of the human story, with its myriad plots and sub-plots in space-time in a bewildering variety cannot be fitted into any definite master-rhythm or super-pattern of history, despite the genius of an Ibn Khaldun, Vicco, Hegel, Marx, Spengler or Toynbee No matter what super-purpose we may identify, the actual historical process does not show any evidence of being a purposeful, rational or systematic movement towards a goal. So great and glaring are the vicissitudes, convolutions, and reversals of trends, tragedies and destruction of values that history appears to be devoid of any super-purpose or cosmic meaning.

History cannot prove or disprove God's existence, even as science and philosophy cannot do so. Nature and history both provide man with experience, which is highly complex and gives contradictory messages or clues, as it were, which completely baffle all human efforts to penetrate into the mystery of being. Like a gigantic Rorsach Stimulus card, both nature and history could be interpreted in diverse ways. Some objective justification or reason could always be traced in the mosaic of the 'empirical manifold' or what is objectively given to us in experience. Thus, many known parts of nature are, in fact, structured with a remarkable mathematical proportion and functional coordination (the epitome of which is the human body). Such structures strongly incline us to the interpretation, that nature is linked with a benevolent purpose or telos, while some other features of nature (enormous waste, nature's circuitousness or trial and error, dead ends, struggle and suffering) incline us towards the interpretation that the cosmic process is blind and absurd. In the final analysis, neither of the two interpretations could be deemed to be a verifiable hypothesis. Both are essentially 'adventures of faith', that could claim existential but not logical scientific certainty.

DOUBTS AND DIFFICULTIES OF HISTORY

It seems to me that existential doubts and difficulties, as presented by nature, in relation to God's existence, are rather less than the doubts and difficulties presented by history. Nature presents the difficulty that it is 'red in tooth and claw' (suggesting that life is a relentless struggle for survival in which the strong devours the weak, rather than a garden in which a hundred flowers bloom to glorify their Creator). The difficulty presented by history is that it is 'blue' in pain and suffering of innocent millions down the ages. Does not the sorry tale of the periodic destruction of cultures and the regression of human societies to barbarism, the untold sufferings of oppressed minorities, the inhuman exploitation of the despised untouchable for millennia mock at our attempts to find the hand of God in history? Does not the tragic story of the sufferings of countless millions of maltreated children, persecuted wives, detested widows, unwanted female children, luckless orphans, mutilated prisoners and slaves, bonded laborers, underfed and emaciated workers, the unattended sick, and last, but not the least, the tortured mute domestic animals, fill our eyes with tears which rather dim the picture of an all loving and all powerful God in heaven? Does not the anguished unrequited prayers of countless millions of innocent sufferers raise a serious question mark against the assumption of the hand of God in history? Is it so easy to dismiss the doubts of an honest skeptic or agnostic in the Divine regulation or intervention in history as nothing more than a perverted or wicked response of a proud atheist or materialist, rather than the anguish of a compassionate and noble soul caught in the antinomies of history. While the brighter side of the tangled and tortuous web of history inclines one towards theistic optimism, the darker side pushes one towards atheistic or agnostic pessimism.

God as Master of History

A person may take the stand that the proper evidence of cosmic purpose should be sought, not in the realm of history, but in the realm of nature, since God has given a long rope to man until the day of final reckoning and chosen, in his Divine wisdom, to withhold His intervention. This does not imply any external or forced limitation of His sovereign power or loving concern as Supreme Creator of nature and Master of the course of history. He may intervene in nature or history whenever He may choose, suspending, as it were, the laws of nature or history, through exercising His sovereign power in His inscrutable wisdom. According to this view, the course of history is a tiny fragment of the cosmic process, with man enjoying almost total freedom of action as part of a Divine plan, which is necessarily opaque to us in historical time but which will become manifest in the eschatological future.

According to this view, history is a game in which players win or lose, not because of any Divine help or wrath, but as a result of their hard work, patience, grit, skill, fraud or other human or natural factors. When temporal history ends eschatological history begins, and it is at this stage of the cosmic process that God's omnipotence and justice will make good the deficiencies and contradictions of temporal history. A person who takes this stand may say that the concept of metaphysical time, as distinct from historical time, though an act of faith is, nevertheless, not an arbitrary response, but a response rooted in man's awareness of the immense and wonderful architectonic complexity and beauty of nature.

It seems to me, this approach is quite valid, though it becomes invalid or unwarranted, the moment it is converted into a sort of an ideological argument, for the existence of God or for the presence of a super-purpose in either nature or history. Faith in a Divine purpose of nature and history may evoke only existential, but never logical or objective certainty.

Let us now reconsider the question whether history moves in a particular direction, even though there is no goal as such. We could answer this question in the affirmative, if we could identify some direction, as such, on pure historical evidence. Identifying the direction means being able to point out some basic beliefs and values, towards which the human family may have been moving over the centuries past, albeit, haltingly, deviously, even reversibly, as the case may be. These ideas and values, if any, may well be called 'Consensus Ideas and Values'.

Grand Consensus of Ideas and Values

It seems to me, the human family has been moving towards an enormously slow but grand consensus. As examples of this consensus one may cite the ideas and values of reverence for life, dignity and equality of man, dignity of labor, gender equality, equality of opportunity, religious or cultural pluralism, secularism or separation of church and state, democracy, scientific attitude and technology, welfare state and planning for social security, family planning, environmental control, political federalism, international controls and standards, and world brotherhood.

The above consensus ideas, which are value judgments, are not capable of any logical, scientific or objective proof. Nor could it be claimed that the consensus has already been reached. Thus, for instance, the issue of the separation of church and state is a highly controversial, rather explosive issue in the Muslim segment of the human family. The concept of the equality of the sexes is also, perhaps, just one shade less controversial. Again, the entire human family is still groping for and, unfortunately violently disputing, about the ideal pattern for reconciling two basic, but highly conflicting human needs—social or economic security and individual freedom and creative self-realization. Even the wisest and most knowledgeable statesmen, philosophers and social scientists of the human family stand baffled and perplexed at the complexity of human affairs. They are not able to lay hands on any simple panacea, for reconciling the above conflicting needs. Nevertheless, it may, justifiably, be said that a consensus is in the process of emerging through the steady interchange and fusion of ideas, the shrinking of space, instant global communication, trial and error, the exposure of illusions, the shattering of politico-economic dreams or expectations from one's favored 'ism' or interpretation of religion, in short, the march of history. The consensus ideas must however be viewed as ever 'open' in the changing human situation.

No Verifiable Hypothesis

Whether the slowly emerging consensus is a willed goal, or is merely the unintended resultant of situational forces cannot be conclusively settled for reasons already given. The 'telos' of the theist, and the 'social dynamics' of the historical materialist, both, more or less, reflect human hopes, fears, attitudes and values. Thus, they cannot claim the status of being verifiable hypotheses. While man can live the good life in a universe without God, or without an immanent Divine purpose, these ideas enhance man's ontological dignity, moral motivation and confidence in success in the midst of undeniably heavy odds and obstacles on the cosmic stage.

Empirical history, thus interpreted, becomes a major pathway to wisdom. By describing and connecting different phases and facets of man's story, understanding human character and cultural patterns through historical research and investigation, history leads man, from the philosopher's abstract theories of mind and spirit, towards a concrete organic vision of man in the universe. While classical philosophy deals with the abstract, formal structure of man, history, like great literature, reveals his concrete psychic depth. Both functions are necessary and complementary. Conceptual abstraction is ever in the danger of getting vitiated by linguistic and conceptual confusions, particularly the fallacy of reification: mistaking a grammatical noun for a metaphysical entity. History, at its best, overcomes this ever-lurking danger by entering into the spirit of an individual's life or age, enabling the reader to 'empathize' with the inner world of different individuals and ages. The reader becomes the living witness of the human drama on the cosmic stage, and is transformed from a historical microcosm into a historical macrocosm. This is, perhaps, the fullest 'humanization' of the individual, and a much higher stage from his earlier 'socialization' through cultural conditioning. This birth of the 'universal individual' as distinct from the 'ethnocentric individual' is the special gift of history, rather than of philosophy, science, mathematics, religion or art. This special gift is wisdom, while the special gift of science is knowledge and the power of technology.

The Distinction between Wisdom and Knowledge

Wisdom is insight into moral good and evil, and the proper attitudes to self, and others, in the concrete conduct of life as a whole. A wise man is, thus, not he who is an expert in logic, mathematics, science or other branches of knowledge, but does not know what to do, when he is betrayed by a friend or loved one, or when his son is killed in an accident, or when old age, disease or danger confronts him with impending death. Wisdom is constituted by proper attitudes to the world, knowledge by the accurate awareness of the world. Wisdom and knowledge are, however, related, since the proper attitude or the right response to an object, presupposes accurate awareness or knowledge of its nature or its properties.

In the pre-scientific era, philosophy itself, in the form of speculative ontology and cosmology, provided knowledge. The different branches of natural and social sciences now perform this task, separately and jointly. And history, in the broad sense, is the source, par excellence, of such knowledge since every scientific discipline has its own history of development.

Limitations of classical Philosophy

Classical philosophy, as the source of wisdom, suffers from some serious limitations. First, it regards cosmological theories as if they were super scientific hypotheses, meant to explain the nature and functioning of Reality at a higher level than that of science. The philosopher further claims his own theory to be true and all other theories to be false. He mistakenly thinks that his technical terms refer to metaphysical entities or essences, whose nature is truly revealed by his own theories, but falsified by rival theories. Thirdly, classical philosophy employs abstract conceptual analysis or reasoning (which is neither logically coercive nor based on any clear cut rules of language), completely ignoring the historical or situational determinants of the rival conceptual systems, which identify and label human experience in a particular way.

The role of hidden value judgments, attitudes and interests, in shaping philosophical theories, is, thus, concealed from him and from others. In other words, the philosopher is unaware of the influence of linguistic, historical, and psychological factors upon the choice of conceptual schemes, which are mistakenly held to be the result of purely rational or logical thinking. The disagreement of other philosophers does not bother him, since he attributes this fact to their crooked thinking. He does not bother to go into the complex causes and reasons for the chronic disease of philosophical disagreement, in sharp contrast with the uniform conclusions of science.

Two Complementary approaches

The linguistic approach to philosophy emphasizes the role of linguistic or semantic factors, while the sociological approach that of values or interests of individuals or groups in the shaping of conflicting philosophical theories or ideologies. In the final analysis, both the approaches complement each other. The proper pursuit of wisdom requires both systematic linguistic analysis (to avoid semantic confusions and errors that generate philosophical controversies) and the study of empirical history to identify the values or interests that mould the thinking of a person, of a social group or of an entire age.

Let us now come to the wisdom, which history teaches us more abundantly than any other discipline. Only a few main themes can be included in this concluding portion of the essay.

(1) Dialectical Movement

The historical approach to the totality of life gives us a width and depth of vision, to see reality in its total career in space-time, instead of reality at any particular phase or stage in its development. We are, thus, enabled to see things whole and see them steady, instead of being carried away by passing fashions of thought, or by a single perspective which might satisfy a vital but narrow need of the hour, but ignore other needs.

Cultural history reveals the changing rhythm of man's sensibility, and its demand for the logic of relativity. The story of man is not a uni-linear sustained progress towards a transcendental goal, but a multi-linear, cyclical or rather dialectical movement. Progress towards ideals creates new positive ideals, as also new negative realities in the ongoing historical process, which rules out final models of excellence. The criteria of excellence are not purely objective norms, to be discovered by pure reflection, but are conditioned by the bi-polar dynamics of action and reaction, thrust and counter-thrust, change and stability, push and pull. Historicism, in the above sense, does not negate the search for norms or criteria of validity in man's eternal quest for values. It only implies giving up certainties that dissolve into illusions in the clear light of history. The study of history gives us existential poise and mature hope, instead of ill-informed certainty and immature expectations that the triumph of our ideas or values is just round the corner, only to find them swept aside in the inexorable flux of history. Neither public acclaim nor short term rejection, neither success nor failure of one's ideas in one's own life time, disturbs the person who looks to history for guidance.

(2) Principle of Recurrence

A major theme of the wisdom, which we learn from history, is the principle of recurrence or the principle of unity in variety and variety in unity, of the human condition down the ages. The characters of kings, statesmen, artisans, merchants, peasants, priests, teachers, poets and artists, and the pattern of events, say, the lust for power, the workings of jealousy, the intrigues of the court, the betrayal of comrades, the fear of reprisal, the inroads of corruption, the rise and fall of individuals, families, or dynasties, and empires—all are repeated again and again like a musical refrain on different instruments and different keys. When we personally taste the above negativities of life, we are apt to be overwhelmed by bitterness and sorrow, and lose our inner poise, thinking our own lot or times to be uniquely bad. But history takes out the sting of our agonized bitterness and the pain of our outraged innocence at the frailties and follies of our contemporaries, or, for that matter, our exaggerated admiration for their virtues and achievements.

The equanimity of the historian must not, however, be confused with moral indifference or insensitivity to contemporary evils. Mature historical vision lends itself, neither to simplistic moral denunciation of evil, nor to its amoral passive acceptance, but rather prescribes resolute and planned ameliorative action, without the certainty of quick or even lasting success, and with the full knowledge, that no remedy will ever root out evil from the human condition.

(3) Slowness of the Movement of History

As mentioned earlier, the course of history appears to be moving in the direction of a consensus of ideas and values. The principle of recurrence is, thus, supplemented by the principle of direction of history. We must grasp the direction of this basic movement or thrust of man's quest for value, as distinct from the deviations and detours, adventurous explorations and fads, exaggerated reactions and rigid responses that are thrown up on the surface of human experience by the inter-play of man's inner freedom, the variety of his cultural and physical environment, and the unintended consequences of his choices.

The wisdom of history teaches us not to get perplexed at or carried away by the contingent reversals or deviations from its basic direction, but to realize the deeper continuity or flow, beneath the surface eddies of the human story, in terms of its halting progress towards the consensus ideas. These ideas and values are the fruit of man's collective and cumulative search for the impersonal summum bonum, as distinct from his group or parochial interests and goals. The making of this distinction requires a critical analysis of man's plural value systems, as they have evolved in history. The realization of the deeper continuity of the historical movement requires the capacity for correctly assessing what shape present conditions and seeming trends are likely to take in the long run, rather than in the immediate future. This foresight or vision into the distant future is sharpened by the study of history. But some individuals may be endowed with historical intuition—the foresight into the contours of the future, on the basis of a 'feel' for the significance of the present.

(4) ILLUSION AND REALITY

History teaches us that our greatest heroes, after all, are not entirely without 'feet of clay', and that human excellence contains some grey areas. History reveals the ever recurring instances of the shattering of ideals by even the noblest, the struggle for power, the reign of self-interest, the brittleness of man's achievements, the tragedies of life, the shifting of loyalties, the miscarriages of justice, the exploitation of the helpless, the reign of the irrational, the persecution of dissent, the arrogance of power, the pride of race, the imperialism of culture, the grip of prejudice, the retreat of value, the corridors of cultural darkness in space and time, the power of the bribe, the corruption of the priest, the callousness of the bailiff, the law's delay, the cunning of the trader. History also reveals, the recurring instances of heroic devotion to duty, unflinching commitment to ideals, drinking the hemlock with smiling lips, eternal love and loyalty of the friend or the spouse, the power of creativity, the strength of faith, the resilience of life, the tenacity of will, the re-emergence of value, the triumph of reason and organization, and the immortality of hope. Such, in short, is the ambivalence of life. And the wisdom of history lies in refraining from passing any one sided judgment, but to be patient and serene in the gathering of evidence and humble in the passing of judgments of probability when the time be ripe. Like great literature, history reveals the complexity, ambiguity and the antinomical structure of man's character. More than any other discipline, it is history, which teaches us that the characters of the human drama are neither white nor black but grey. This insight lifts us from the cave of darkness into clear daylight, in which we can survey the human condition free from distortion.

(5) The Oneness of the Human Family

History teaches us that mankind is one indivisible family; despite the diversity of race, religion, language and culture, and that there are no chosen races or peoples. History is not subject to our hopes and pious wishes or prayers to an omnipotent God Who is partisan to His chosen people; history is a movement governed by sociological laws. These laws, however, leave ample scope for human creativity and freedom of choice between different existential interpretations and of action.

The realization of the essential oneness of the human family leads to a humanistic sympathy, transcending man's sense of belonging to narrow groups. The rise and fall, achievements and failures, glory and decline of different branches of the human family, at different points of time, appear to the historian as parts of a single story, whose heroes and villains, priests and teachers, soldiers and leaders, gladiators and showmen, poets and bards, harlots and slaves, patricians and plebeians are, after all, the flesh of his flesh and the bone of his bones.

The variety and treasures of man's culture—different languages, religions, art forms, political and social patterns—all are seen as the fruit of man's creative response to the essential mystery of the universe, worthy of our respectful attention or study, for enabling us to make our own well informed and free choices, instead of being prisoners of an ethnocentric approach. Every human, thus, learns to rejoice at the achievements of, say, the ancient Chinese, Indians or Greeks, as much as an ethnocentric Englishman would at Clive's victory at Plassey or Nelson's at Trafalgar, or Shakespeare's literary triumphs, or as an ethnocentric German would rejoice at the achievements of Bismarck or Goethe.

Likewise, the tragic disunity of the Greeks, the decline and fall of the Roman empire, the dismemberment of the Mauryan empire into warring districts, the sufferings of the Jews down the ages, the destruction of Baghdad and Cordova, and the present humiliation of the Arab peoples move the universal man with almost the same historical pathos, since they repeat almost the same story with different characters. The smiles or tears, nobility or sordidness, success or failure, good or evil of the characters is seen as a human phenomenon and not from the perspective of an Arab or Jew, Muslim or Hindu, European or Asian.

The victory of Akbar over Rajput Kings, the successful defiance by Shivaji of the might of the Mughal empire, the crushing of the 1857 rebellion against foreign rule in India, the heroic saga of Stalingrad, the humiliating defeat of Mussolini and Hitler, etc., are judged as happy triumphs or sad defeats, not in terms of the racial or religious affiliations or the interests and aspirations of the protagonists, but in terms of their historical role in promoting universal values. Likewise, the martyrdom of a Socrates, Bruno, Gandhi, and Martin Luther King, or the sufferings of a Galileo, Priestley, Freud, and Karl Jaspers, purify and inspire the universal man, no less deeply than the martyrdom of a Husain or Sarmad or the sufferings of Hambal or of Abul Kalam Azad.

The universal man explains the vicissitudes of the human family, not as the wages of sin or as the favors of an anthropomorphic God, or as the trials and travails of a chosen people, who have betrayed their Lord but who are destined to conquer the non-believers at a time of God's own choosing; the universal man tries to understand the ups and downs of the human family, as a doctor tries to understand human health and disease, free from praise or blame, pride or prejudice, anger or hate. The historian who has humanistic sympathy and cares for historical veracity explains the vicissitudes of the human family in terms of universal social dynamics, which does not preclude his faith in God or in any particular Divine revelation.

Faith in the oneness of God does not necessarily imply 'one God, one Church', that is, cultural monism; faith in one God implies man's unity in diversity and diversity in unity. History teaches us not to feel hurt or displeased at the pluralism of language, religion and culture, but to view them all as the flowering of man's creative responses to the mystery of being. When the historian-philosopher truly and deeply realizes this he shares, partly, if not wholly, the joy of the mystic at the contemplation of the unity of all being.

(6) Mystical Dimension of History

Historical contemplation, thus, has a hidden kinship with mysticism. The awareness of the oneness of the human family, and the transience of the characters and events of the human story, add a fresh dimension to man's response to the human condition down the ages.

The decline of great men and empires, the defeat of ambitions, the eclipse of power and glory, the withering away of luxury, the silent eloquence of imposing ruins, the decay of culture and death of creativity, on the one hand, and on the other, the rise to power and greatness of the once lowly, the vindication of the once oppressed and despised, the transfer of power and culture from 'master races' to 'barbarian hordes', the growth of despised and vulgar dialects into the language of learning and culture, the rise of new ideas and values, the emergence of new vistas and horizons, the spectacle of fresh conquests, the entry of new heroes on the center stage of action from the backbenches of humanity, in short, the contemplation of the transience of life and the ever changing wheels of power and cultural glory, lead the historian-philosopher to perhaps the greatest liberating truth man can contemplate: *"everything perishes save the countenance of the Lord."*

(7) THE ANTINOMY OF HISTORY

In the final analysis (as far as empirical history is concerned), power turns antinomically into weakness and weakness into power, knowledge into ignorance and ignorance into knowledge, light into darkness and darkness into light. It is precisely this dualistic process of history, or the antinomical structure of man's life, that constitutes his existential freedom to choose how to respond to his own unique historical situation. He may will to change the darkness in him and around him into light, as far as lies in his power, in the given situation, or he may allow whatever dim light may be present to be swallowed into the enveloping darkness, within and without.

Realizing that the light, which active and dedicated souls help to create in history, with their 'blood, sweat and tears', shines for but a few fleeting moments in the vastness of time and space, before being blown out in dark and stormy nights of the soul, the historian, nevertheless, does not give the counsel of despair to himself or others, since history tells him that the light, which was extinguished in Babylonia did shine again in Athens, Nalanda and Taxila, Baghdad and Cordova, Padua and Paris, Oxford and Cambridge, Konigsberg and Heidelberg, Petersburg and Harvard, Benares, Aligarh and Shantiniketan.

Should the historian have an existential faith that nature and history move in some direction that partakes of good even if there be no verifiable goal as such, he can very well cherish the hope that ultimately light would prevail over darkness. The historian need not despair at the many noble failures to set right a world, ever out of joint. In the final analysis, the active existential pursuit of good leaves man with little energy or inclination to debate intellectual proofs whether God has created man or man has created God.

Essay 6

Towards a Humanist Interpretation of History and Politics

Facts of History and Their Interpretation

If one looks at history from the humanist perspective the political or religious conflicts of the human family in the past turn into humanity's march (in circuitous and halting stages) towards a global federal unity. The victory of an Alexander and the defeat of a Porus in India, the almost total destruction of Baghdad by a Halaku and the devastations in north India by a Nadir Shah, the compassion of an Asoka, the statesmanship of an Akbar, the aberrations of a Hitler, all become the achievements or failures of the human family. With charity for all and malice toward none, the historian passes judgment on the deed, rather than the doer. His standards remain consistent, but he takes into account that human ideas and ideals are subject to the law of evolutionary growth. In short, his range of sympathy gradually becomes universal instead of remaining congealed at a particular parochial level determined by his birth or early conditioning.

It is significant that the data of history are not given to the truth seeker, as are the data of nature to the scientific investigator through sense perception or experiments under controlled conditions of observation. The data of history are themselves, in part, constructs out of surviving remains of past things or events. Moreover, no two historians select exactly the same set of data out of the total range available. Historians select their own unique 'effective' data for a systematic narrative and analysis of the past. The historian fits these data in his favored framework of ideas and values out of several alternatives available. No such framework, as such, can be proved as conclusively true or valid. Yet, one must have some basic frame of orientation (as pointed out by Erich Fromm) in order to understand or existentially respond to the human situation in totality. Religions and philosophies, in different ways, perform this function. They hold their effective data together and enable one to arrive at a total perspective on the human situation as such. Thus, a historian having a *Hindutva* frame of orientation would tend to view Sultan Mahmud's destruction of the Somnath temple, Gujrat, in the 10th century as an Islamic attack on Hindu India. A historian with a humanist sociological orientation would view the same episode as a medieval Sultan's lust for booty. This admission, however, does not amount to unrelieved relativity of historical interpretation as such. Let me explain this point further.

A reliable contemporary Persian record of Mahmud's time states that after returning to his capital, covered with glory and laden with booty, the Sultan sent some valuable gifts to a venerated divine of Ghazna; Qazi Abul Hasan Baulami. The Qazi returned the royal gifts and severely chastised the Sultan for violating the *shariah*, which prohibited the desecration of any place of worship. Obviously, the honest and bold response of the Qazi had no effect upon the Sultan and the general course of events in medieval time. However, the above authentic story makes it quite clear that the primary '*leitmotif*' of the medieval Sultans was personal aggrandizement and expansion of power, not the promotion of Islam or forcible conversion. In this sense and to this extent, therefore, the humanist interpretation of history becomes more valid than the *Hindutva* interpretation that rejoices in Muslim baiting and distortion of the past. By the same token those Muslims who glorify Sultan Mahmud as an Islamic hero misinterpret or distort Islam and also harm Muslims and entire humanity.

The liberal humanist approach looks upon the conflict between Shivaji and Aurangzeb in the 17th century as a confrontation between a well established, but declining imperial Delhi and a rising regional power in the Pune region of India. The destruction of some Hindu temples during the medieval period, according to the humanist perspective, was essentially an exercise to contain political rebellion or defiance, rather than an attack on the Hindu faith. Is there any justification for preferring one perspective to the other, or is each perspective merely arbitrary? Well, I submit valid reasons can be advanced in support of the humanist approach.

These facts are well documented in reliable contemporary sources. Even the Mughal-Sikh relations during Aurangzeb's long reign were far more cordial than came to be believed in later times, primarily, due to Ahmad Shah Abdali's plundering raids in the Punjab region and other political developments in India after the decline of Mughal power. Ranjit Singh, again, inaugurated an era of religious liberalism and tolerance in his Lahore Kingdom, but his successors failed him woefully. The Muslims of north India lost their self-confidence and *elan* and withdrew into a fundamentalist shell, under the impact of steadily growing British domination throughout the land.

As said above, the historical interpretations are organically related to still more basic existential interpretations of the total human situation and such interpretations do not admit proof in the conclusive scientific or logical sense. It is incontrovertible that the Arab or Turkish tribes who invaded India were Muslim by religion. Therefore, if one insists upon emphasizing the religious identity of the invader, the invasion will always appear as an attack of Islam upon Hinduism. However, the dispersal of peoples and races on earth, and struggle for power and wealth is universal and an integral part of the human story as such. Before Mahmud and Babar had turned their attention to India they had conquered or tried to conquer lands in central Asia that were inhabited by their own co-religionists. The Aryans and other Hindus, in earlier times, had done the same in vast stretches of the Indian subcontinent. So have all other races and peoples the world over, be they Egyptians, Greeks, Romans, Chinese or Europeans. Now this awareness can and usually does liberate the impartial and careful observer of the human situation from the habit of seeing every person or event under a religious label. He then becomes open to the concrete quality of life as it flows in history and judges men and matters accordingly. The humanist does not divide humans into permanently hostile in-groups and out-groups. He looks at the conflicts of the past as stages in the slow growth of the human family and the progressive realization of cherished ideas and ideals in history.

HUMANISM AND SECULAR DEMOCRACY:

Humanism implies giving primacy to man's sense of wonder and mystery when he confronts the universe. Secular democracy, as a political concept, flows from humanism. Every religion attempts to unravel the mystery of birth and death, good and evil, joy and sorrow, final release from pain and suffering. Answers to such questions can never be proved and different people at different times are bound to give different answers to such existential questions. Such matters should, therefore, not be dealt with by the state and should be left as matters of individual preference or conscience. Secularism holds that the state should not advocate or oppose any attempt at resolving the existential mystery of the universe. The state should concern itself only with matters of law and order, security, political, economic, educational and administrative arrangements, framing and administering of civil and criminal laws and so on. When Secularism is combined with liberal Humanism this adds up to Democracy. This implies that the state should perform all the above functions with the consent of all its citizens according to previously agreed procedures so that law becomes the ruler, rather than any person or persons. It is, however, inevitable that law will be interpreted and enforced by the persons concerned, and, thus, will reflect their personality and national character in the framing and the application of the laws as such.

A serious complication, however, arises in the above definition of Secularism, if and when any organized religion claims that it is more than an existential perspective on the inscrutable mystery of the universe, and that it is a complete 'blue print of the good life as a whole', and further, that it is the religious duty of the believer to live strictly in accordance with the prescribed code as such. Some believers might be convinced that it is also part of their religious duty to convince all other to do the same. Now, if the state has a mixed population this approach creates tension and conflict. Even if the citizens belong to one religion they may, well, be members of different sects or have diverse views on creedal and social matters. This was the actual situation in medieval Christianity and Islam, and the idea prevailed that the church and state ought to be one.

As we all know, after centuries of doctrinal and also armed conflict the Christians in Western Europe outgrew doctrines that directly or indirectly produced conflict between the church and the state. *The Treaty of Westphalia*, Germany, signed in 1648, was, in essence, the recognition of the principles that:

(a) the church and the state have their respective proper jurisdiction, and neither should encroach upon the other; and

(b) the state should be neutral and impartial to all its citizens, irrespective of the church to which they belong.

The Treaty of Westphalia, thus, initiated the era in which the English philosopher, John Locke, wrote his famous letters on tolerance and *The Glorious Revolution* took place in Britain in 1688. This was the beginning of the story of religious tolerance in Western Europe, but the story took two centuries to reach a happy ending when Disraeli, Jewish by blood, became Prime Minister of Great Britain.

The founding fathers of the constitution of free India were inspired by the idea that every citizen of a sovereign state stood equal in regard to basic rights, responsibilities and opportunities, irrespective of religion, caste, region or gender. This approach implied that the Indian republic had no official religion. It will be agreed that this ideas was very laudable and also courageous at a time when extreme passions had been aroused due to the unfortunate partition of the country in 1947 on religious lines.

THE HINDU AND MUSLIM RESPONSES TO SECULAR HUMANIST POLITICS:

When the Constituent Assembly was carrying on its deliberations and also subsequently some Hindu quarters raised voices (perhaps in all sincerity and good conscience) that the term, Secularism, was an unnecessary borrowing or imitation of Western ideas, under the influence of Nehru and that the secular ideal should be displaced by the ancient Hindu ideal of equal respect for all religions (*sarva dharma sadbhava*). They argued that the idea of Secularism was an understandable response of the Western humanitarian reformers to the never-ending religious intolerance and conflicts between different religions or sectarian groups in Christian society. Since Hinduism was intrinsically free from the virus of intolerance and was committed to the doctrine of free choice of Deity (*Isht Devata*), free India, having an overwhelmingly Hindu population should substitute the borrowed Western secular idiom with the ancient traditional idiom of *sarva dharma sadbhava*. They confidently claimed that a true Hindu state would guarantee and fully protect all fundamental human rights as the secular dispensation does today. They held that the stress on secularism not only diluted national pride but also diluted the distinctive spiritual basis of the Indian value system that was her glory from time immemorial. Perhaps, these quarters had in mind the example of several Muslim countries, recently liberated from colonial rule, which became Islamic states and commanded influence and power in the comity of nations without having imitated Western secular democracy. I submit this reasoning is sophistry and illusion.

The definition of Hinduism, or any other religion, for that matter, is a matter of choice and opinion. The basic question, 'what is Hinduism/Islam?' or, 'who is a good Hindu/Muslim?' elicits plural answers. Both Gandhi and Hedgewar were good Hindus, but their idea of Hinduism differed. Likewise, Sir Syed, Maulana Azad, and Mawdudi were all good Muslims, but their idea of Islam differed. Gandhiji remarked that if untouchability were an integral part of Hinduism he was not prepared to call himself a Hindu. He, obviously, believed that untouchability was not integral to Hinduism. However, I personally know some Hindus who honestly hold that a good Hindu ought to follow Manu's laws to the letter. I may add that I honestly respect these Hindu friends for their sincerity and integrity though I freely express my disagreement with them. The same remarks apply to some Muslim relatives or friends. I admire them for their integrity without agreeing with their idea of Islam.

Despite the fact that India is a secular state the country has to face serious problems in controlling communal passions and maintaining inter-group harmony. These problems arise due to political or economic factors, but interested parties give a religious or communal color to them as a matter of strategy. A secular state, therefore, would always be better placed than a Hindu state to provide an even ground to players belonging to diverse religions, castes and regions. The same remarks apply to Islamic states whose citizens belong to different religions or sects.

Many Indian Muslims feel uncomfortable with the idea of de-linking politics and Islam. In their hearts they continue to hold that the *shariah* applies to every aspect of life, but they, reluctantly, reconcile themselves to the realities of the Indian situation. This approach is a halfway house, rather than a full or unqualified commitment to humanist secularism and liberal democracy. But, then inner attitudes require centuries to grow and evolve in the minds and hearts of men enjoying security and freedom. Gandhi and Nehru understood the human condition and showed patience and generosity to all. Perhaps, the votaries of *Hindutva* today are impatient and their insight into the human condition is blurred, and this makes it hard for them to arrive at a proper and balanced evaluation of the genuine Muslim response to the Indian situation.

The doubts and fears in *Hindutva* quarters arise more because of Islamic terrorism outside India than because of religious fundamentalism among Indian Muslims. Since Muslim terrorists in Pakistan and elsewhere carry on the heinous crime of killing innocents in the name of Islam, non-Muslims are led to accept this claim at is face value. But the truth is entirely different. Religious fundamentalism, as such, springs from cultural isolation and a closed society that hampers free enquiry. Political terrorism, on the other hand, springs from existential anxiety and despair in the face of perceived injustice and the tyranny of the strong over the weak. Moreover, political terrorism cuts across different religions and regions.

Muslims in fairly large numbers in India may have demanded and loudly cheered the birth of Pakistan in the forties of the last century, but the fateful partition, certainly, traumatized those who were left in the lurch in India by its creation. Now they suffer from a growing sense of insecurity in India due to the rising Hindu fascist trends in Indian politics. The Hindus, on the other hand, constitute eighty-five percent of the population and, more or less totally, control the politics and economics of the land. Yet, they do not feel inwardly secure and in full control of the situation in India. They are scared of the dangers latent in Islamic fundamentalism and terrorism.

The Muslim logic is that Hindus do not behave like a 'big brother', as they should towards the Muslim or the Christian minority. The Hindu logic is that far from being this case, Indian Muslims, in fact, are members of a mighty and potentially extremely rich Islamic power bloc stretching from North Africa to South East Asia. In other words, the Hindus do not perceive the Muslims as a weak younger brother but as a potentially larger and more powerful world community. A fear seems to lurk in the depths of the Hindu psyche that neither the Western world, nor the Islamic wants the peace loving and patient Hindu community to live in peace under their own sky. And fear is the mother of hate and aggression. This is also the root cause of the rising incidence in recent years of physical violence against Indian Christians in several parts of the land.

Whatever Christian missionaries may or may not have done in the past to save lost souls in India the Christian Church has nothing to do with the theory or practice of forcing Christianity on infidels or bribing them to join the flock of Christ. The plain truth is that the vast majority of Christian missionaries in India today are models of selfless service, piety and religious scholarship. Even the Pope has accepted plural paths to salvation. The adversarial approach to other religions has undergone an internal revolution in the contemporary Christian value system. On this point all the major religions of the world are fast converging. It is a pity that some *Hindutva* quarters still nurse or air old grievances against Muslims and Christians.

There is no dearth of compassionate and fair-minded Hindus and Muslims in India and Pakistan. They are, in fact, the silent majority. However, a vocal minority among the Hindus and Muslims may be said to have hijacked the role of spokesperson for Hinduism or Islam, as the case may be. But I submit, it will not be long when the relative supremacy of good over evil in the human heart, armed with the advantages of modern communication technology, will empower the liberal humanist vanguard, within each community, to initiate interfaith dialogues. And this is bound to produce very fruitful results in terms of mutual understanding and appreciation of the spiritual wealth found in every religious tradition. This will pave the way for removing ignorance and prejudice in each in-group against other out-groups. This will dilute the present adversarial relations between the different religious groups in India and elsewhere.

This is how modern intellectual and savants such as Newton (d. 1727), Gibbon (d. 1794), Goethe (d. 1832), Carlyle (d. 1881), and Browne (d. 1926) *et al* came to respect and admire Sufism, while others, such as, Schopenhauer (d. 1860), Max Muller (d. 1900), and Romain Rolland (d. 1944), *et al* came to respect and admire Vedanta and Yoga. The same was the case with Ram Mohan Roy (d. 1833) in the late 18th century and M.N.Roy (d. 1954), Bhagwan Das (d. 1958), and Tara Chand *et al* in the 20th century. They all greatly appreciated the historic role of Islam in world history.

The theory and practice of organized Hinduism in modern times does not regulate or control every sphere of human life to the same degree or extent, as does Islam through *shariah*. Hindu society has been rather permissive and tolerant of plural interpretations of both creed and law. In ancient times it accommodated Jain and Buddhist ideas and values within the wider *Brahmanical* culture. According to judicious historians, due to this conceptual openness of early Hindu society Buddhist agnosticism, more or less, completely came to overshadow *Brahmanical* orthodoxy in several parts of the county. This lasted till the rise and spread of Shankarcharya's revivalist movement of pure *Brahmanism* in the early 9th century. Thereafter, both Jainism and Buddhism declined or rather withered away and the contours of Hinduism, as we understand it today, emerged. Scholars have viewed this crucial process differently. Some regard it as the result of persecution of dissent. Others say it happened due to the extreme 'porosity' of Hindu thought and culture. Due to various factors the Hindu population absorbed the conceptual and social innovations of Jain and Buddhist reformers, and took the wind out of the sails of these early reform and protest movements in ancient India.

By the 10th century *Brahmanical* thought became rigid, as Al-Beruni points out in his monumental work on Indian thought and culture. Hindu creativity had become a spent force, as generally happens in the human family. Political in-fighting between the Hindu chiefs and a vicious social stratification had resulted in a shocking dehumanization of the lowest class. At the same time the Islamic revolution in the 7th century had grown into a mighty world current. This, rather than the sword of Islam, acted as a catalyst in different parts of the then known world. In India the creative impact of Islam led to the ideas of ethical theism and bhakti. A little later in Western Europe it led to the Protestant and Humanitarian versions of Christianity.

The Islamic message of social equality, however, was qualified by the idea of the brotherhood and equality of all Muslims, rather than of all men, irrespective of religion or faith. Not only this, the Islamic idea of equality and fraternity remained entangled with the thorns of racial pride and kingly authoritarianism. To make matters worse, the Sultans in India and the entire nobility could not emancipate themselves from the evil of a vicious caste system in India. Thus, the seed of early Islamic republicanism and democracy lay fallow and dormant for several centuries before they flowered and flourished in the representative democracy of modern times, first in England and subsequently in Western Europe and America. As we all know, this consummation took place in the Christian rather than in the Muslim world. The scientific and technological revolutions that took place in Western Europe from the end of the 18th century onwards were, thus, the complete flowering of the early spiritual and intellectual creativity of early Islam. Paradoxically, Islamic creativity led to a glorious cultural reconstruction in Europe, but not in the regions of Islam itself. Indeed, as the West continued to rise and soar even as Muslim lands continued to decline and sink into decay.

Conclusion:

Western creative modernity reached India via Bengal in the late 18th century. Under its impact as well as the earlier influence of Islamic values Ram Mohan Roy (d. 1833) redefined Hindu spirituality. Almost a century later Sir Syed (d. 1898), leader of the Aligarh movement, did the same for Islam. The liberal Hindu vanguard has retained till today the considerable advantage of their early lead. Moreover, the flame that Ram Mohan ignited soon lighted several other lamps in other parts of the great land. The *Brahmo Samaj Movement* stirred a new vision before the Hindu psyche leading to the Ramakrishna mission and produced luminaries such as Vivekananda (d. 1902), Rabindranath Tagore (d. 1941), Aurobindo (d. 1950), Krishnamurti (d. 1986) *et al* and Gandhi (d. 1948), Rajagopalachari and Nehru (d. 1964) himself.

Sir Syed, on the other hand, to the misfortune of Indian Muslims, in spite of his laudable creative work in the field of Islamic liberalism, merely founded the *Muhammadan Anglo-Oriental College* at Aligarh that produced good cricketers, Deputy Collectors, and of course Muhammad Ali (d. 1931), the President of the Indian National Congress in 1923. As also Altaf Husain Hali (d. 1914), the poet, Allama Shibli (d. 1914), the liberal historian and the impartial biographer of Prophet

Muhammad ﷺ, Chiragh Ali, the social reformer and a few Westernized, forward looking and progressive men of letters. But no corresponding rethinking on Islam or Islamic Reformation (parallel to the massive Christian and Hindu Reformations of earlier times) emerged in a big way from the efforts of Sir Syed and the Aligarh Movement. To my mind, Sir Syed's followers failed him. He died in 1898 and the partition of India, fifty years after his death, was the nadir of this failure. The responsibility for partition however, falls not only on his followers but also on several exclusive Hindu quarters, both individuals and groups that failed to appreciate the larger inclusive vision of the top ranking Congress luminaries.

The partition of India in 1947 has greatly slowed down the cultural interaction between Islam and Hinduism that had begun in medieval India. However, it is patently clear that the process cannot be arrested, no matter what the political constraints and short-term interests of India, Pakistan and Bangla Desh may demand. None of these independent countries can insulate themselves from the pressures and pulls of cultural modernity, economic interdependence and a growing globalism. They are all faced with problems and challenges of overpopulation, corrupt politicians, misuse of religion or caste for short term political gains, poor political will and discipline, irresponsible trade unionism and a host of similar other problems. Yet, it is a fact that the common man everywhere yearns for mutual understanding and peace and is moved by the simple goodness of the heart, above all talk of religion or politics in the name of jihad, *Hindutva* or Communism.

Through trial and error, blood and tears the human family is reaching out for the 'religion of the spirit' without any call for converting people to any theological creed or tradition. This approach to religion leaves intact the distinctive idiom and symbols of each historical religion, but unites them all in a common search for values. This is the interfaith approach of all enlightened and noble souls in the world today. Gandhiji was the prophet of the religion of the spirit. He remains the most outstanding combination, in modern times, of mass political leadership, conceptual creativity, statesmanship and sainthood. The RSS has different ideas and sources of inspiration. Persons, like Bal Thackeray, look up to Shivaji for inspiration and guidance. I will respect all sincere devotees and believes even though I may not agree with them. But I strongly protest the behavior of the VHP, Bajrang Dal, Shiv Sena and others when they resort to violence for promoting their vision and values. If militancy or terrorism is evil in the case of jihad it is also evil in the case of *Hindutva*. There can be no double standards. This is the crux of the matter.

The United Nations is a great step in this noble direction. But super powers are ever tempted to turn the august body into a tool for promoting their own interests. This, again, is quite natural and understandable. It is, therefore, imperative not to lose faith but to persist in doing what is right and avoid what is wrong.

Essay 7

Mughal–Sikh Relations in Medieval India

Introduction

The purpose of this essay is to make a critical survey of Mughal-Sikh relations from the inception of the movement of radical reform in Hinduism, the stages of its growth leading to the rise and glory of the Lahore Kingdom of Maharaja Ranjit Singh, and its end a few years after the death of Ranjit Singh in 1839. I am not a historian, but I hold that historical enquiry holds the key for opening the lock of truth and wisdom of life in general. I have already discussed the theory, philosophy and wisdom of history in my essay of the same title above. Here I propose to apply my theoretical approach to the theme of Mughal-Sikh relations in medieval India.

This subject is of utmost importance if one wants to understand the past as well as the present internal conflicts in Indian history in the proper perspective. As we all know, humans just cannot live without entertaining some image of the past and some dream of the future, just as they cannot survive in the present without some pattern of power relations within some social organization. The struggle for supreme power is, thus, the inseparable shadow of the substance of human life and relationships. Any distortion in the image of the past or confusion/or illusion in the dream of the future has a spill-over effect upon human attitudes and actions in the present. That is why history matters so much for living the good life in the present.

In the context of Indian history and politics the struggle for power very easily comes to be looked upon as the conflict of one religion with some other or others. But nothing could be further from the truth than this conception. The impartial study of history based on reliable historians (whose reliability is not assumed but ascertained as critically as humanly possible) gives us a sound basis for making sense of the movement of history. The entire narrative or purely descriptive portion of my essay is based on Khushwant Singh's two-volume History of the Sikhs and the History of Ranjit Singh. I have consulted other standard works also. But I shall not name them since Khuswant Singh's narrative is based on a remarkably judicious and balanced selection from these older and larger works. The important thing is whether, or not, the narrative one accepts as one's base takes into account all interests and points of view. I think Khushwant Singh's narrative passes this test with flying colours.

Guru Nanak

Guru Nanak was born in a village, near Lahore, in 1469 in a middle class *Khatri* family of Punjab. His father, Meha Kalyan Das Bedi, was an accountant in the village. The Punjab was under the stable rule of Turkish Sultans for more than 200 years and the gradual peaceful Islamization of north India was already far advanced in the region, as well as in the entire Gangetic plain down south under the successive Turkish dynasties starting from the Ghorids of central Asia.

The *Sufi* movement had already reached India after the victory of Sultan Muhammad Ghori in the battle of Tarain in 1191. The premier saint of north India, Al-Hujwari, popularly known as Data Sahab (d. 1079) lies buried in Lahore. He was soon followed by Khwaja Moinuddin Chishti (d. 1235) of Ajmer. The movement grew by leaps and bounds specially among rural folk cutting across the religious divide between Muslims and Hindus. The thrust of the *Sufi* movement lay in pietism and absolute trust in an all-loving and all-powerful Creator who responded to the prayers of sincere devotees, irrespective of distinctions of creed or caste. The *Bhakti* movement in the pale of Hinduism was the counterpart of, essentially, the *Sufi* approach, and it made great headway all over the country ever since the advent of Islam in India. However, the basic concepts and values of *bhakti* were already embedded in the far older Indian religious and spiritual tradition.

The Hindu tradition, however, always possessed an 'umbrella' character that permitted internal diversity and flexibility, including polytheism and idol worship, while the Islamic tradition did not allow plural forms of worship and theologies. The orthodox Muslim theologians just could not appreciate this enduring pluralist temper of Hindu spirituality and religion. But the *Sufis* were liberal and tolerant from the very beginning. They were very good and devoted practitioners of the prescribed Islamic code of conduct in all matters, spiritual and worldly, yet they did not object if other believers found solace and satisfaction in idol worship. The orthodox *ulema*, to date, find idolatry extremely repulsive and repugnant. The *Sufis* kept at a safe distance from the Sultans and were totally averse to interfering in state policy or in administrative matters. They respected all faiths and creeds as different paths to one God. They stressed on cultivating piety rather than pressurizing the Sultan to follow the *shariah* in both private and public life as was the wont of the *ulema* on the ground that the *shariah* was all embracing. The *Bhakti* and *Sufi* movements were functionally similar, though each was rooted in a distinct cultural tradition.

The unique contribution of Guru Nanak is that he blended the two streams in a captivating spiritual synthesis that had an organic unity. The Guru had the intellectual penetration, moral courage and foresight to Islamize Hinduism or to Indianize Islam. As an intellectually honest and sensitive observer of the Indian scene, where the state was dominated politically by the Muslims, but numerically by the Hindus, the Guru knew very well the strengths and weaknesses of both. As a free seeker of truth he appreciated and assimilated truth wherever the search led him. He deeply appreciated the Islamic form of Monotheism, the simple mode of worship almost devoid of rituals, the social equality and brotherhood of all men, the absence of gross superstition and myths, the moral and physical courage of its followers, while he abhorred the superstitions, the spate of rituals and rites that permeated religious worship, the extreme social gradation and also the caste system (including the morally repugnant prevalence of 'untouchability' and the ban on temple entry) and other forms of gender inequality in Hindu society. Guru Nanak was led to accept that what ultimately mattered to the one single human family was social harmony, goodness of character and righteous action, just as the *Sufis* did and Gautama Buddha had done long ago. Probably Guru Nanak's extensive travels all over the country and also central and west Asia had completely liberated him from the pull of ethno-centricity, which is the general lot of the common man. The saint, Kabir (d. 1515) in the heartland of the Gangetic plain, had spoken the same language of the spirit a little earlier before the Guru. However, Kabir was not as proactive as Guru Nanak in the task of fighting against various forms of social injustice and evils that had crept into Indian society. Kabir also did not have the extraordinary organizing skill of Guru Nanak.

Guru Nanak decried not only the weaknesses of his own Hindu tradition but also of rigid Islamic orthodoxy that preached the concept of exclusive salvation. He never imitated or blindly accepted any belief or practice. He continued to accept the ancient Aryan or Hindu concept of '*karma*' or repeated rebirths as retributive and reformative punishment for moral wrongdoings. He did not give up his inner conviction in this core Aryan belief in favor of the Semitic belief in one final Day of Judgment. This demonstrates, to my mind, the power and depth of the Guru's spiritual autonomy and the profound integrity of his character.

In the final analysis, Guru Nanak was a universal man, not a spokesman. His was a perennial vision, not a time-bound code. His message transcends, not constitutes any sect. He would have said, '*I am not a Nanakvadi*'. Guru Nanak belongs to the category of great prophets and seers who are the joint architects of the ever-evolving human spirit that yearns to transcend all temporal particularities of the human situation. Buddhism and Jainism were creative protests against some features of the *Aryan Sanatana Dharma*. This *Dharma* responded creatively in the form of Shankara's inclusive and permissive synthesis of Vedism and Buddhism/Jainism. This synthesis is the core of what we understand by Hinduism today. Similarly, *Nanakvad* was a creative protest against some features of the Hindu *Dharma* as it developed after Shankara. Just as Buddhism was the catalytic agent that acted as a leaven for the internal growth of the Aryan thought and value system, Islam was the catalyst in the case of *Nanakvada*. Guru Nanak's all-inclusive vision became the turning point in Indian history that triggered several 'shakings of the foundations' of the Hindu mind ever since the cry from the heart of Kabir in Kashi and Guru Nanak in Lahore. Ram Mohan Rai, the father of the Indian Renaissance, stands on their shoulders, but his arms had a far wider reach than the two because his vision was further enriched by the knowledge and wisdom of the modern West.

Not content with the high spiritual level he had attained Guru Nanak set out to help others to do so. He wanted to liberate the masses from ignorance, superstition and fanaticism. His simple but profoundly moving poetry in Punjabi was his mode of communication. His Muslim disciples were not apostates from Islam but Muslim believers who genuinely admired the elevated spiritual status of the Guru. Under his inspiration they concluded that the highest level of Monotheism had the capacity to accommodate its various historical versions, whether Indian or Semitic.

Guru Nanak totally rejected the idea or institution of hereditary succession in the sphere of spirituality. He nominated a very close and highly evolved disciple, Angad, as his spiritual successor. Angad became the Second Guru in 1539; Amar Das the Third Guru in 1552. He nominated his son-in-law, Ram Das, as the Fourth Guru in 1574. His son, Arjan Mal, under the name Arjan Dev, became the Fifth Guru, in 1581. It will be seen that the criteria of nomination of the Second and Third Guru were purely spiritual with no regard for hereditary succession. The hereditary or family principle of succession started from the Fourth Guru onwards and remained operative till the end of the line of Gurus with the death of Guru Gobind Singh in 1708.

The anointment of Arjan Dev is a landmark in the history of Sikhs. A poet and man of letters, and dynamic leader he collected the scattered poetic compositions of Guru Nanak and his immediate successors and his own poems in one volume. He included the poetic writings of selected *Sufi* poets such as Kabir, Guru Nanak, Baba Farid, and *Bhaktas* like Namdev, Ravi Das, Jai Dev and others in the same collection, called the *Adi Granth Sahib*. It contains approximately five thousand hymns and, understandably, the largest number of poems (about 975) are by Guru Nanak. The Fifth Guru also built the *Harimandir* right in the center of a sacred tank, Amritsar that had been dug earlier by the Fourth Guru. It is widely believed (though many reliable historians are doubtful) that Mian Mir, the much-venerated *Sufi* saint of Lahore, laid the foundation stone of the Golden temple at the invitation of the Guru. This fact or myth (whatever the truth) symbolizes the catholicity of Sikh spirituality like the institution of free community meals (*langar*) inside the *gurudwara* without any distinction of caste, color or creed.

MUGHAL-SIKH RELATIONS:

The Sikh reform movement Guru Nanak initiated in the Hindu tradition in the 15th century had the full support and blessings of Emperor Akbar (d. 1605). He donated land in Amritsar for the construction of the *Harimandir* and also met the Fifth Guru, Arjan Dev. However, within a few months of Jehangir's accession his son Khusro rebelled against his father, the Emperor. The rebellion failed and all supporters of Prince Khusro were executed or severely punished. It is well established that the erring Prince had sought blessings and material aid from the Guru. It is also certain (as certain as any historical certainty in such cases) that the Guru had obliged the Prince. But to what extent he went is not clear. However, in pursuance of the law of the land Jehangir ordered the Guru to be tortured to death.

Jehangir had inherited the religious liberalism of Akbar, but he could not tolerate sedition. The Emperor did not listen even to the plea of the highly venerated saint, Mian Mir, of Lahore. All those who supported Khusro were executed with the sole exception of Shaikh Nizam of Thaneswar. Jehangir granted his plea that he be allowed to migrate to Arabia as a permanent exile. One may well question the Emperor's wisdom in rejecting Mian Mir's intercession on behalf of the Guru, but it is difficult to hold that the Emperor was intolerant or a fanatic. Jehangir did not hesitate to imprison the famous theologian and saint, Shaikh Ahmad Sarhandi, in the Gwalior fort for a year or more when the Shaikh started opposing the religious liberalism of Akbar and dabbling in politics.

On Guru Arjan's death in 1606, his eleven year-old son, Hargobind, became the Sixth Guru. At the very outset the young Guru chose to challenge and confront the Mughal authorities. He refused to pay the fine of two lackhs that had been imposed upon his father, enlarged his small bodyguard into a private militia, including gunners. He built a throne, approximately twelve feet high (*akaal thakht*) facing the *Harimandir*, in the manner of a ruling chief, and also adopted other symbols of royalty. He put forward the doctrine that the Guru was not merely the spiritual head, but also the political head of the Sikh community, which could not accept any other authority. This was known as the doctrine of '*peeri*' and '*meeri*'. He started wearing two swords, one symbolizing spiritual authority (*peeri*) and the other (*meeri*). It is, therefore, understandable why Jehangir decided to imprison the Guru in the Gwalior fort for about two years. After the period of internment was over the Guru was left in peace for the next twenty years or so.

The situation again changed after Jehangir's death and the ascension of Shahjehan. The Guru re-embarked upon political activism of sorts. Most probably, some grudges developed between the Mughal authorities and the henchmen of the Guru who was passionately fond of horses and the hunt. There were reports of skirmishes between the Guru's militia and the imperial forces between 1628- and 1634. The militia did not fare badly in such encounters. However, the Guru himself realized the futility of such aggressive postures and ordered his militia to abandon militancy. He also shifted his headquarters from the centrally placed Kartarpur to Kiratpur in the interior of the Himalayan foothills. There he passed away peacefully in 1644. There was no hostility from the Mughal side.

The Seventh Guru, Har Rai, occupied the apostolic office from 1644 to 1661. Very different from his predecessor, he reverted to the purely spiritual and quietist stance of the earlier Gurus. Aurangzeb ascended the throne in 1658 and had some misgivings about the Guru's role in the war of succession between Aurangzeb, Dara Shikoh and other sons of Shahjehan. The Guru thought it proper to remove all doubts on this score and sent his eldest son, Ram Rai, to pay his respects to the Emperor. Ram Rai was well received and an amicable relationship sprang up between the two. However, the Guru became unhappy with his son when, subsequently, he was led to believe that during his audience with the Emperor Ram Rai had knowingly mistranslated some verses from the holy *Granth Sahab* with a view to pleasing the monarch. Thereupon the Guru decided to exclude his eldest son from succession and nominated his younger son, Hari Krishen (who was then a minor child) as his lawful successor to the spiritual office. Ram Rai naturally resented this and a clear rift was created between father and son, and brother and brother.

Guru Har Rai died in 1661. His nominee was even then a minor, but he had been nominated successor by the Guru himself. The elder brother, Ram Rai enjoyed the patronage of the Emperor, and had not reconciled to the perceived injustice done him by his father. But Sikh public opinion very strongly favored the Guru's nominee. There was considerable suspense and delay in deciding the matter. Finally, public opinion prevailed and the child Hari Kishen was accepted as the Eighth Guru. The elder brother, Ram Rai established a dissident sect and *gurudwara* at Dehra Doon, which functions to date as a minor sect within the wider Sikh fraternity. The child Guru, Hari Krishen, however, shortly afterwards died of small pox at Delhi in 1664.

Just before his death the Eighth Guru (still a minor) nominated his grand uncle from Bakala the Ninth Guru. There was considerable confusion and suspense about the exact identity of the nominee. Eventually, the elders of the community agreed that the person was Tegh Bahadur who was then 43. Before his elevation he lived a life of seclusion, meditation and spiritual discipline. After he became the Ninth Guru in 1664 he became proactive and traveled a lot in the eastern parts of India. His son who was to become the Tenth Guru was born at Patna in 1666. In 1672 the Guru all of a sudden left his family at Patna and returned to Punjab. He became a roaming preacher and prophet of courage and virtue ever exhorting the common man to resist evil in any shape or form. He went to Delhi in 1675 and the same year he suffered martyrdom.

Until very recently the exact circumstances and background of this tragedy was steeped in controversy. A superficial but rather common view was that this was the consequence of Aurangzeb's anti-Hindu and anti-Sikh temper and policies, and that he was bent upon the forcible Islamization of the people, while the Ninth Guru was equally bent upon preserving the freedom of belief and the dignity of the Hindus. These quarters further stated or implied that some Hindu opportunists advised the Emperor that the best way to spread Islam in India was to concentrate on the conversion of *Brahmans* at the main centres of Hindu learning and culture such as Kashi, Hardwar, Kurukshetra etc. If the top *Brahmans* got converted the rest of the population would follow suit. The story goes on that this strategy appealed to the Emperor, while the common Hindus became alarmed. Since they had no courage to face the mighty and haughty Mughal establishment they appealed to the Ninth Guru to help them. The Guru willingly agreed, but advised them not to enter into any arguments with Muslim missionaries, but merely take the stand that they would just follow the lead given by the Guru.

The story proceeds that Aurangzeb invited the Guru to Delhi and tried to convert him, but did not succeed. The Emperor then asked the Guru to show some miracle (*karaamat*) to prove the truth of Sikhism, but the Guru refused. Aurangzeb then imprisoned him and gave him the option to choose either Islam or death. The Guru gladly chose to die.

Kushwant Singh rejects this story. But Dr. Trilok Singh gives a graphic description of the alleged dialogue between the Emperor and the Guru just prior to the execution. Trilok Singh even adds that while the Guru was calmly waiting for the execution a disciple sought the Guru's permission to perform a miracle to satisfy the Emperor's demand made earlier. But the Guru again refused.

I have no doubt that the story is a patent fabrication since as, Khushwant Singh rightly holds on the basis of clear evidence, Aurangzeb was not present at Delhi in 1675. Moreover, the story fits neither with Aurangzeb's character, nor his intelligence. Aurangzeb firmly adhered to the *shariah* and the *shariah* just does not permit forced conversion. Aurangzeb was also too intelligent and prudent to float such a preposterous option before the Guru when he, as the sovereign, had innumerable highly competent, and loyal, non-Muslims occupying some of the top assignments in the army and civil administration of a mighty empire. What Aurangzeb could, possibly, have done in this case and what he actually did in a few cases was to waive a serious penalty when the person had been lawfully proved guilty but was willing to convert and reform himself, if pardoned.

On the basis of a reliable contemporary Persian work, '*Siyaar ul Muthaakhareen*' Khushwant Singh holds that, in fact, there was a formal charge that the Guru was instigating the peasants in Punjab to withhold revenue payments to the Mughal collectors to protest against local corruption and non-action on the just grievances of the poor tillers and farmers in Punjab.

It is worth exploring the truth of this line of thinking. It is established that prior to his elevation as a Guru, Tegh Bahadur was a person of saintly character and a quietist way of life. However, after he became a Guru he was exposed to the stark realities of life and gradually turned into a pro-active social reformer. He spent five years or so traveling extensively in eastern India and then returned to Punjab. When in Bengal and Assam he was closely associated with Raja Jai Singh, one of the most distinguished luminaries of the Mughal establishment and extremely close to the Sovereign. What brought about this profound change is not clearly evident. Perhaps, he realized that the Jat peasants were passing through very harsh times due to local conditions and the callous indifference of the local establishment. Bribery and extortion, indeed, have ever plagued the life of the poor tiller of the soil. It is quite likely that Jat Sikhs were hard pressed to pay revenue dues when they had to pay for the upkeep of *gurudwaras* and the free 'langars' and also gratify the corrupt petty officers. Known for his rectitude and moral courage the Guru may well have encouraged the peasants to 'non-cooperate' with the local staff as a tactics of moral pressure. In short, the hard line of the Guru may have prompted the intermediate higher authorities of the empire to take a hard line against the Guru himself. It is also likely that some sections (known to have opposed the elevation of Tegh Bahdur in the first instance) may have given a twist to the Guru's honest and bold moral support to the weaker sections.

If we look at the tragedy from the above perspective the Guru's martyrdom was not the result of any clash between Hinduism/Sikhism and Islam, or the fanaticism and irrational hatred of Aurangzeb towards the Hindus. It was the result of Aurangzeb's political failure to prevent social unrest and to thwart court intrigues due to his military pre-occupations in far-flung Deccan and Maratha areas, and the consequential rise in levels of corruption, intrigue and aggrandizement in the heart of the empire. Even if the leader of the moral fight against social evils or injustice had been a Muslim saint like Sarmad (who sympathized with Dara Shikoh in the war of succession) he would have fared the same way under the then conditions of the empire.

The Tenth Guru, Gobind Singh, succeeded his father, Tegh Bahadur in 1675. He was at Patna and only nine when he received the severed head of his dead father. His first act, as a Guru, was to vow to avenge his father's murder. This decision signified both filial loyalty and moral indignation against a miscarriage of justice due to intrigue and corruption. The young Guru soon returned to the ancestral residence at Anandpur, Punjab, and forthwith raised a battalion of five hundred paid Afghan fighters as the nucleus of his militia.

The Guru's short but eventful life of forty-four years may be divided into five distinct phases since he became Guru in 1675. The first phase, 1675-1685, lasted ten years. During this period the young Guru resided at Anandpur in perfect peace without any harassment or persecution by the Mughals. He was a gifted and precocious child and his personality blossomed, spiritually and intellectually.

The second phase, 1686-1687, lasted for two years. Alarmed at the growing military build-up and the radical thinking of the Guru, the hill Rajas combined to eject the Guru from Anandpur, which fell in the territory of Bilaspur. The Raja of Bilaspur and his allies bought off the five hundred Afghan mercenaries of the Guru just before they began the attack. Outnumbered, as was the Guru, he fought valiantly at Bhangani, near Paunta in 1686, and repulsed the Rajas. The shock of this defeat made the Rajas take a u-turn in their strategy. They befriended the young charismatic warrior Guru and decided to use his fighting talents for defying Mughal authority. They refused to pay the revenue due to the Mughal government and this led to the battle of Nadaun, 1687, against a small Mughal force. The Guru and his men fought valiantly and repulsed the imperial troops. But apprehending the arrival of Mughal reinforcements the Rajas appealed for a cease-fire and agreed to pay off arrears of revenue. Sadly disillusioned with such fickleness and lack of courage, the Guru, forthwith, broke off from the Rajas and took to a life of tranquil study at Anandpur.

The third phase, 1687-1699, lasted for twelve years. Abjuring all politics and military involvements the Guru engaged himself at Anandpur in pure meditation, study and writing. He also collected a number of *Brahman* scholars (*nirmalas*) for religious studies and research. This is the most creative period, spiritually and doctrinally, in the Guru's life. On the first day of *Baisakhi*, 1699, at the Guru's invitation a vast gathering of his followers collected at Anandpur. The Guru performed the *'Panch Piare'* ceremony, formed the *Khalsa*, formulated the doctrine of the *Panth* and the *'Rahat'* (code of conduct), conducted the ceremony of mass baptism and finally solemnly declared armed resistance to evil as a religious obligation of the true followers of Guru Nanak. In a planned manner and with remarkable insight into human psychology the Guru brought to full fruition, as it were, the seed planted by the first Guru two hundred years earlier. The call given by the Guru was a blend of continuity and change.

The fourth phase, 1700-1704, lased for five years, and during this period also the Guru stayed at Anandpur. But peace was no more. The momentous developments within this period, inevitably, raised very serious apprehensions in the minds of the hill Rajas who were least inclined to appreciate the new militancy of the Guru and all its implications. Not at all interested in throwing off Mughal suzerainty (which was mutually beneficial) the Rajas again combined to evict the Guru from Anandpur by force, if necessary. However, all their efforts proved futile and the Guru stood like a rock against the combined armed attacks. At last, on the appeal of the Rajas, the Mughal forces came to their rescue. In 1703-1704 Anandpur was put under a total siege from all sides. Food stocks ran out and the Guru was in desperate straits. The Guru thought it prudent to accept the offer of safe conduct and leave Anandpur. But no sooner did the Guru, with a small party, leave Anandpur than he was attacked. Escaping to Chamkaur, thence to Machiwara, he found himself in dire peril. Luckily, the stratagem of two loyal Pathans saved his life. The Guru escaped to Jautpura where he learnt the shocking news of the murder of his two minor sons at the hands of the Mughals. Eventually, the Guru reached Kot Kapura camp where he was joined by a large number of the *Khalsa* troops. Once again, from a position of strength the Guru turned the tables on the Mughals and their hill allies. The place of victory came to be known as Muktsar (the place of deliverance). After the dispersal of his pursuers the Guru retired to the village, Talwandi Sabo, later named Dam Dama. This place soon became the centre of Sikh studies and remains so till today.

The fifth and final phase, 1704-1708, lasted five years. During this period the Guru once again withdrew himself from military activities and devoted his time to meditation and writing. He moved about in the Muktsar area of the Malwa region of Punjab. The Jats of Malwa joined the Guru in large numbers during this period. Dam Dama, also called *'Guru ki Kashi'* became a hub of religious studies. Mani Singh, the scholarly and devoted companion of the Guru, re-edited the Adi Granth and also worked on the collected works of the Guru himself (*Dasam Granth*).

While moving about in the Muktsar area in the atmosphere of peace the Guru was led to believe that Aurangzeb had no hand in the sordid murder of his two sons. He dispatched a letter to the Emperor by special messenger and sought an audience with Aurangzeb who was then in the Deccan. The Guru had come to entertain some hope that Aurangzeb might be persuaded to take action against the real culprit, namely Wazir Khan, Governor of Sarhind. Aurangzeb was in a mood of reconciliation with the Guru and agreed to a meeting. While the Guru was on the way (in Rajputana) the Emperor passed away in the Deccan. This was in 1707. The Guru then proceeded to Agra and met the new Emperor, Bahadur Shah, who created a good impression upon the Guru. The Guru began to entertain some expectations from the Emperor, but the sovereign was too insecure and pre-occupied with his own problems to be willing or able to take any step against Wazir Khan. Bahadur Shah rushed to Deccan where a rebellion had broken out. The Guru also proceeded south and reached Nanded. It seems he had a desire to keep up moral pressure on the new sovereign to rectify the wrongs done by Wazir Khan. It was here that he met the Hindu tantric, Banda Bahadur, who came into the limelight of Sikh politics, shortly after the martyrdom of the Guru in 1708 because of a dastardly act of two Pathans hired by Wazir Khan.

It will be seen from the above account that out of the five phases of the Guru's life three: the first phase lasting ten years, the third phase lasting twelve years and finally, the fifth phase, lasting five years were all peaceful without there being any suppression or persecution of the Guru or the Sikhs. Confrontation took place only in the second phase, lasting two years and the fourth phase lasting five years. Now in the second phase the *causus belli*, clearly, came from the side of the hill Rajas rather than the Mughals. In the fourth phase also the same holds good. In no case, however, the armed conflict had even the remotest connection with issues of religion, nor was the conflict a confrontation between Islam and Hinduism/Sikhism.

The chapter of violence by the Mughals against the Sikhs opened only when the Guru took to the politics of violence against the central government or the Rajas of Bilaspur, Nahan, Mandi, Seymore etc, under Mughal suzerainty. The Raja of Bilaspur, Bhim Singh, always had an ambivalent relationship with the Guru. The Raja admired and patronized the Guru and was also antagonistic towards him on account of the Guru's military prowess and radical rejection of traditional Hinduism. The Guru's sincere and active championship of the weaker sections of society, irrespective of religion or caste, was perceived as a potential threat to the higher castes. Both the Guru's valour in battle and his social radicalism and egalitarianism were a threat to the Rajas and the upper classes in general.

Assuming that the above account is factually correct, the Mughal government did not harass or persecute the Sikhs or resort to violence unless the Sikhs themselves threw an armed challenge directly to the Emperor or to the hill Rajas under Mughal suzerainty. And no sovereign in pre-democratic times ever tolerated any challenge to royal authority.

MUGHAL–SIKH CONFLICT (1708-1799)

No Guru ever displayed any communal hatred or bitterness towards the Mughal establishment. The Gurus fought for truth and honor, but were never averse to just reconciliation with the secular powers. The Gurus combined courage and integrity. They stood for constructive justice, not terror, for harmony, not dominance, dignified self-assertion, not aggression. But Banda Bahadur who rose to a position of pre-eminence soon after the death of the Tenth Guru had a totally different personality and outlook. Though extremely audacious, resourceful and charismatic his complex personality had a streak of abnormality, rather than of genuine spirituality and humanitarian love.

Banda Bahadur opened a new chapter in the history of Sikh agrarian revolt against Mughal rule right in the heart of north India. Emerging from Nanded soon after the Tenth Guru's death in 1708 Banda Bahadur inflicted several humiliating defeats on the imperial forces in pitched battles between 1709 and 1715. He also committed atrocities on peaceful Muslims as part of his terrorist tactics. It took considerable time and well organized effort by the Mughal Emperor, Farrukh Siyar, to contain and finally defeat Banda. Abdus Samad Khan, Governor of Lahore, and his son, Zakarya Khan, performed this difficult mission. Banda and approximately seven hundred of his men were executed in 1716. But intermittent and surreptitious violence continued and the Mughal authorities were compelled to resort to stern measures against Sikh terrorists. Many Sikhs thought it prudent to clip their hair to evade preventive and deterrent retaliation for killing innocent citizens. Other Sikhs who wore their hair long moved into remote areas, and from there carried on their guerrilla activities. All this violence and counter-violence was, however, political and would have taken place even if Banda's followers were Muslims.

Zakarya Khan who succeeded his father as Governor of Lahore tried an entirely different strategy in 1733. To win over the Sikhs he offered a land '*jagir*' to Kapur Singh who, along with Jassa Singh Ahluwalia, was highly respected among the Sikhs. But this reconciliatory approach failed to check violence. Zakarya Khan was forced to confiscate the '*jagir*' and his energetic and trusted minister, Lakhpat Raj, severely punished the *Khalsa Dal*. Mani Singh, the aged manager of the *Harimandir* at Amritsar was also executed in 1738.

In the same year a new threat arose from Nadir Shah of Persia, who entertained a grudge against the Mughal emperor, Muhammad Shah, for giving protection to some enemies of Nadir Shah. The Mughal emperor thought it prudent to appease Nadir Shah by giving him a handsome cash amount to avert the threat of invasion. Asaf Jah

Nizamul Mulk was deputed to negotiate the amount and other details with Nadir Shah. The success of the mission aroused the jealousy of another prominent noble in Delhi, Burhanul Mulk, who secretly met Nadir Shah and advised him to raise the cash demand by several millions. Nadir Shah went back upon his word. Eventually he sacked Delhi and subsequently Lahore. Most of the victims were Muslims. After extracting immense booty Nadir Shah returned to Persia leaving the Mughal authorities badly demoralized. The Sikh problem grew even more intractable.

Zakarya Khan was unable to control and contain Sikh terrorism until his death in 1745. Till then the Sikhs carried on their terrorist activities with the help of bands (*Jathas*) each of appointed twelve guerillas. In 1745 Kapur Singh organized these numerous Jathas into twenty-five regiments, each under an able commander. Hari Singh Bhangi, Naud Singh Sukerchack, Jassa Singh were some of the most noted commanders of the time. A no-tax campaign was initiated and terrorist activities intensified against the public. Lakhpat Raj's brother was killed and the government was forced to intensify repressive measures. This led to the death of seven thousand Sikhs and another three thousand were made prisoner and executed at Shahid Ganj, Lahore in 1746.

Zakarya Khan died shortly afterwards and was succeeded by his son, Yahya, to the Governorship of Lahore. His right hand men were one Sahajdari Sikh, Kura Mal and an unscrupulous power seeker, Adina Beg Khan. Shortly afterwards a far more serious event took place –Ahmad Shah Abdali's first invasion of Punjab in 1747. Mir Mannu, the young Governor of Punjab, fought with remarkable tenacity and repulsed the attack. Adbali decided to withdraw, but to carry along with him the immense loot he had collected. The Sikh freebooters then attacked him from the rear and made good with a substantial part of the spoils. It was at this time that Jassa Singh came into great prominence as successor to Kapur Singh. Jassa Singh later defeated Adina Beg and regrouped the twenty-five regiments, (earlier formed by Kapur Singh) into eleven consolidated '*misls*'. This was a crucial stage in the further consolidation of Sikh power in Punjab. The Arabic word '*misl*' which means 'equal' signified the complete equality of the status and power of each *Sardar*.

The union of eleven '*misls*' became a proto-state and continually resisted the persistent Afghan efforts to establish their hegemony over Punjab. The '*misls*' fought a long drawn out guerrilla war against the Afghans and also maintained internal law and order within their respective areas in accordance with Jat customary law. The '*misls*' also resisted the expansion of Maratha's power in the Punjab. At times the Jats themselves made adventurous forays into the *Jamuna-Gangetic Doab* to loot the Mughals and Marathas.

Following the strategy once adopted by Zakarya Khan, Mir Mannu again tried a policy of appeasement to contain the steadily growing Sikh power under the '*misldari*' system. Kaura Mal, once the trusted aide of the dissident Shah Nawaz, had by now joined Mir Mannu's camp. Adina Beg too changed his loyalty to Mir Mannu, just after Adbali's second invasion in 1749-50, and the third invasion on 1751-52. During this period Kaura Mal brought about an understanding between Mir Mannu and Sikhs apart from inflicting a crushing defeat upon his former, master, Shah Nawaz. Indeed Kaura Mal dispatched the severed head of Shah Nawaz to Mir Mannu. Mir Mannu on his part, heaped honours on several '*misldars*', assigned the revenue of twelve villages to the *Harimandir*, appointed Kaura Mal as governor of Multan and conferred upon his Sikh aide the title of Raja Bahadur. This success, however, was transient.

Abdali besieged Mir Mannu's forces and Kaura Mal fell fighting, while Adina Beg managed his escape. Mir Mannu surrendered and the Mughal emperor had to cede Lahore and Multan to Adbali in 1752. As Abdali was returning in triumph to Kabul, the Sikh guerillas and freebooters attacked his force form the rear and captured their spoils. But the more serious consequence was that the link forged between the Sikh and the Mughal ended with the death of Kaura Mal. Mir Mannu reversed his recent policy of appeasing Sikhs who reverted to their terrorist methods. Thus while the military victory accrued to the Afghans the real gainers were the Sikhs. Mir Mannu died shortly afterwards in 1753.

Adina Beg now became the principal actor on the almost chaotic scene in Punjab. Adbali launched his fourth attack in 1756. Abdali was very successful in the first phase of the attack and he garnered immense spoils from Lahore, Delhi and Mathura. But he had not reckoned with Adina Beg's strategy of befriending Jassa Singh and appealing to the Sikh to fight against a common foe – the Afghans. A combined force under the Jassa Singh and Adina Beg routed the Afghans near Hoshiarpur in 1757 when the Afghans were on their way back. Infuriated at this unexpected reverse Ahmad Shah Abdali pounced upon the *Harimandir* at Amritsar and blew it up before finally crossing over to Kabul. He left his son, Prince Taimur, to manage Punjab. Adina Beg now made a volt face. Realizing that the Sikhs may now create trouble he turned towards the Marathas for help against the Afghans. The Maratha general, Raghunath Rao, was received in Punjab with great enthusiasm in 1758. The formation of the united front of the Mughals, Sikhs and Marathas was enough at that point of time to make the Afghans evacuate Punjab. Adina Beg thought it was an opportune time to get rid of the Sikhs whom he had so recently made his allies against the Afghans. The Sikhs were furious. But before any major confrontation could take place Adina Beg died in 1758.

Ahmad Shah Abdali was not the man who could be cowed down by Adina Beg's diplomatic offensive and victory. Abdali attacked for the fifth time and this time his force was substantially bigger. In 1761 Abdali decisively defeated the Marathas at the third battle of Panipat. The Afghans triumphantly left for home, but the real gainers were the Sikhs. No soon had the Afghans left Jassa Singh occupied Lahore. The infuriated Abdali attacked the very next year in 1762. This was the sixth attack.

This time the Sikhs had to pay an extremely heavy price in a terrible massacre of their men near Lahore in 1762. This is called '*Vada Ghallughara*' in Punjabi. Ala Singh, of Patiala remained neutral. The *Harimandir* was blown up for the second time. However, the resilience of the Sikhs enabled them to establish their power once again in the greater part of Punjab. Shortly after Abdali left Punjab, leaving Kabuli

Mal as governor of Lahore, the Sikhs started to dictate terms to the Governor as if Jassa Singh rather than Abdali had appointed him.

Abdali's response was predictable. He launched his seventh attack in 1764. This time the Sikhs made a tactical withdrawal to areas completely out of reach of Abdali's army. He gave vent to his rage by ravaging the *Harimandir* for the third time. After conferring the title of Raja upon Ala Singh of an enlarged Patiala under his suzerainty, Ahmad Shah set for his return journey to Kabul. Once again the Sikhs repeated their favourite tactics of emerging from the jungle retreats, plundering the Afghans on their way back and finally occupying Lahore. The popular and able, Lehna Singh, was made Governor of Lahore, and he succeeded in winning over the Muslims of Punjab to his side.

Abdali attacked again for the eighth time in 1766. The Sikhs repeated their old tactics and Abdali was frustrated once again. Abdali's ninth and last invasion was in 1769 but it was abortive. Soon afterwards Abdali's health broke down and he died the same year.

Abdali's son, Taimur, was ineffective. Punjab was now under the de facto rule of the Sikh '*misls*'. There was a brief period in which Bhagel Singh and Zabita Khan forged a Sikh-Rohilla alliance, and extended their sway into Delhi and *Gangetic Doab*. Later Bhagel Singh joined hands with the Rohilla adventurer, Ghulam Qadir, and looted Mughal and Maratha territories.

The '*misls*' grew in strength. However, with the decline of Afghan pressures after the death of Ahmad Shah Abdali and due to other internal factors the system itself began to decline after 1774. The '*misls*' fell prey to petty intrigues, murders and organized infighting. Maha Singh of the Sukerchakia '*misl*' played a highly destructive role. But before strife could turn into total chaos, the same '*misl*' threw up a young leader – Ranjit Singh (1780-1839). This natural youth leader of nineteen not only restored unity in the factions but founded the Kingdom of Lahore in 1799. Shah Zaman, the Afghan claimant of hegemony over Punjab, the Mughals, the Punjabi Muslims and the

East Indian Company all tacitly accepted this new kingdom: the fruit of a century of hard struggle by the *Khalsa*. The *'misls'* of the Malwa region, chief among whom was Patiala, remained outside the Kingdom. Two years later in 1801 Ranjit Singh officially declared himself Maharaja of Punjab at a simple but dignified coronation ceremony at Lahore.

The Role of Ranjit Singh:

Punjab lay bleeding as a result of the repeated attacks by Abdali. The third battle of Panipat in 1761 destroyed the prospect of Maratha hegemony in northern and western India. However, the dream of Afghan hegemony also failed. It was Ranjit Singh who filled the power vacuum. He founded and ruled the Kingdom of Lahore for full forty years from 1799/1802 to 1839 as a great ruler. His administration was a model of 'functional secularism' like that of Akbar. There was equality and opportunity for all religious groups. Religion was viewed as a personal matter and Persian was the official language. Tolerance, equality and prosperity prevailed all over the realm. Multan, Jammu, Kashmir and Kabul became integral parts of the Lahore Kingdom. The Malwa region of Punjab (the area between Satluj and the Jamuna) never merged into the empire, despite having a substantial Sikh population in Patiala, Nabha, Jind, Faridkot, and Maler Kotla. These states, however, accepted Ranjit Singh as the suzerain until 1809. Thereafter, the East India Company manipulated to displace Ranjit Singh as the suzerain.

The functional separation of religion and politics in the Lahore kingdom worked well in Punjab. But the champions of the traditional Islamic idea of the supremacy of *shariah* in all spheres of human activity could not accept any non-Muslim as a legitimate ruler. These forces launched a '*jehad*' against Sikh rule. The crusade failed and notable religious figures such as Shah Ismail of the house of Shah Waliullah of Delhi and Syed Ahmad of Bareilly died fighting in the famous battle of Balakot in 1832. To my mind, this was a tragic failure of the traditional *ulema* to appreciate the forward-looking vision of Ranjit Singh who was honestly following the example of Ashoka and Akbar. This is not to say that the evils of intolerance, corruption and exploitation of the weak had been eliminated. No state or reign has ever been all golden without any chinks of baser metals.

Ranjit Singh died in 1839. It is tragic that he did not have able successors. Dissensions about succession began immediately after he passed away. One camp favored his eldest son, Kharak Singh, another camp favored Kharak Sing's son, Nau Nihal Singh, while still another camp favored Sher Singh, another son of the late Maharaja. Eventually Kharak Singh ascended the throne, but he died just after a year in 1840. Almost immediately after his cremation his son, Nau Nihal, also died of a fatal accident. Kharak Singh's widow, Chand Kaur, managed to succeed, but civil war broke out. Her chief supporter, Gulab Singh of the Dogra clan, could not sustain her position, and Sher Singh emerged as the final winner. He appointed Dhian Singh Dogra as the Chief Minister, but dissensions grew. Sher Singh and his minor son were murdered while they were watching a show. The culprit, Ajit Sigh Sandhawala, then assassinated the Chief Minster and his close supporters. He was now poised to usurp the throne, but his plan failed. In utter disgust and after another bout of violence Prince Daleep Singh, the youngest son of Ranjit Singh was put on the throne. Daleep was then a minor of seven and his mother, Rani Jindan, was proclaimed as Queen mother, and Hira Singh Dogra as the new Chief Minister. But once again the plan misfired. Jalla, the *Brahman* tutor and mentor of the Chief Minister started interfering in the administration and this was not acceptable to Rani Jindan as well as the powerful Gulab Singh. Soon afterwards the new Chief Minister, Hari Singh, was murdered.

This was the last straw on the camel's back and Gulab Singh decided to end the nefarious merry go round of the politics of murder. Gulab Singh secretly negotiated with the East India Company to intervene in this internal chaos. Rani Jindan and some others also got into secret touch with the Governor General, Lord Harding. The

Company declared war against the Lahore Kingdom in 1845 and several battles took place. The battle of Sabraon in 1846 was decisive and the Sikh power was broken. The Kingdom was trifurcated into three separate regions. One region, the *Jullandar Doab* was ceded to the British, another was made into a separate state of Jammu and Kashmir under the rule of Gulab Singh Dogra under British suzerainty, and the rest remained under the rule of Dalip Singh with Rani Jindan as the Regent. Thus, within seven years after the great founder of the Lahore kingdom died, only a stump remained. But even this did not work. Rani Jindan was banished to Benares, and her power gravitated to one Sher Singh Attariwala who was an important member of the Regency Council. He tried level best to rally the old and loyal Sikh Sardars and to make one supreme effort to get rid of British interference.

The British, meanwhile, had become too strong for the much-weakened Kingdom. The new Governor General, Lord Dalhousie, was happy to get some excuse for invading the shrunken state. The British won the battle of Gujrat in 1849 and annexed the state. The Sikhs fought with superb valor but to no avail against British tactics, technological skill and discipline. Almost all sections of the Kingdom accepted defeat in good grace. Indeed, this defeat in 1849 turned them into enduring admirers of things British, and Punjabis, in general, remained loyal supporters of the East India Company during the great Indian rebellion of 1857 against British rule.

The Punjabi response to defeat at the hands of a superior adversary, to my mind, is comparable (in terms of social depth psychology and the sociology of change) to the much earlier defeat of the Bengal kingdom at the battle of Plassey in 1756. Raja Ram Mohan Rai was among the earliest Indians to understand the shape of things to come and became the prophet of a reconstructed liberal Hinduism to his countrymen.

His vision represented a great advance over the categories and values of a rigid and stagnant Hinduism and Islam. Much after him the Urdu poet, Ghalib, who survived the great Indian rebellion of

1857 began to see things from a fresh perspective. Sir Syed, in his early period, was still groping in the mists of a pre-scientific outlook when Ghalib had seen the light of a new dawn. But Sir Syed soon followed suit and responded to the call of modernity by founding the Aligarh Movement.

Concluding Remarks

Aurangzeb died in 1707 and the tenth Guru a year later. The substance of Mughal power had dwindled almost immediately after the Emperor's death; its shadow lingered on until 1857. The Indian people were helpless victims of the sheer corruption, intrigue and adventurism of the Indian ruling class, and the tragic failure of the traditional Hindu and Muslim religious establishments to respond creatively to the situational challenges. The power vacuum at the Centre peaked in the third quarter of the century when central Asian marauders entered the fray. Only the consolidation of British power in India terminated the prolonged power struggle as it used to be conducted in pre-democratic times in India.

In the final analysis, the Mughal power declined due to the phenomenon of 'territorial overstretch' (as the Oxford historian, Paul Kennedy, defines it) due to the expansionist policy of Aurangzeb. His authority and law-enforcing powers became increasingly inadequate in relation to the requirements of empire. All sorts of ambitious individuals joined the game of seeking power without any ethical or principled motives. It became the order of the day for allies to change sides or repudiate solemn contracts at crucial moments.

Contemporary sources lament that the common man had deep grievances against petty local authorities—the *'patwari'*, the *'darogha'*, the *'sarpanch'*, the *'mahajan'*, and the landlord, who harassed the weak, irrespective of religion. The weaker sections had little hope of redress, despite their faith in the personal goodness of the sovereign. Those who could took law into their own hands. Those who had contacts with the rich or the mighty sought help from them. The idea of 'accountability' of the executive to the people and of peaceful elections and transfer of power was absent and the only hope of the people was in the benevolence of the king after the religious faith in Divine justice. This was the common condition of the weaker sections without any differentiation between Muslim or Hindu and this existential faith was shared by both.

From a sociological point of view, however, the Muslims were, relatively, better placed for the obvious reason that their chances of access to the king, the ruling nobility or the wealthy were greater. The imperial court at Delhi and the capitals of the provinces were all arenas of sordid intrigue, conspiracy, and unscrupulous play of personal ambitions. The Jats of the Punjab took to highway robbery and extortion as a way of life. Local satraps in Bengal, Avadh, Maharashtra and other places became semi-independent. However, these challenges were political and social. And the players belonged to all religions.

The challenge from outside was from Nadir Shah (d. 1747) of Persia and later from Ahmad Shah Abdali (d. 1772) from Afghanistan and both were invited by dissident Indian Muslim nobles or religious leaders to try their luck in India. The invitation was a desperate attempt more to check the growing chaos in the land than to serve Islam. Nor did the invaders have any mission of service to God and Islam since they knew full well that their intended victims of loot and plunder were their own co-religionists in a good measure and even, predominantly so, in numerous places. Thus their aim was to fill their coffers, not to save souls.

The Sikh strategy was to commit highway robbery, extort money from traders and the peasants, raids on towns, hit and run surprise attacks at well timed moments. The Afghans tactics was lightning cavalry attacks and the striking of terror. The rulers and administrators used bribery, false allurements, planned rumors, intrigues and disruptive techniques against enemies as well as rivals. The monarchs had only one super strategy: to utilize the services of anybody (irrespective of his religion, caste or morals) who could get things done according to the wishes and commands of the sovereign. The aspiring status or wealth seekers were ever ready to change loyalties without any remorse. This willingness brought about strange bedfellows, and allies suddenly changed into adversaries.

The ethos of the rural Jats in Punjab was tribal. They relied so much on hit and run methods that they just could not turn their rebellion into a freedom struggle and establish a state. Organizational maturity was absent. In fact, after the death of the Tenth Guru in 1708, it took the Jat Sikhs almost a full century to produce the charismatic figure of Maharaja Ranjit Singh who founded the Sikh Kingdom of Lahore in 1799. There were several phases in this long process.

In the first phase Kapur Singh consolidated innumerable Jat bands (*jathas*) of about twelve each into twenty-five regiments. In the second phase Jassa Singh Ahluwalia consolidated the rural Sikhs into eleven '*misls*': administrative cum military units. The Phoolkia '*misl*', under the leadership of Ala Singh of Patiala was separate and had an undefined status. This was a great step forward in the evolution of the Lahore Kingdom. The devastation wreaked by Abdali on the Mughals was poison for their empire, but meat for the Jat Sikhs. This is the regular pattern of history.

Ahmad Shah Abdali invaded India nine times in twenty-two years between 1747 and 1769. After decisively defeating Mir Mannu in 1752 Abdali began to regard Punjab and Kashmir as integral parts of his empire to be governed by his viceroys. His also was more interested in seeking loyal lieutenants and followers than in serving Islam or God. Indian history is full of instances where co-religionists have fought each other while those professing different religions have proved their loyalty even in death. Dewan Kaura Mal was loyal to the Mughal governor, Mir Mannu. Ala Singh of Patiala and the Abdali greatly trusted each other. The Sikh leader, Baghel Singh, fully cooperated with the Rohilla Chief, Zabita Khan. Baghel Singh also joined Ghulam Qadir in jointly plundering Mughal territory, near Agra and Delhi. In 1788

Ghulam Qadir committed atrocities in Delhi and even blinded the Mughal emperor. The Marathas were so shocked at this crime that they executed him after defeating him in battle the next year.

It is true that Abdali's troops thrice desecrated the Golden Temple at Amritsar. But this was the result of helpless indignation and frustration at the Sikh tactics of avoiding direct battles in Punjab and resorting to sudden rear attacks just when the retuning Afghan soldiers were nearing Kabul, laden with loot but tired and weary and not prepared to fight back. The Sikhs mauled them near Kabul and fled back into the safety of their own homeland, to regain their political and military initiative against the Abdali's regime. This just infuriated the Afghans who vowed to attack again. This, rather than any hatred against the Sikh religion, explains the repeated desecration of Sikh or Hindu places of worship on Indian soil. Likewise, Abdali raised slogans of '*jihad*' to raise the morale of his army. He conveniently forgot that he was attacking his own co-religionists along with others, and that Islam prohibited killing innocents.

Abdali's decisive victory at the third battle of Panipat in 1761 crushed the Maratha confederacy and much pleased the upholders of the theocratic approach to politics. But the winners of the battle lost the war against the rising Sikhs under the leadership of Ranjit Singh.

The above sociological analysis clearly confirms that the primary determinant of political and military conflict is not religion but the search for power. Migration, conquest, pursuit of worldly wealth rather than pursuit of the pleasure of God propel the migration and movement of peoples on the earth, be they Aryans, Greeks, Romans Arabs, Pathans or Turks. From time immemorial different ethnic groups and races have undergone periods of heightened dynamism and creativity at different times. During such periods of horizontal expansion vertical growth may also take place, specially, when some charismatic leader emerges on the scene of action. At times extreme adversity and suffering of the group may also bring about 'inner development through crisis' as in the case of the Jews and the early Christians. The history of the human family presents several instances.

While humans who really strive to promote fundamental ethical and spiritual values (through the right means) never produce strife and conflict in society, those who desire to extend Divine power over the earth unconsciously seek to exercise power over others. This invariably leads to fears, tensions and conflicts. Religious fanatics always use religion as an ally or tool; they hardly serve it as a master. Religious establishments also are drawn into exercising power when they loudly proclaim that religion should direct and regulate every sphere of human activity. The struggle, therefore, does not lie between alternative religions as such, but between aspirants for power unconsciously seeking to use religion as an ally or tool.

The story of India is a chapter of the long and unfinished drama of the human struggle for power. In this unending struggle for ascendance new races or ethnic groups, rise from relative obscurity and cultural backwardness and succeed in dominating other more cultured and better established groups of the human family. That Babar was a Muslim does not mean that his attack was an Islamic onslaught against Hinduism. After all, Babar had fought against several Muslim rulers in Central Asia before turning his attention to India. One Muslim ruler fought against another Muslim in Central Asia in the medieval period, and one Hindu ruler against another Hindu in ancient India. Likewise, Greek fought against Greek no less than he fought against the Iranian or Roman in the ancient period. The same is the case today in the Arab world and also among others.

According to the Hindu *Dharmashastras*, every king is duty bound to enlarge his dominion and fighting is the highest duty of the warrior caste. The Raja fought both to enlarge and to defend his territory, but the '*praja*' pursued the prescribed life goals in the normal manner, unmindful of who won or lost in the struggle for power. This social ethic was also applied to Muslim warriors. The Hindu populace did not grudge Muslim rule, provided the ruler did not interfere in '*dharma*'. The legitimacy of the ruler was not dependent upon his race or religion; it flowed from victory in battle.

The falsity of interpreting the struggle for power in medieval India as a confrontation between Islam and Hinduism becomes all the more glaring after the advent of Babar. The antagonists, clearly, become a mixed lot on either side of the fence. Thus, Babar fought against the combined armies of Ibrahim Lodi and Rana Sanga, Humayun struggled against Sher Shah. The power of the Mughals flowed from a firm and lasting alliance between them and the Rajputs, and their adversaries were Muslim princes no less than Hindu. Muslims manned the entire artillery of Shivaji. Both Hindus and Muslims were despoiled of their wealth when Shivaji attacked and looted the prosperous Mughal port of Surat. The same holds good of Nadir Shah and Ahmad Shah Abdali, as already mentioned.

Shivaji's opposition to the Mughal emperor was certainly not directed against Islam or the Muslims. Given the restless energy, daring, and ambition he possessed, Shivaji would have defied any central authority, Muslim or Hindu. Shivaji's father, a '*mansabdar*' under the Sultan of Bijapur, was rather unhappy at his brave son's defiant conduct. The son, after a brief interlude at Aurangzeb's court, rebelled against the Mughal emperor and established himself as an independent ruler in the Pune region. He avoided regular battle against the imperial army and opted for guerrilla tactics, which ruined the Mughal exchequer. As a king Shivaji was well disposed to his Muslim subjects and his artillery was manned by Muslims. The struggle between the decaying Mughal power and the Marathas, Jats, Sikhs, Rohilla Pathans etcetera was, likewise, a struggle for power rather than a religious confrontation.

In the southern region Tipu Sultan (d. 1799) emerged as the hero, both of Muslims and Hindus of Mysore. The Nizam retained the loyalty of all his mixed subjects in Hyderabad. However, Mysore and Hyderabad always remained political antagonists. Coming to more recent times, the great princely states, Gwalior, Indore, Baroda, Jaipur, Patiala, Kapurthala, etcetera (all ruled by Hindu or Sikh kings) gave liberal patronage to Muslims who rose to the highest positions in the state.

As prudent statesmen the Muslim Sultans and emperors did not mix religion with politics. They adopted a policy of non-discrimination between their subjects the overwhelming majority of whom were Hindus. A section of the *Uuema* were not happy at this state of affairs. They held that in an Islamic state the Sultan was bound by the law of the *shariah*, which, according to them, prescribed harsh treatment against the non-believers. The friendly relations, which obtained between the Muslims and non-Muslims and the power and position enjoyed by Hindu nobles and top administrators, irked the narrow minded section of the *ulema*. The expression of these views in the writings of some contemporary divines has misled some scholars into thinking that this was the general view and the actual practice. But this was far from being the case.

ESSAY 8

THE CONCEPT AND ROLE OF TOLERANCE IN INDIAN CULTURE

INTRODUCTION

Indian culture, being a continuing process, cannot be reduced, without remainder, to any particular stage in its long history, though for the purpose of intensive study or analysis we may well limit ourselves to a particular period or aspect. For the purpose of this Seminar we may confine ourselves to the ancient and medieval periods of Indian culture.

In the medieval period, Indian culture cannot be reduced to its territorial stem, whether pre-Aryan or Aryan minus the cultural career of Islam in India. Indeed, the cultural history of the Muslims of the subcontinent is an integral part of Indian culture. By the same logic pre-Islamic Indian culture is as much the heritage of the Muslims of India as of the Hindus or others. Ideally speaking, neither the cultural elements of Indian origin predating the Muslim presence, nor the cultural elements of Islamic origin, developing and flourishing in the Indian environment, can be viewed as alien or dispensable elements of the highly complex and still growing entity or process called "Indian culture".

The analysis of the concept of tolerance is a philosophical task, but the description of the role of tolerance in Indian culture is a complex analytical-cum-historical task. If the skills of the philosopher be satisfactory, but the data supplied by the historian be incorrect or distorted, the philosopher's conclusions would go wrong. Again, the purely historical question itself comprises two distinct questions which should not be confused with each other:

(a) what ideals, teachings or sentiments concerning tolerance exist in the culture, i.e. are found in the works of its philosophers, saints, poets, scriptures and folklore? And;

(b) what has been, the actual behavior of individuals or groups in that society, i.e. how far have the ideals been put into effect? Even highly educated persons frequently confuse the two questions with disastrous results.

THE MEANING OF "TOLERANCE"

Let us first analyze the word "tolerance", as the sponsors of the Seminar have used it, and let us call it the Seminar's use or meaning of the word. This sense is best conveyed by a quotation from a Standard English dictionary:

"... the disposition to tolerate or allow the existence of beliefs, practices or habits differing from one's own; now often freedom from bigotry, sympathetic understanding of others' beliefs, etcetera, without acceptance of them..."

The above sense of the word which is now the main or usual sense became prominent perhaps only in the 17/18th centuries when Western Europe first saw the dawn of the age of tolerance.[1] The original uses of the word referred to tolerance of metals, gold or silver coins, of bridges to bear stress, or the capacity of a person to bear pain and suffering, i.e. the quality of endurance or the ability to bear irritants or pressures, etc. These uses have all become the specialized meanings of the word. The Seminar's use of "tolerance" has now pushed aside other uses into the conceptual background, as it were.[2]

The diverse meanings or uses of the word in different contexts show the futility of trying to discover the meaning of a word with a capital 'M', or, to put it differently, to discover or identify the essence of concepts in the abstract, say, truth, justice, good, beauty, courage, and tolerance, etc. What is needed is a survey of the concrete spectrum of the uses of a word. However, this analysis, which may well be called contextual analysis, may and should be supplemented by a phenomenological or conceptual analysis in the sense of identifying the bare minimum connotative meaning of a word in a specific context and then differentiating it from cognate or related concepts. Contextual analysis is best done by translating the analysandum into expressions, which are simpler and/or clearer and easier to use, according to current rules of the language concerned as compared to the original expression or statement.

Applying the above method of contextual analysis, let us analyze the statement, "Ram is a tolerant person". Most English speaking persons would agree that the above sentence is true or the word "tolerance" has been rightly used under the following conditions. These conditions are illustrative rather than exhaustive.

> **(a)** Ram befriends or is willing to befriend those who differ from him, but are otherwise honest.
>
> **(b)** Ram tries to understand the other's point of view with sympathy.
>
> **(c)** Ram does not believe, unless there be clear evidence that those who differ from him are dishonest, or ill-motivated, or perverse.
>
> **(d)** Ram realizes that beliefs, attitudes or approaches other than his own could possibly be right or justifiable.
>
> **(e)** Ram realizes that while judgments of fact or of logic can be settled conclusively, judgments of value cannot be so settled, making disagreement almost unavoidable and understandable.

(f) Ram does not allow his differences with others to cloud his judgment concerning their good points, or to be vindictive or hostile to them in other matters or situations.

Likewise, the statement, "Indian society is tolerant", may be analyzed as follows.

(a) Most Indians are tolerant persons in the above sense.

(b) All Indians, irrespective of caste, color, creed, or sex, have equal rights, duties and opportunities both in theory and in fact, though the ideal may not be perfectly realized due to human limitations.

(c) The Indian way of life does not directly or indirectly adversely affect the self-realization, recognition, and reward of Indians on the basis of their caste, color, creed or sex.

Let us now attempt to supplement the above analysis with a phenomenological or conceptual analysis of "tolerance". Tolerance, as a basic attitude towards others or as a moral value, usually develops under the following conditions:

(a) awareness of plural truth-claims,

(b) experience of existential perplexity,

(c) spiritual autonomy or inner freedom,

(d) awareness of distinction between subjective and objective truth,

(e) awareness of man's historicity or cultural contingency,

(f) respect for other minds or persons,

(g) capacity for empathy.

Awareness of plural truth-claims, inner questioning, and perhaps a measure of existential perplexity constitute the seed which grows into the tree of tolerance, provided the seed is watered by inner freedom and intellectually nourished by two basic concepts, (a) truth as subjectivity and (b) culture as historicity or contingency. Respect for the other and the capacity for empathy, though perhaps not strictly essential for the genesis of tolerance, do in fact greatly facilitate its birth and growth, since existential perplexity is intensified, when a person realizes that someone whom he deeply respects holds different views or values. When the difference pertains not to matters of taste, but concerns moral, religious, political or philosophical issues, respect for the other predisposes a person towards tolerance as a way of life, or style of personality orientation. It may be said that existential perplexity is also merely helpful rather than being an essential condition for the genesis of tolerance, or an essential element of the concept of tolerance. This is a plausible view, since we can well imagine a sage or spiritual genius who is the picture of deep commitment to values and of complete tolerance without having known the tensions or pains of existential perplexity. Such points, however, do not matter much even if they cannot be settled.

Let us now distinguish the concept of tolerance from some other psychologically related or cognate concepts with which it is liable to be confused.

(1) A tolerant person may, but need not, be a skeptic or atheist. Indeed, tolerance is perfectly compatible with the most passionate and profound religious faith or commitment to basic values as also with skepticism.

(2) A tolerant person may, but need not, be indifferent to religion. Even if he is indifferent himself, a truly tolerant person would respect a person who is genuinely religious, and if the tolerant person be also brave enough, he would stand up for the rights of the religious person. "*I do not believe a word of what you say, but I shall give my life to defend your right to say so*", admirably sums up the matter.

(3) A tolerant person may, but need not, be secular in the current sense of keeping the functions of the church and of the state apart. If a religious person upholds the organic unity of the church and of the state and if his religion does not demand any discrimination against other groups or within his own group, the practice of tolerance would be quite possible in consonance with his religion. Since, however, most religions do, in fact, have some in-built elements of inter-group or intra-group discrimination (in some form or other), tolerance cannot be put into practice without separating the church from the state and viewing religion as primarily a moral-spiritual experience rather than a set of political and socio-economic laws binding upon its followers. But secularism is neutral with regard to belief in God and the hereafter, and commitment to secularism does not imply or even suggest that the secular person is a theist, atheist, or agnostic, though it certainly does imply de-linking the respective spheres of religion and state.

(4) A tolerant person may, but need not, be apathetic towards persuading others to his own values or beliefs. Apathy is not any index of tolerance, but only unconcern for others. But the concern of a tolerant person for others is always tempered by sympathy and tender humility instead of being a conceited imposition of one's own values as the one and only truth.

(5) A tolerant person may, but need not always or habitually, practice a discreet silence in the face of conflicting truth-claims. Tolerance is not passive acquiescence to opposed views for fear of giving offence to others or the fear of communication. Tolerance is perfectly compatible with free communication and spontaneous self-expression in an atmosphere of mutual respect and good will. In the long run, communication helps to promote tolerance and greater harmony despite making unbridged differences clearer or more articulate.

(6) A tolerant person may, but need not, be given to habitual appeasement of those who disagree with him. Tolerance is an intrinsic value like love or beauty, while appeasement is a strategy for avoiding conflict and achieving success. It may lead a man to voluntary risks and sacrifice for impersonal ends, while appeasement implies expediency and following the least line of resistance. Indeed, a tolerant person may well be extremely firm and unbending in discharging his moral obligations and in resisting moral evil.[3]

To round off the above conceptual analysis, it must be added that tolerance, like truth, love, power, has several dimensions, and further that each dimension has a scale. Thus a person or society may be tolerant in one sense, but not in another and may show different degrees of tolerance on any particular dimension. A person may tolerate, i.e. willingly accept a close political relationship with a person of a different race, religion or caste, but not be prepared for close friendship or marriage. Again, a person may be tolerant of differences within a cognate group, but not of inter-group differences. Likewise, a person may fall short of full tolerance even on a single dimension, as Locke failed to tolerate atheists, or Madan Mohan Malaviya failed to tolerate *non-Brahmans* on the dining table.

In view of the different dimensions and degrees of tolerance, no individual or society may properly be judged as tolerant or intolerant on an either or basis. Rather the elements and degrees of tolerance or intolerance should be identified. Even if no society be perfectly tolerant, it could be graded.

CONCEPT OF TOLERANCE IN INDIAN CULTURE

To the best of my knowledge, there is no exact equivalent of the word "tolerance" in the Seminar's sense in Sanskrit. The word "*ksama*" which has been used in the Gita and other works means endurance, which was also the original sense of the English word. Likewise, the Sanskrit word "*sahana*" also means endurance or forbearance, while the derivative "*sahanashilata*" means the trait or character of endurance. The word "*ksama*" as used in modern Hindi means forgiveness. The expression *"sarva-dharma-samana-bhava"* has been coined in some quarters for secularism in the highest sense. But, as we have seen, tolerance, in the Seminar's sense, is a wider concept than "equal respect for all religions", since tolerance applies to much that is not religion, say, art, literature, manners, morals, and taste, etc. or even opposed to religion, like Marxism, Freudian psycho-analysis, and nihilism, etc.

The absence of a Sanskrit word, however, does not mean that the attitude or value of tolerance was not known in ancient India.[4] The Jaina doctrine of *anekanta-vada* and the Hindu approaches of *adhikara* and *ista-devata* capture the spirit of tolerating plural truth-claims in all walks of life. Viewed as a methodological concept, *anekanta-vada* is a subtle and fruitful analytical tool. Likewise, the Hindu meta-theory of philosophy that philosophers give us different partial views or perspectives (*darsana*) of one and the same reality, which accommodates all the partially correct views, none of which is, however, totally true, also makes the same point and serves the same purpose.[5]

The concept of *adhikara* in the sense of "level of competence of a person", and the doctrine of *adhikara* that truth should be formulated in accordance with the level of understanding or competence of different persons who all differ from each other also serve to promote tolerance.

The twin concepts of *adhikara* and *isht-devta* allow worshipping the essentially formless divine Being in any form of one's own choice. This implies that no one form can claim to be intrinsically more desirable than another, so that the desire to convert others or bring about uniformity in belief and worship is uncalled for. It is difficult for a non-specialist in Indian philosophy, like myself, to say whether the concept of *ista-devata* could logically be, or has actually been, extended to embrace agnosticism or atheism. But perhaps this extended use may be deemed plausible, since belief in God or Isvara is not an essential element of Hindu orthodoxy. As we know, Hindu orthodoxy means essentially belief in the infallibility of the Vedas. Again, if a person denies this belief, could it be said that this denial is his *ista-marga* and that he should be permitted to take to this path without attracting any penalty in any form? As we know, the Jains and Buddhists did deny the sanctity of the Vedas, and most probably no human bodies were put on stakes to save souls.

The concept of *anekanta-vada* and the twin concepts of *adhikara* and *ista-devata* or *ista-marga* thus jointly do the conceptual job of the word "tolerance" in the Seminar's sense. Whether this concept was translated into practice or not, and if so, to what degree and at what time and place, whether there were periods of tolerance followed by intolerance or a primitive intolerance gradually evolved into tolerance (as happened in Western Europe from the late 17th century onwards): all these questions are matters for historical enquiry. Thus initial intolerance by Aryan victors over non-Aryan or Dravidian people may have led later on to an extended period of cultural fusion resulting in classical Hinduism. The point is that the period of Indian pre-history is so long that a suspension of judgment becomes methodologically essential. However, the full implications of authentic scriptures, law books, literature, folklore, and reliable social-cultural records should be used to answer the historical question concerning the role of tolerance in Indian culture.[6]

RELIGIOUS TOLERANCE AND THE CASTE SYSTEM

Tolerance, in the fullest sense, embraces differences in the total spectrum of human life, language, dress, customs, food habits, morality, religion, art, politics and social institutions. I shall confine myself to politics and religion in this paper, as it is precisely these two, along with language, which provide the stage or scenario in most societies for the demon of intolerance whenever it casts its evil shadow over humans.

The struggle for political power leading to military conflicts is a universal feature of the human situation, and Indian society has been no exception. Rather the struggle for power was even more pervasive and incessant because of the ambition or aspiration of each and every ruler to become the *"Chakravartin"* or the overlord, the king of kings ruling in their own smaller territories. And the whole of the Indian subcontinent from the Himalayas to Kanyakumari, and from Dwaraka in the west to Puri in the east was the *Chakravartin's* legitimate jurisdiction as the first step towards a universal commonwealth based on *dharma*. Wars and battles were, however, the sport and the business of kings and their warriors who won and lost without seriously affecting the lives and fortunes of the common man in the territory of the victor or of the loser in the tournament of kings. This was also more or less true in other parts of the world until medieval times, apart from the great risk of religious persecution of the subjects of the vanquished prince. In India, however, this sort of persecution hardly ever occurred.

Indian history does not point to any massacres, forcible mass migrations, religious bans, forced conversions. The movements of reform or spiritual renewal, like Jainism and Buddhism, which were roughly contemporaneous, were based on free exchange of ideas and challenging the authority of the Vedas. It is significant that this challenge was made in the name of reason, the right of free enquiry and the ethic of large-hearted tolerance, and further that this challenge was met by the Vedic orthodoxy, not by the sword, but by the pen. Both Mahavira and Gautama Buddha initiated an era of peaceful change, shifts in meaning of basic concepts and values, new cultural symbols and practices and an inner spiritual renewal to cure the hardening of the spiritual arteries of the Vedic priests (lost in the esoteric intricacies of *mimamsa*) and to improve the spiritual and moral health of the vast populace sunk in the torpor of ritualistic conformism and the prison of caste.[7]

After centuries of cross-fertilization of ideas and an extended dialogue between Indian classicism (represented by Vedanta) and the then modernism (represented chiefly by Buddhism), Hinduism (represented by the Gita) displaced Buddhism from the land of its birth. Meanwhile, Buddhism itself had undergone considerable inner transformation in the course of the extended peaceful dialogue. As we all know, the presiding muse of this super-Marathon cultural dialogue was Sankaracharya who died in the 9th century.

In the course of later centuries when *Mahayana Buddhism* and Hinduism developed or degenerated into *Tantrism*, the process was again peaceful. The socio-cultural dynamics of this interesting phenomenon is perhaps not fully grasped, but in any case, no coercion of the populace was involved.

The study of history and psychological analysis of human nature both show that intolerance and persecution, never lead to genuine conversion, but merely to spiraling violence or a superficial uniformity of belief and practice destroying the very soul and purpose of religion. The vast cultural diversity of India in the form of different languages, religions, cults, laws, marriage and inheritance customs, manners, food habits, all testify to, and are explainable only on the basis of, a widespread tolerance rooted in the concepts of *anekantavada, adhikara, ista-devata* or *ista-marga*.

Having surveyed the impact of the above basic concepts, let us now analyze the implications of another fundamental principle or postulate of Hindu society, viz., the caste system. Social gradation by caste has been not only the de facto social reality in Indian society from time immemorial, but is also a de jure and sacred institution sanctified by all her scriptures, and traditionally deemed to be the very foundation or backbone of the Hindu religion (*varnasramadharma*).[8] Philosophers, historians, and social scientists must, however, discuss this concept with the utmost intellectual honesty without any admixture of apologetics.

Both actual social reality and plain scriptural texts make it evidently clear that the Hindu fourfold classification of men is not a psychological classification of personality types cutting across religion, race, and social status, but a classification based on heredity and the accident of birth. The duties corresponding to each caste (*varnadharma*) do not flow from the person's actual traits (*gunas*), but from his predetermined caste (*varna*). It is, therefore, misleading and futile to try to assimilate the caste system to the concept of class or of social gradation, as it exists outside Indian society. It is equally misleading to hold the caste system as some sort of anticipation of the modern psychological theories of human types or to assimilate the concept of *varnadharma* to the ethical theory of self-realization or Bradley's concept of "my station in life and its duties." Indeed, the caste system is a unique style of social gradation without any strict parallel in the rest of the world.

Some modern Hindu thinkers and writers (including Radhakrishnan) are inclined to hold that the caste system was originally a function of the actual endowment or personality structure of a person who acquired the status of a *Brahman* or *Ksatriya* or lost it, instead of being born as such. This is certainly a logically possible situation. But it seems to me there is no evidence to support this historical claim, which, for all we know, might well have been the case. But even if we do accept this line of thinking, only a measure of occupational mobility was allowed to the upper or twice-born castes leaving the Sudras and the out-castes patiently to serve the higher castes as expiation for their sins (*karma*) in previous generations.[9]

The conclusion of the above evidence is that, while Indian culture admirably tolerated doctrinal differences, it failed to develop the idea of toleration into the concept of humanistic respect of man as such. The humanistic protest of Jainism and Buddhism against caste could not be assimilated by Hindu orthodoxy, despite the spiritual renewal produced by these movements and the legacy left by Ashoka. The tremendous latent power and hold of the caste system obstructed the growth of fresh dimensions in the concept of *ista-devata* and *adhikara*. The idea of tolerance remained confined to the choice of the form of deity without developing into *ista-dharma* or the choice of vocation on the basis of one's ability and aptitude rather than one's pre-determined status by birth. It is both astonishing and tragic that the philosophical theory of the identity of *Brahman* and the *Atman*, (of *Advaita Vedanta*) giving such high ontological status and dignity to the human soul (*jiva*) as it does, did not lead to the simple ethical ideal of the dignity and equality of man, irrespective of caste, color, creed, or sex.

Hindu thought evolved the concepts of *ista-devata*, *ista-marga* and *adhikara*, which promoted religious tolerance. But it could not evolve the concept of *ista-dharma* (based on one's actual ability and aptitude) as distinct from *varnadharma* (based on birth within a caste). Likewise, Hindu thought could not evolve the concept of *adhikara* in terms of a humanistic right to self-realization. Thus equality of status is absent from the Hindu concept of man, and equality of opportunity from the Hindu concept of justice. If tolerance remains incomplete without equality of status, the Hindu concept of tolerance has only one leg to stand upon.

CONCEPT AND ROLE OF TOLERANCE IN MEDIEVAL INDIA

To the best of my knowledge, the Arabic and Persian languages also do not have an equivalent word for tolerance in the Seminar's sense. The words; "*tahammul*", "*hilm*", "*burdbari*", "*bardasht*"; all mean endurance, steadfastness, or patience. However, the ideal of tolerance is certainly present in the *Quran* and also found in the conduct of the Prophet ﷺ and the pious Caliphs.[10] But some of the schools of Islamic law (*shariah*) have unfortunately developed on lines (allegedly based upon the *Quran* and the sayings or practice of the Prophet ﷺ) that certainly negate the concept of tolerance towards both Muslims and others. For instance, according to the classical or traditional Muslim view, a Muslim who repudiates Islam or commits apostasy (*irtidad*) attracts the death penalty. Again, if a Muslim does not repudiate Islam, but competent authorities deem his views or actions to amount to apostasy, the unfortunate Muslim may be held to be guilty of heresy and executed.[11] However, no school of Islamic law upholds the permissibility of coercing non-Muslims to accept Islam or to give up their faith, though inviting them to Islam is upheld as highly desirable for the Muslim. We must remember that the above views are not *Quranic* textual injunctions, but only interpretations or inferences (rightly or wrongly) drawn from the text.[12]

Some Muslim theologians or jurists have expressed the view that the *Quran* and the sayings of the Prophet prohibit Muslims from befriending and trusting non-believers. An under-current of suspicion and prejudice does exist in the popular Muslim consciousness side by side with the inspiring humanism and tolerance of the great *Sufi* saints and poets.[13] Many non-Muslims also honestly believe that the *Quran* actually does prohibit Muslims from trusting and befriending non-Muslims just as it prohibits inter-marriage or idol worship. It must, however, be noted that a careful and honest reading of all the relevant *Quranic* texts (as distinct from the gloss or interpretation) in the light of the situational context of the *Quranic* verses makes it clear beyond any doubt that the *Quran* is free from such repugnant intolerance and anti-humanism that some Muslim interpreters unfortunately have projected into the *Quranic* text or deemed to be the correct Islamic view.[14] In any case the Muslim political establishment in India, i.e. the kings or sultans unhesitatingly rejected such interpretations. And this holds good, not merely of such eminently liberal and humanistic kings or princes as Akbar, Tipu or Dara Shikoh, but also of Muslim rulers in general.[15] The very, very few exceptions only confirm the general rule. It was precisely the religious liberalism and practical secularism of the kings that led to repeated tensions or conflicts between the Muslim political and the religious establishments in India.[16]

The position of the *Sufi* saints was different from the theologians or jurists. Barring the *Nakshbandiya* order and some other individual mystics, the *Sufis*, in general, stood for liberalism, universal tolerance and love. Muslim sovereigns understandably felt closer to the *Sufis* than to the theologians who were patently unhappy with the worldly-wise secular approach of the kings. However, there was a liberal section among the theologians as well, and it would be grossly inaccurate and unfair to paint them as monsters of intolerance and the *Sufis* as the paragons of Humanism.[17]

The populace, Hindu and Muslim alike, deeply venerated the *Sufi* saints as the embodiment of religious piety, though the puritanical

Muslim elements, especially among the urban middle classes, tended to look up to the Muslim theologians and scholars who were apt to frown upon the predilection of the *Sufis* towards music, *yoga* and Vedanta, their tendency to practice different types of innovations and give esoteric interpretations of the *Quran* which clashed with the plain and simple puritanical approach of the theologians. Thus a measure of innocuous tension existed between *Sufis* and theologians.[18]

Political tensions and the struggle for power obviously went on during the medieval period as in the ancient. The only difference was that sometimes the royal antagonists and the warriors professed religious faiths of different origin instead of professing one common faith or its different variants as happened in the pre-Islamic period. But the struggles were always political and not religious wars between Hinduism and Islam. Often the teams of the antagonists were mixed groups, though perhaps the regiments or battalions were composed of single communities. It is not sheer accident that the *Mughal* general who defeated Shivaji in the beginning was a Hindu, while the person who helped Shivaji to escape from the *Mughal* fort in Agra was a Muslim.[19]

It is also deeply significant that the loyalty of subjects to their kings and princes cut across the distinction between Hindu and Muslim so long as the king could command military success by defeating his rivals. The warrior class helped and freely gave their lives for the king's cause, and their code of honor made them pledge their loyalty to the victor irrespective of his religion. Cases of revolt, rebellion, treachery, disloyalty, bribery, and corruption were human responses of the participants and not actions calculated to help the cause of Islam or Hinduism. This was secularism in action without bothering whether the state was secular or religious, or whether sovereignty rested in the people or in God.[20] This pragmatic secularism was rooted in the following social realities of the age:

(a) the voluntary extension of the concept of *ista-devata* to the followers of Islam,

(b) the voluntary extension of the *ksatriya-varna-dharma* to the Muslim warrior class and the princes, thereby viewing them as honorary or functional "Rajputs" and as an integral part of those who dwelt in India as their home (*Bharatavasis*), and

(c) the firm and unwavering principle and policy of the Muslim sovereigns (barring very few exceptions) to keep the church and the state separate and distinct in practice, even if not in theory, despite the pressure of the orthodox theologians and their lobby in the corridors of power or in the counsels of the king. With one or two exceptions, the Sultans in North India, in general, and particularly the Sultans in the South and the *Mughal* emperors succeeded in rising above the din and dust of communal or sectarian slogans. Perhaps the sound political instinct and practical wisdom of the ruling class enabled them to see that the talk of "Islam in danger" was an unconscious strategy for obtaining maximum material gains or defending existing vested interests which were perceived as threatened by rivals professing a different faith. [21]

Coming to the cultural aspect, the medieval Indian society was a period of intense spiritual searching leading to the rise of the *Sufi* and *Bhakti* movements. The Hindu and Muslim saints held loving surrender to God (rather than external practices) to be the breath of true religion, and they preached and practiced love of God and love of man as two sides of a single coin. Holding universal kindness and goodwill and devotion to duty as the common ethical teaching of all religions, they repudiated all barriers of caste or creed.

The humanist message of Jainism and Buddhism thus came to life again in the framework of a simple, easily understandable, and emotionally moving theism, both Hindu and Muslim. The symbols of this movement are Kabir and Guru Nanak in North India and Ramanuja in the South, but there are numerous other great souls who inspired and elevated Indians of all castes and creeds, helping the common man in the villages and the cities to share the common joys and sorrows, and hopes and fears of life, the ceremonies of birth and death, the festivities of the season, of marriage and of religious occasions, the pleasure of folksongs and the wisdom of folklore — all cutting across the distinction of Hindu and Muslim.[22]

The emotional integration mentioned above, however, did not lead to a full-blooded and mature humanism which accords unconditional worth and dignity to the individual qua individual, irrespective of his caste, color, creed, or sex, and which also prescribes a multi-dimensional tolerance. The concept or ideal of humanistic tolerance, rooted in the study of world history and critical philosophy, entered the Indian cultural scene as a stable and effective factor only with the advent of Western liberal values in the 19th century.

Perhaps the most important single factor, which historically has inhibited the flowering of the ideal of the humanistic brotherhood of man on the Indian scene, was the traditional ban on both inter-caste and inter-religious marriages. Even when the British rulers legally provided for civil marriage, irrespective of the caste or religion of the contracting parties, an express declaration was required from them that they did not profess any religion. Evidently, this was a reluctant concession to both Hindu and Muslim orthodoxy. This irrational condition has now been removed, and conditions, political, cultural, and economic, are slowly arising which bear the promise of the growth of tolerance in all the spheres of Indian life and culture.

Notes To Essay 8
The Concept And Role Of Tolerance In Indian Culture

1. The birth of religious tolerance in Western Europe dates back to the Renaissance in the 15th century, which drew inspiration from the wisdom and humanism of ancient Greece. The Christian Reformation, which led to plural versions of Christianity, created the need for tolerance, but the parallel authoritarian approaches of Luther and Calvin indirectly led to intolerance. The rise of the Counter-Reformation brought about the darkest era of intolerance in the Western world, which was soon to see the horrors of the Thirty-year War (1618-1648), which remains unparalleled in the annals of history for mass destruction and religious persecution. Perhaps the horrors of protracted violence for the sake of saving souls mentally and emotionally prepared Western Europe to listen to the philosophy of tolerance preached by John Locke of Oxford, the father of British democracy and the humanistic conception of the dignity and rights of man as such. However, even Locke was ill-prepared to tolerate atheists and also had some reservations against Roman Catholics. The idea of tolerance took almost two centuries for its maturity and application by John Stuart Mill in the third quarter of the 19th century, though it was fully present in the thought of Spinoza, Kant and Voltaire much earlier.

2. This shift of meanings is a regular feature of living languages and cultures. Different meanings or uses become prominent due to social and cultural changes. The mature critical philosopher or historian of ideas must try to understand the situational genesis of these changes and not remain content merely with linguistic and phenomenological analysis.

3. Politicians and administrators often practice appeasement but claim the virtue of tolerance. In some cases the appeasement leads to a tragic-comic intolerance and pseudo-religious piety, as happened

some time ago in Tamil Nadu and Andhra. It was reported in the press that some Harijans notified local politicians that if the grievances of the Harijans were not rectified within a time bound period, they would embrace Islam. It was reported that the demands were promptly met. Evidently, the Harijans did not care for Islam, nor the politicians for Hinduism. The Harijans were motivated by expediency, and the politicians were guilty of appeasement.

4. Man's experience can be identified, described and classified in more ways than one. In view of the fact that human experience both resembles and differs from age to age or society to society, man's linguistic responses also both resemble and differ from each other.

5. This is also what Karl Jaspers appears to mean by saying that the philosopher ought to 'glide' over conceptual space, which is sought to be mapped by philosophical theories. This also resembles John Wisdom's view that philosophical theories are neither true nor false, but illuminating and misleading and reflect both intellectual penetration and confusion in some form or other.

6. The following few quotations from innumerable Hindu, Jain and Buddhist sources will illustrate the spirit of tolerance found in Indian culture:

As men approach me, so do I accept them: men on all sides follow my path, O Partha (Arjuna).
(Gita, 4:11)

Even those who are devotees of other gods, worship them with faith, they also sacrifice to Me alone, O son of Kunti (Arjuna), though not according to the true law.
(Gita, 9:23)

Whatever form any devotee with faith wishes to worship, I make that faith of his steady.
(Gita, 7:21)

Whatsoever being there is endowed with glory and grace and vigor, know that to have sprung from a fragment of My splendor.

(Gita, 10:41)

(All from Radhakrishnan's translation of the Bhagavad Gita)

Cows are of many different forms and colors. Their milk is always white. The path of virtue, like milk, is one. The sects that teach it are manifold. (*Naladinanuru* quatrain 118)

All paths of realization, though manifold and different according to (different) traditions, flow to you only, even as all streams of Ganga flow into the ocean. (Kalidasa in the *Raghuvamsa* as quoted in V. Raghavan, *The Great Integrators*. Publications Division, Ministry of Information and Broadcasting, New Delhi, 1966, p. 76)

In You, O Lord! Arise all viewpoints, even as all rivers rise out of the ocean and just as the ocean cannot be seen in those rivers so long as they remain separate, even so, You cannot be seen in the separate viewpoints. (Siddhasena Divakara as quoted in *Raghavan,* op.cit., p. 78)

The Beloved of the Gods... honors members of all sects... by gifts and various honors. But he does not consider gifts and honors as important as the furtherance of the essential message of all sects. By doing this one strengthens one's own sect and helps the others, while by doing otherwise one harms one's own sect and does a disservice to others. Whoever honors his own sect and disparages another man's... does his own sect the greatest possible harm. (From *Twelfth Rock Edict* of Ashoka).

7. It is held in some quarters that the near complete disappearance of Jainism and Buddhism from the land of their birth proves mass persecution of their adherents by the *Brahman* establishment. But this inference is based on *a priori* reasoning rather than empirical evidence. There is some evidence of Jains having been persecuted and of the destruction of their temples in South India in the Pallava and Chola period, in Gujarat, and also in Kashmir (See A.B.M. Habibulla, *The Foundation of Muslim Rule in India*, Allahabad, 1961). Also, there is some evidence of inter-sect violence in the south. But the scale of such happenings is trivial in relation to the violence in other parts of the world. According to Voltaire's calculations, approximately ten million souls lost their lives in the space of about two hundred years due to religious persecution in Western Europe. The record of medieval Islam does not bear any such blemish, and Jews and Christians enjoyed security of life and property and opportunities of material progress in Muslim countries, but the degree of tolerance of dissent within Islam was appreciably less than in India, or classical China and Japan. Western Europe, however, became the nursery of a progressively growing tolerance from the late 18th century onwards.

8. The Gita (3: 35) is unmistakably clear on this point:

"Better is one's own law though imperfectly carried out than the law of another carried out perfectly. Better is death in (the fulfillment of) one's own law, for to follow another's law is perilous."

9. The provision that the caste position of a Hindu could be upgraded or downgraded after seven generations under specified conditions does not disprove the essentially hereditary basis of caste. The dozen or more categories of intermediate or mixed castes (depending upon the original caste of the male or the female parent) as also the social stigma attached to a child born of a *Sudra* father and a *Brahman* mother show the true nature of the concept of caste. Radhakrishnan quotes one or two instances of a sage in the remote antiquity having taught philosophy to a lowborn pupil. Even if this had actually happened, this does not go to show the functional nature of caste in remote antiquity.

10. The following verses of the Quran may be noted:

(2: 256)
There is no compulsion in religion...

(6: 108)
...We have not sent thee (Muhammad) as a keeper over them (non-believers), nor art thou responsible for them...

(10: 99)

And if thy Lord willed, all who are in the earth would have believed together. Wouldst thou (Muhammad) compel men until they are believers?

(16: 125)

Call unto the way of thy Lord with wisdom, and fair exhortation, and reason with them in the better way. Lo! Thy Lord is best aware of him who strayeth from His way, and He is best aware of those who go aright.

(42: 48)

But if they (non-believers) are averse, we have not sent thee (Muhammad) as a warder over them. Thine is only to convey (the message)...

(109: 4-6)

And I (Muhammad) shall not worship that which ye (poly-theists or heathens) worship. Nor will ye worship that which I worship. Unto you your religion, and unto me my religion.

Also noteworthy is Caliph Umar's refusal to pray within the premises of a church in Palestine after the Muslim conquest on the ground that this may be made an excuse later on for converting it into a mosque. The Quran repeatedly refers to all places of worship as sacred and worthy of respect.

11. The story of the martyrdom of Mansur Hallaj and of Sarmad is well known. But perhaps the most tragic and shameful instance of the penalty is the execution of Buddhan Brahman, a learned saint of the 16th century, during the time of Sikander Lodi. As a Hindu, Buddhan could not have attracted this penalty. Since, however, he had happened earlier to praise Islam, the establishment (on some perverse logic) gave him the option either to embrace Islam or face death. The tragedy took place a few years before the advent of Babar in India. Most probably, political motives were the real cause, as in the cases of Mansur and Sarmad.

The traditionally approved death penalty for apostasy (*irtidad*) is the height of intolerance and is patently incompatible with the

Quranic verse that there is no compulsion in religion. The fear of internal disruption of the nascent Islamic church-cum-state may have led the early Muslim jurists to this indefensible view. But unfortunately this approach was never repudiated even when Islam had achieved a dominant position, and there was no question of any threat of internal disruption or external attack. This provision still remains part of the Islamic religious law (*shariah*), and may be invoked by the religious establishment (whenever it may so choose) for stifling free enquiry or suppressing honest dissent. It is this law which has produced self-alienation and fear of authentic being in the Muslim mind or psyche, and obstructed the growth of spiritual autonomy and the spirit of free enquiry, and also a large hearted tolerance of honest dissent within the fold of Islam, as distinct from a rather condescending tolerance of other faiths.

12. It must be conceded that some theologians strangely maintain that force is permissible for creating external and psychological conditions for eventual inner conversion to Islam, though they have never stood for coercion leading to death. The belief that Islam gave to the conquered peoples the option between annihilation and conversion to Islam is, however, an exercise in pure imagination on the part of either misinformed historical innocence or perverse hostility.

13. The spirit of tolerance found among the *Sufis* is beautifully illustrated by the following anecdote from the poem, *Mantiq-ut-Tair* (*The Logic of the Birds*) by the famous *Sufi*, Fariduddin Attar (d. 1229).

"Once the angel Gabriel came to know that God was especially pleased with, the adoration of some devotee. Gabriel tried to trace the privileged soul, but all in vain. He then approached God for information. And lo! God directed Gabriel to proceed to a temple in Rum (Turkey) where he found an idol worshipper absorbed in worship. Shocked, Gabriel went back to God, only to be told that the idolater was worshipping God himself, though traces of ignorance were present in his heart."

As regards prejudice and suspicion among Muslims against non-Muslims, even such eminent figures as Ghazzali (d. 1111), Ahmad

Sarhindi (d. 1624) and Wali Ullah (d. 1763) are guilty of such irrational sentiments and views.

14. The relevant Quranic verses have been analyzed by me in my paper, "*How I see the Quran?*". I now give a few revealing quotations from some eminent Indian Muslim theologians. Unless Muslim scholars and public men *suo motto* express their unqualified disapproval of such anti-humanistic interpretations and sentiments that unfortunately passed muster in the medieval period as true Islam, no honest and well-informed person could repudiate the charge of intolerance against Islam, or claim that it preaches true dignity and brotherhood of man. Here is a specimen of the twenty conditions for permitting Hindus to acquire the status of **zimis** according to Shaikh Hamdani of Kashmir in his *Zakhirutul Muluk*.

1. They (Hindus) are not to dress like Muslims.

2. They are not to give each other Muslim names.

3. They are not to ride on horses with saddle and bridle.

4. They are not to possess swords and arrows.

5. They are not to build their houses in the neighborhood of those of the Muslims.

6. They are not to mourn their dead with loud voices.

7. They are not to pay Muslim slaves.

(Folios 94a-95a, as quoted in Wm. Theodore de Bary, Sources of Indian Tradition, New York 1956, p. 490)

"Pious Muslims should be posted to the provinces so that they may collect taxes in accordance with the principles of *shariah*. No *Kafir* should find any office or employment in the *Diwan* of Islam as well as in the Capital of Islam. Posts of *Amirs* and *Amils* should be barred to them. Furthermore, in conformity with the principles of *shariah*, they should be subjected to all types of indignities and humiliations. They (the *kafirs*) should be made to pay revenues, and *jizya* and *zakat* on their goods should be levied as prescribed by *Shaura*. They should have no parity with the Muslims in matters of dress, and should be forced to keep their *kufr* concealed, rather than be allowed to perform ceremonies of *kufr* openly and freely. Stipends should not be paid to them from the *Baitul Mal* of Islam, but they should confine themselves to their own professions. They should not be allowed to consider themselves equal to the Muslims, so that the glory of Islam may reach its zenith".

(Letter of Sh. Abdul Quddus of Gangoh, letter No. 169 to Emperor Babar as quoted in S. A. A. Rizvi, Muslim Revivalist Movement in Northern India, Agra, 1965, p. 245)

"Everyone has some desire in his heart. The desire of this *Faqir* is that the enemies of God and Prophet Muhammad ﷺ should be dealt with severely and these wretches and their false gods should be insulted. You should rest assured that no action is more laudable before God than this one... We should strive hard to insult and condemn these wretches and their false gods... I would have come to you and persuaded you personally to do this act and might have utilized the opportunity by spitting on that idol and might have regarded it as my good fortune".

(Sh. Ahmad Sarhindi's letter to Murtaza Khan. Maktubat, Vol. I, letter No. 269 as quoted in Rizvi, op. cit., pp. 303-307)

"The honor of Islam is in insulting *kufr* and *kafirs*. One who respects the *kafirs* dishonors the Muslims. To respect them does not merely mean honoring them and assigning them a seat of honor in any assembly, but it also implies keeping company with them or showing consideration to them. They should be kept at an arm's length like dogs... If some worldly business cannot be performed without them, in that case only a minimum of contact should be established but without taking them into confidence. The highest Islamic sentiment asserts that it is better to forego that worldly business and that no relationship should be established with the *Kafirs*".

(Maktubat Imam Rabbani, Vol. I, letter 163, as quoted in S.A. A. Rizvi, op. cit., p. 248)

"The real purpose in levying jizya on them (the non-Muslims) is to humiliate them to such an extent that on account of the fear of jizya, they may not be able to dress well and to live in grandeur. They should constantly remain terrified and trembling. It is intended to hold them under contempt and to uphold the honor and right of Islam".

(Mujaddid's letter No. 163, Vol. I to Sh. Farid as quoted in Rizvi, op. cit., p. 249)

"Cow-sacrifice in India is the noblest of Islamic practices. The *kafirs* may probably agree to pay *jizya*, but they shall never concede to cow-sacrifice".

(Mujaddid's letter No. 81 to Lala Beg as quoted in Rizvi, op. cit., p. 249)

14. The Muslim sovereigns in India right from the Arab dynasties in Sind to the *Mughals*, including the Turkish Sultans, firmly and consistently practiced tolerance towards their non-Muslim subjects who formed the vast bulk of the population, no matter what the stand of the religious establishment. The very few exceptions, Sultan Sikander (d. 1410) of Kashmir, Firoz Tughlaq (d. 1388) and Sikandar Lodi (d. 1517) only prove the general rule. Much earlier, in the tenth century, Sultan Mahmud's hit and run ransacking of Hindu temples was unmistakably a search for gold rather than any devotion to Islam. Indeed, Qazi Abdul Hasan Baulami, the famous divine of Ghazna, openly disapproved of the Sultan's despoliation of temple wealth in India as anti-Islamic, and refused to accept the rich presents Mahmud sent him after one of his adventurous exploits in India.

It is also noteworthy that there was no mass destruction of Hindu temples in the medieval period, though some temples were destroyed, as the Mahakala temple in Ujjain and other temples in Delhi, Ajmer and Jaunpur. In some cases the material of the demolished temples was used in mosques. However, the construction of new temples was discouraged without being prohibited. In any case, no restrictions were placed on public Hindu worship or celebration of festivals. Indeed, Hindu festivals were also celebrated by the Muslims, to the displeasure of some Muslim puritanical quarters, while Hindu masses showed great reverence and devotion to *Sufi* saints, both living and dead.

It may be said that Muslim Sovereigns were influenced consciously or unconsciously by the approach of Al-Beruni; one of the greatest savants of all time and the author of *Kitabul Hind*, wherein he had stated that the prima facie idolatry of the Hindus was quite compatible with the monotheism of Islam. The Muslim sovereigns stood for justice and tolerance and took their main task to be the efficient governance of the state and the protection of its territorial integrity rather than the spread of Islam or the reform of Hindu society. However, those who professed Islam did enjoy a privileged position by the very nature of the case in the then religiously oriented and hierarchical society. The earlier advantageous position of Muslims (especially of Turkish, Persian and Pathan origin) in the competition for power and prestige in the court and society in general gradually lost its weightage by the time of Akbar. Mutual sympathy and a genuine dialogue in the field of religion marked his long and prosperous reign. As also a creative synthesis in art, music, and literature, and the spirit of humanism and composite nationalism in politics.

Akbar's ideal of universal concord (*sulah-e-kul*) was not a new approach for the Muslim rulers in India. The essential novelty in Akbar's approach was his concern to give Islamic legitimacy to the de facto liberal approach of Muslim rulers in India. In other words, Akbar was, probably, interested in a sort of philosophical reconstruction of religious thought in Islam, like say, Sir Syed, Iqbal or Azad. This understandably provoked the theologians and some others (who could not appreciate the need for continuous growth in the concepts and values of a living cultural tradition) to charge Akbar with unwarranted interference in religious matters (*mudakhilat-fi-deen*). However, the launching of the *Deen-e-Ilahi* as an independent religion, rather than merely as a reinterpretation of Islamic thought, was an ill-conceived adventure, which proved to be stillborn. Reliable historians tell us that only approximately twenty persons (both Muslim and Hindu) joined the royal cult. But to be fair to the Emperor there was absolutely no coercion and no withholding of royal patronage from those who politely but firmly declined to embrace the royal cult.

The prima facie deviations of Akbar's successors were politically motivated. Even Aurangzeb functioned within broadly the same parameters with some qualifications (namely, the re-introduction of the *jizya*, restrictions on state appointments at the lower level and discriminatory rates of taxation). However, the style of Aurangzeb's Islamic piety, as also his political perception, was different from those of Akbar or Dara Shikoh, though he was far from being a fanatic or bigot in the derogatory sense of the term. His demolition of one or two temples must be judged in the light of his endowing others. Aurangzeb's grandson, Jahangir Shah, was deeply interested in Indian culture. *Tuhfatul Hind*, an encyclopedic work on Hindu sciences and fine arts, was especially composed for the benefit of the Prince. Mirza Raushan Zamir who was appointed Bakshi of Surat by Aurangzeb translated a Sanskrit work (*Parijatica*) on music into Persian. Liberal *Sufis* remained quite influential during Aurangzeb's rule. However, it remains true that Aurangzeb's approach to religion was not humanistic and philosophical, but rather authoritarian and theological.

16. The following quotations from Ziauddin Barni's *Tarikh-i-Firozshahi* show the sense of helplessness of the religious establishment to influence state policy.

"How can piety and righteousness be established when philosophers and heretics (*bad-mazhaban*) who prefer Greek rationalism to the *sunnah* and who disbelieve the physical existence of heaven and hell, are allowed to openly spread their doctrines? How can the religion of God triumph when these people, the enemies of God and His Prophet ﷺ, live in the capital with dignity and ostentation and are not afraid to express their views?"

(Barni, Tarikh-i-Firozshahi, pp. 42-72, as quoted in A.B.M. Habibullah, op. cit., p. 333)

"...How will the true faith prevail over other religions, if the kings of Islam, with the power and prestige of Islam which has appeared in the world... permit the banners of infidelity to be openly displayed in their capital and in the cities of the Muslims, idols to be openly worshipped and the conditions of infidelity to be observed as far as possible, the mandate of their false creed to operate without fear? How will the true faith prevail if rulers allow the infidels to keep their temples, adorn their idols and to make merry during their festivals with beatings of drums and dhols, singing and dancing?"

(Folios 119 a-b. Barni, Fatawa-i-Jahandari, as quoted in de Bary, p. 489).

17. There was no watertight division between theologians and *Sufis* as was the case before Ghazzali's classic reconciliation of theology and mysticism in Islamic thought through his life and works, particularly his magnum opus, *Ilhya ul ulum din* (*Revival of the Religious Sciences*). Thus several theologians were also practicing *Sufis*, though not all *Sufis* were scholars. The degree of tolerance practiced by theologians or *Sufis* ultimately depended, not on the *Sufi* order (*silsalah*), or the level of piety, or the scholarship of the person, but upon his personality type. Thus Sheikh Ahmad Sarhindi, one of the foremost *Sufis*, was conspicuous for his intolerance while Abdul Haq Mohaddis, a great theologian, had a liberal approach, though not so pronounced as that of Amir Khusro, Nizamuddin Auliya or Sharafuddin Yahya Manyari. In general, the Indian Muslims were attracted to the liberal *Sufism* of Nizamuddin Auliya, Sharafuddin Yahya Manyari, Sheikh Aman Panipati, Miyan Mir, Shah

Mohibullah, Sheikh Burhan Shattari rather than the extreme puritanical *Sufism* of Sheikh Ahmad Sarhandi whose views remained confined to a very narrow circle. Indeed, even the sons and other close followers of his spiritual preceptor, Khwaja Baqi Billah of Delhi, disagreed with Sheikh Ahmad Sarhindi's approach.

18. The tension between the religious approaches or attitudes of the saint and those of the theologian is one of the moving themes in much of classical Persian and Urdu poetry. Poetic license enables man's deeper feelings and attitudes to be fully expressed without the fear of censorship or the risk of giving offence to the orthodox.

19. Muslim kings acquired military victories because of superior artillery and reliance on cavalry. But they acquired political legitimacy and emotional acceptance by the common man because of the spirit of tolerance inherent in Indian culture. This tolerance in the sphere of politics may be called macro-tolerance as distinct from micro-tolerance in the religious sphere. Despite his vigorous opposition to the *Mughal* Empire, Shivaji stood for tolerance in his own affairs. His army had numerous Muslim soldiers, specially his artillery, even as the *Mughal* army had a substantial Rajput component. His conflict with the Emperor was basically political and populist rather than religious. His continual attacks on *Mughal* territory were in accordance with the then princely code of invading or looting neighboring territories for spoils or for territorial expansion. During his sack of Surat twice, Shivaji did not spare its prosperous Hindus because of any religious sympathy or bond.

20. It is true that, after the end of the *Abbaside Caliphate* in Baghdad, some Indian Muslim rulers looked up to the *Fatimide Caliphs* of Cairo to confer spiritual legitimacy upon the Sultans who regarded themselves as "shadows of the Caliph", the successors to the Prophet of Islam ﷺ. But this was a pious fiction, which satisfied the religious establishment without depriving the Sultan of even an iota of his sovereignty in favor of a distant *Caliph*. Thus, the Sultanate was essentially a political rather than a religious institution. Even this pious fiction of "recognition" by the *Caliph* was formally discontinued by the *Mughal* emperors; who regarded themselves the shadow of God (*zille Illahi*) and who vied in power and glory with the *Fatimide Caliphs* of Cairo.

21. The resentment shown by Muslim beneficiaries of state grants to theologians and scholars against Akbar's decision to extend the scheme to non-Muslim scholars and Akbar's move to remove the abuses of the system well illustrates the tendency of vested interests to invoke the theory of religion in danger. It is both amusing and significant to hear the cry of "Hinduism in danger" in some quarters in contemporary India.

22. Among the mystics, saints, and poets of this period notable for their tolerance and humanism, mention must be made of Raidas (15th century), Mirabai of Rajasthan (16th century), Sankaradeva of Assam (16th century), Dadu of Rajasthan (d. 1603), Tulsi Das (d. 1623), Ramdas (d. 1680) guru of Shivaji, Raskhan (17th century), Bullhe Shah (d. 1758), and Tyagaraja (d. 1847).

The following two quotations, one from Kabir (in Tagore's translation), and the other from Ramdas, well illustrate the spirit of the religious sensibility of the above saints who have been termed "the great integrators" by Raghavan.

(a)
"... I do not ring the temple bell:
I do not set the idol on its throne:
I do not worship the image with flowers.
It is not the austerities that mortify the flesh which
are pleasing to the Lord".

When you leave off your clothes and kill your senses,
you do not please the Lord.
The man who is kind and practices righteousness,
Who remains passive amidst the affairs of the world,
Who considers all creatures on earth as his own self,
He attains the Immortal Being, the true God is ever with him.

I want not wealth, nor wife, nor rebirths,
I want not in me the pride of knowledge.

By the path of worship (bhakti) lead me to a life of goodness.
O Ram, this is all I ask of Thee now...
I have no skill of mind, no power of thought, no wisdom,
or strength of reason.
I am Thy ignorant bhakta, give me an understanding heart, O Ram.
I know not how to talk or act. I do not understand my duties.
I am greatly troubled in my relations with men.
Give me an understanding heart, O Ram...

(b)
As I listen to the explanation of scriptures, a good thought
enters my mind;
"But it soon passes away as the time of giving up the fruit arrives.
But what shall I do, O Ram, I am unable to do what I ought.
O Ram, I cannot endure life without Thee".

(Ramdas in Dasabodh quoted in Raghavan, op. cit., p. 138)

Apart from the *Sufi* and *Bhakti* movements within Hinduism and Islam in medieval India, the extended religious and cultural dialogue between these two great traditions of the human family led to the birth of the Sikh Reform Movement, which has gradually developed, into a distinct organized and institutional religion with a scripture and priesthood, rituals and also sects. Originally rooted in tolerance and humanistic brotherhood of man, Sikhism later on shrank to a rather narrow fraternity of those prepared to fight against the *Mughals*. Nothing, however, reveals the original catholicity of the Sikh Gurus better than their asking Mian Mir, the famous *Sufi* saint of Lahore, to lay the foundation stone of the Golden Temple at Amritsar in the 17th century. Likewise, the *gurudwara* has always offered hospitality to all without discrimination. The later militancy of the Sikhs against the Muslims was a political development whose genesis need not be analyzed for our purpose here.

The following quotation from Guru Gobind is noteworthy:

Notes to Essay 8

As out of a single fire
Millions of sparks arise;
Arise in separation
But come together again
When they fall back in the fire.
As from a heap of dust
Grains of dust swept up
Fill the air, and filling it
Fall in a heap of dust.
As out of a single stream
Countless waves rise up
And, being water, fall
Back in water again.
So from God's form emerge
Alive and inanimate things
And since they arise from Him
They shall fall in Him again.

(Guru Gobind Singh, Dasama Granth, Akal Ustat, p. 269, as quoted in Raghavan, op. cit., p. 156)

ESSAY 9

CRITIQUE OF ASTROLOGY

INTRODUCTION

Many highly educated and professionally accomplished Indians (including eminent scholars and thinkers) believe that Astrology is a science and its practitioners make correct predictions on the basis of theories propounded by ancient seers and sages in India and elsewhere. In the recent past full-fledged departments and state sponsored programs of research have been instituted in several Indian universities.

The central astrological thesis is that astral configurations and movements that are the subject matter of Astronomy are 'independent determinants' of physical, social psychological and historical phenomena on the earth. Theoretical Astrology is the systematic map of these invariable connections or correlations. Astrologers further hold that some therapeutic practices alter these otherwise invariable correlations between the stars and their earthly effects. It is believed that Theoretical Astrology is an exact science and that the occasional errors of prediction are the result of either arithmetical errors the individual astrologer makes in the process of lengthy calculations, or the wrong factual information or data the individual client supplies to the astrologer. Numerous people (especially) in India believe that if these two possible sources of error could be removed Astrology would become as accurate and certain as, say, Physics or Chemistry. This truth-claim is quite different from the much more modest claim that some individual or individuals can see into or read the past and future without using the normal methods of enquiry or discovery. Indeed, most of us can testify to have witnessed this remarkable phenomenon that leaves us quite baffled. In the following pages I propose to examine (impartially and critically) the restricted central thesis that astral configurations and movements determine earthly events in the manner of a cause-effect relationship. In other words, that Astrology is a scientific or rigorous discipline just like Astronomy.

Let us begin with briefly explaining the concept of science. Well, science is accurate and quantitative description of what is the case in terms of actual or possible sense experience, supplemented by verifiable explanations of why such and such is the case. If and to the extent that the explanation cannot be checked or verified in the strict sense of direct or indirect verifiability, the explanation becomes speculative or metaphysical rather than scientific in the strict sense of this term. In other words, even if the putative explanation is not directly verifiable (for some reason or other) but it implies or suggests some states of affairs and these states can be cross-checked for their presence in the total picture of 'what is the case' the explanation can be (provisionally) accepted as 'scientific'. If this cannot be done at all the explanation stands disqualified for being considered or regarded as 'scientific'. Science is, thus, a highly provisional but progressive body of truth-claims needing continual verification. If, therefore, one believes or claims that Astrology is a scientific discipline he must be able to explain the exact sense in which it is scientific and also why astrological predictions go wrong so frequently as they actually do.

To give some concrete examples, an astrologer predicts that the marriage of 'P' with 'Q' will fail within a year because of such and such astrological configurations or incompatibility between their stars. Such predictions together with astrological explanations are indeed, the stock in trade of astrologers. But when we question the astrologer why is such and such a configuration inauspicious, we find that the astrologer just reiterates this truth-claim and confines himself to citing venerated ancient authorities who were the founding fathers of astrological science in the hoary past. One may well, in all honesty, accept the intuitive wisdom or knowledge of the great 'rishis' and sages of India and even go on to accept that their ideas or theories about the benign and evil consequences of specified configurations and movements of the stars as true and, therefore, reliable guidelines for human choice and action. However, the issue concerning the status of Astrology will remain unanswered until such time as the presumed correlations between astral configurations and earthly events can be explained in the proper scientific sense, namely, as instances of a general verifiable theory of the universe as a whole.

Scientific knowledge starts with accurate observation, experimentation, description of regular correlations and interconnections of events but ends with the formulation of laws of wider and still wider generality based not on induction alone but on verifiable theories that connect the maximum number of events in a broad and internally coherent conceptual framework. The ceaseless search for verifiable laws of wider and still wider generality keeps the motor of science in perpetual motion and continually expands the frontiers of knowledge. Even if it be true that astrological predictions are found to be correct in a very large number of cases, this fact, by itself, does not prove that Astrology is a science, in the above sense. The fact is that the critical enquirer of the real status of Astrology must have before him the statistics of success and failure of prediction on a far bigger scale than what is presently available to us.

Astrology, Astronomy and Mathematics

The votaries of Astrology take keen delight in pointing out that when an astrologer predicts the future he does not speak out of his hat but on the basis of exact figures, axioms and derivative formulas in the manner of a mathematician. I respectfully submit that this self-image follows from two confusions, **(a)** equating Astrology with Astronomy, and **(b)** equating astrological calculations from unproved premises with mathematical calculations that are based on logical necessity and rigorous deduction from self-evident truths or axioms.

There is a radical distinction between the truth-claims of Astrology and Astronomy. The latter is akin to Mathematics and Physics. In fact, Astronomy is Mega-Physics, and its truth-claims are restricted to the parameters of science or the scientific method. Its predictions are subject to scrutiny and verification in the scientific sense. But it does not claim that the writ of the stars runs the fate of marriages, the fortunes of tycoons and sovereign states or governments. Its truth-claims are more or less like those of other natural or physical sciences.

Astrological calculations, however, are radically different from mathematical calculations. The latter deal with analytical truths based on strict logical implication without any reference whatsoever to what is the case at the factual level. When, for instance, one says that 3+2=5, there is no reference to any physical object or objects, nor to the actual or factual situation right now. The mathematical truth-claim merely states a necessary or logical implication of adding up two numerals. No factual evidence is called for to test or establish the mathematical truth-claim concerned. On the other hand, the truth-claim that the boiling point of water is 'X', while that of milk is 'Y' does need empirical evidence for its final acceptance as true. In short, mathematical inference is the pure explication of the inherent implication of either a self-evident truth or any initial assumption for that matter, quite irrespective of the actual truth of the base assumption. Modern Mathematics has, thus, reduced mathematics to the science of pure logical implication without any reference to the self-evidential status of the starting axiom or axioms. However, the truth-claims of the natural sciences do require and will ever continue to require sound and adequate empirical evidence for their final acceptance or corroboration.

Let us now consider to which category astrological truth-claims belong. It should be obvious to any critical student that they are neither self-evident nor logically deducible from any self-evident truth or truths. They are, really speaking, assumptions or beliefs held in good faith, on the basis of long cultural conditioning or faith in a hallowed and sacred tradition. Predictions are based on a person's horoscope or the configuration of the heavenly bodies at the time and place of birth. The horoscope, in turn, flows from basic astrological truth-claims, say; configuration 'A' brings good luck while configuration 'B' bad luck. But this truth-claim is, obviously, not self-evident. Then why should one accept it as true unless there is empirical evidence for its truth? Now what sort of evidence, possibly, could have established the truth, if not conclusively, but at least, as reasonably probable, beyond a shadow of congenital doubt. To me, a mega statistical survey of the total life-chart or biography of persons born in different astrological configurations would have sufficed for the purpose of reasonably satisfactory evidence. But this evidence is not there. What is there is merely faith in the unerring wisdom of the ancient seers and sages. This faith can and does survive in millions of adult men and women. And the fact is that faith can and does act as an anchor and source of consolation and strength for the human species. We all know that even the well established theories of Physics and Chemistry are not certain in the 'logical sense of certainty' but only in the sense of 'very, very probable' and also extremely fruitful for further research and exploration of other factual truths. However, it is very important and necessary for human growth and welfare to remove one's inner confusions and bring to light one's hidden and unexamined assumptions in general.

THERAPEUTIC ASTROLOGY

This term refers to practical Astrology that prescribes remedies for removing or reducing the bad influence of astrological configurations or stars on the life course of different individuals.

The human individual is a born 'activist'. The child is 'active' even when in the mother's womb though his awareness and activity are severely limited. As he grows so does his awareness of his or her needs, of communicating them to others. His power of manipulating objects and satisfying his needs also grows and in the fullness of time he becomes an adult. If the adult is thirsty he does not touch or see water, he gulps it down; if he wants to buy food or sweets he goes to the proper shop; if he wants to go out of town he travels by train or bus or by car, and so on. In short, he takes the world to be a system of causes and effects though he may still continue to believe in an all-powerful Creator who could do whatever He willed. Now the point is that Therapeutic Astrology encourages or propels humans to shift the gear from natural cause-effect activism to dependence on some sort of substitute occult action to satisfy their normal needs, desires and goals. The therapeutic actions astrologers prescribe include such acts as feeding *Brahmans*, or needy persons or animals, burning some specified oils, burying some specified articles or any object of some specified color under the earth or throwing it in a river, reciting some mantra, etc. If one accepts the basic astrological thesis that stars cause good luck or bad for humans on earth, how come that such completely unrelated earthly remedies modify or cancel the inherent power of stars on human destiny. *Prima facie*, the basic thesis of theoretical Astrology, as such, and the practice of therapeutic Astrology appear to be incompatible.

It seems to me that astrological theory affirms that stars are all powerful while human will and aspiration are helpless, and if the astral configuration is unlucky every effort will go wrong despite every human ingenuity and planning, while astrological practice affirms that rather strange remedial acts (prima facie quite unrelated to the issue concerned) can break the power of the stars. This lands us in a sort of predicament. If we accept theoretical Astrology, therapeutic Astrology collapses. If we give more weight or importance to the latter the former seems to crumble.

THE TRACK RECORD OF ASTROLOGY

Let us now briefly review the actual success record of Astrology in history. I submit this is a purely factual question whose proper answer depends upon an impartial descriptive survey (based on reliable statistics) of the success/failure in life among the practitioners of

Astrology, on the one hand, and non-practitioners on the other. If the survey shows that pro-Astrology individuals or groups have done consistently better than anti-Astrology ones this should be regarded as a pragmatic argument in favor of Astrology. If the survey shows no significant difference in the two groups this should be regarded as seriously weakening the case of Astrology. Moreover, if the survey shows that a large number of highly successful and inwardly happy individuals do not worry at all about the stars but follow scientifically confirmed techniques of self-improvement, positive thinking and *yoga* this would further weaken the case of Astrology.

There are no reliable statistics at present. However on the basis of everyday observation it seems to me that, in the final analysis, the key factor that determines the success graph of both individuals and groups has little to do with acceptance or rejection of Astrology, and much to do with self-understanding, intellectual and emotional maturity, integrated personality and the active cultivation of good and productive habits of honest hard work and patience. If we closely examine the lives of outstanding happy and successful individuals in different societies all over the world we shall find that they all share certain traits of personality and character, no matter what they think about Astrology. Likewise, the failures would be found to share some other negative or destructive traits, no matter what they think or do about the good or evil power of stars.

ASTROLOGY AND SOCIOLOGY

Whether stars determine or influence the life story of individuals or not, it is absolutely certain that social cultural factors and the personality type jointly shape the life history of the individual. Diseases related to malnutrition, over-crowding, lack of medical care are far more common among the poor than among the affluent classes, quite irrespective of their presiding stars. It is significant that marital discord and breakdowns of marriage increase when both the partners happen to be economically independent, no matter what their horoscopes might be. Even if we accept that stars matter, reducing the tremendous complexity of human life to the astral dimension (quite clearly beyond human control) and ignoring the social, cultural, economic and technological determinants of the quality of human life (considerably under human control) is the height of un-wisdom. Likewise, the concept of individual fate or predestination (*taqdeer*), as an immutable Divine decree, is also a tragic misinterpretation of Monotheism, Islamic or Christian.

Concluding Reflections

Is it possible to redefine or reconstruct the old and persistent Indian astrological tradition in the light of modern scientific knowledge? I leave this task to those who feel powerfully drawn to Astrology even though they are intellectual giants and eminent academics. I, personally, do not have this inner fascination for Astrology. However, it seems to me that this task is, in principle, possible. In the realm of theoretical Astrology one could replace 'hard astral determinism' with 'soft astral influence', while in the realm of therapeutic Astrology one could replace the traditional, rather, arbitrary prescriptions with modern clean cognitive and meditative therapy without any admixture of superstition. In this reconstructed sense an auspicious astral configuration would mean a 'favorable wind' or weather, while an unlucky configuration would signify 'running against the wind or current'. It is obviously implied that a 'favorable wind' is no substitute for the actual process of running, while an 'unfavorable wind' is no excuse for abandoning an otherwise rational and desirable choice or project. In short, the astrological concepts of 'auspicious' and 'inauspicious' may well be interpreted as 'downstream swimming' and upstream swimming' without any power to veto well considered and rationally sound choices or decisions in the sphere of personal, family, business or state undertakings, as the case may be.

Whether the above approach to Astrology would be practically feasible cannot be asserted at present. The reason is that we do not have enough data to confirm the idea of 'soft astral influence' as such. A colossal amount of statistical data would be needed for clinching this issue. On the other side, the universal success of the standard scientific method and technology (without any aid whatsoever of Astrology) in the arts of peace and war is already well established. To my mind, therefore, it is far more prudent for all individuals and groups to rely on the scientific method and apply policy recommendations made by competent psychologists and sociologists for achieving their well-considered goals of life. Reliance on science, however, by no means, implies neglecting or devaluing the proper roles of morality and spirituality in the good life.

Essay 10

Reincarnation and the Modern Mind

Introduction

The doctrine of *karma* (literally action) together with its corollary, *punarjanam* (rebirth or reincarnation) rather than *Ishwar* (Personal God), or in *Brahman* (Ultimate Self-Existent Being) is the common substratum of the Indian religious tradition. Thus, even Jainism and Buddhism, which are agnostic, and do not accept the authority of the Vedas, still accept the doctrine of *karma*. So does Sikhism. It is significant that several reform movements within the fold of Hinduism, even though they, jointly or severally, repudiate idol worship, the eternity and infallibility of the Vedas, and the caste system, yet they all accept the doctrine of *karma*.

This doctrine is passionately held by millions of Hindus, Buddhists, Jains, and other metaphysical thinkers and should not be brushed aside as a mere clever strategy of priests, kings and the rich to justify their own power and privileges in the present life. To my mind, the doctrine is an attempt to discover some order and justice in the cosmic process with the view to explaining or accounting for pain and suffering that extends even to apparently highly upright and virtuous people.

The Doctrine of Karma

The self-existent eternal Reality underlying or overarching the ever-changing cosmos is *Brahman*—the Supreme Eternal Spirit. The nature and functioning of *Brahman* is beyond human comprehension. All that can be said is that *Brahman* is the ultimate Source of the ever-changing finite existents. These existents comprise living individual beings (*jiva*), and inert objects of different types. Living beings are of different grades, the human *jiva* being in the apex grade, next only to the Supreme Spirit. This is so because *Brahman* is present in the human *jiva* in the form of *Atman*. The relation of *Brahman* and *Atman* may be likened to the relation between the sun and its numerous rays of light. In the final analysis, it is no more explicable than the nature of *Brahman*, as such.

The *Atman* constitutes the higher self of the *jiva*. Thus, the human *jiva*, as the locus of *Atman* has the potential to relate oneself to *Brahman*, as such. This is God-realization and is the highest vocation and the differentia of the human *jiva*. Death is the temporary release of the *Atman* from the bondage of the psychophysical organism, while birth is its temporary incarnation. Every individual is a link in the infinite chain of birth and death (*sansar*). This continual process comes to an end as and when the individual organism overcomes the last trace of inner tension and restlessness that are inseparable from human life. This state is termed *moksh* in Hindu thought and *nirvana* in Buddhist and Jain.

The theory of *karma* is the view that every act, whether overt behavior, or attitude of mind, affects, for better or worse, the human agent. Every act of an agent may be likened to a stroke of the artist's brush, which alters his painting, howsoever imperceptibly. Every good act improves the spiritual health of the agent, bringing him nearer inner goodness and delivering the soul from the '*karmic*' necessity of rebirth, as a penance for his acts of commission or omission. Every bad act has just the reverse consequence. These effects, good or bad, follow in the present life or in the successive incarnation or incarnations, and just cannot be wished away. However, sincere repentance and prayer quicken the pace of spiritual purification and growth.

Suffering follows when, under the sway of blind desire (*ichha*), or temptation, an individual fails to do one's proper duty (*dharma*). Uncontrolled desires are thus, the womb of suffering. The total extinction of desire, rather than merely controlling or regulating it, is the necessary condition for final deliverance from the sway of desire and the cycle of birth, death and rebirth, *sansar*. Every birth is, thus, not only a '*karmic punishment*' but also a fresh opportunity to redeem the past failures and to attain complete salvation.

It follows from the above conception that *karma* must take its own course. Indeed, the Indian conception of final salvation has no place for forgiveness of sins, since there is neither Law-maker, nor Punisher apart from the Law as such. The individual must master his base desires and acquire positive spiritual merit in a measure that could more than compensate for the faults of commission and omission in his previous births. Salvation, therefore, must be assiduously earned by the individual himself, rather than granted by God as a gift in response to man's supplication. According to the religions of Indian origin, the Law rather than the lawgiver is supreme. The view that the lawgiver could suspend the law in special cases is deemed to be an anthropomorphic refraction of the objective truth.

According to the Indian view, every individual strives after perfection and is bound to achieve perfection, which is the same as the extinction of his finite distinct self. The Indian view rejects the belief that only people who profess a particular religion or creed will be saved, while all others will be eternally doomed.

EVALUATION OF THE DOCTRINE OF KARMA

The doctrine of reincarnation is, strictly speaking, not a hypothesis put forward in the spirit of disinterested enquiry. The child is indoctrinated to believe in it just as he or she learns the mother tongue. However, a little reflection will show that the cycle of birth, death, and rebirth is one particular form of the antecedent belief or faith that the universe is not a chaos but a cosmos. Indeed, the belief that there will be a final Day of Judgment when the Supreme Creator would right all wrongs is an alternative semitic version of the same basic belief that as a man sows so shall he reap.

The basic belief that the universe is not chaotic but is a cosmos tries to explain why the innocent or the seemingly innocent suffer in this world. It also motivates man, confronted by prima facie undeserved suffering, to abstain from evil and keep up striving for final salvation despite such pain and suffering. However, to my mind, the Indian doctrine of rebirth hardly fares any better than the doctrine of a final Day of Judgment to explain the pain and suffering of prima facie virtuous people. The struggle between religious faith and atheism goes on.

Consider a bright young boy who loses the sight of one eye when it is hit by a stone an urchin throws at a moving train during the *Holi* festival. Or, think about a plane crash killing a scientist, poised to make a break-through in a great humanitarian project. The scientist dies, but a crippled patient sitting next to him (for whom death would have been a welcome deliverance) survives. Among the papers destroyed in the crash is the only copy of the scientist's findings, while an old railway timetable remains intact.

In the case of the stone throwing the suffering is, patently, due to the irresponsible prank of the urchin. Why should we infer, on the strength of an, avowedly, unverifiable hypothesis, that the injured boy must have deserved this punishment, say, because in his previous incarnation he had, perhaps, mocked at a half blind child, or had deliberately blinded a dog or cat, or because his father, a tyrant landlord had blinded a poor serf? Would this not amount to abandoning a simple and straightforward verifiable explanation, and turning to an extremely complicated doctrine to explain the injury suffered by the boy?

Why may we not say that the injury was due to blind chance, rather than due to the operation of the law of *karmic* punishment on the boy? In fact, doing so would amount to assuming that every event has some moral purpose, whether we humans understand the purpose or not. But where is the evidence that this assumption is correct?

Next consider the case of a young student who embarks on a cycle tour of India to spread the message of world brotherhood. While on a lonely stretch of the road he is struck by lightning. The destruction was caused by a natural phenomenon whose laws are not fully known to man. There are several other instances of, prima facie, unmerited human suffering. Earthquakes kill thousands of people including numerous children and infants. Their lives are cut short without their getting an opportunity to redeem their past sins, if any. It may be said that they would get another opportunity in their next incarnation. But, then, this particular incarnation appears uncalled for.

A young boy falls prey to leukemia, and after a painful illness, passes away. When the cause of leukemia is unknown *karmic* punishment may be acceptable. However, the ever-advancing frontiers of human knowledge continually alter the knowledge-map. Thus, whatever plausibility the reincarnation view might have in such cases recedes once again. Advances in modern medicine, surgery and macro-hygiene are progressively reducing the incidence of physical pain, premature death due to infection, disease, epidemics and physical injuries.

An able and devoted wife has a tyrant husband whose callous behavior drives the long-suffering wife to suicide. But the attempt fails and deepens the tragedy. A competent and honest manager refuses to cooperate with his superiors in an ongoing racket. He is severely made to suffer by being falsely implicated in some crime. His wife falls critically ill and the family is ruined. This is micro-suffering. It is macro suffering when their employer, or landlord, for exercising their right to vote freely, victimizes a group of landless laborers. The helpless victims are forced into bonded labor for a long time to come. Hitler's atrocities against millions of innocent persons are well known.

It is pretty clear that such macro suffering is the result of attitudes and actions of the wrongdoers here and now. The suffering flows from evils inherent in the political, economic and social system. Micro-suffering can be explained, quite adequately, in terms of personality dynamics, and macro-suffering in terms of social dynamics, Why, at all, inject '*Karmic dynamics*' to explain prima facie undeserved suffering of innocent people? Why should not the autonomous truth-seeker just accept that the world is imperfect and contains much ignorance, fear, hatred, selfishness, tyranny, and tragedy apart from goodness and beauty? Man is called upon to resist and conquer pain and evil, no matter how arduous the task. Indeed, the struggle against evil and suffering has always gone on with partial success and fluctuating fortunes. And this struggle will continue.

Why should we complicate the human situation by saying that the oppressed wife of today must have been a tyrant mother-in-law or husband in her previous incarnation, or by saying that the oppressed manager must have been a cruel dacoit in his previous life, and the bonded laborer a tyrannical landlord? Why should we not just say that evil, suffering and tragedy flow from faults in the system as such rather than merely consequences of one's own evil deeds in this or previous births?

A good deal of human suffering is the by-product of the unthinking and selfish behavior of human agents engaged in the irresponsible pursuit of their own good. Now, just as science and technology have reduced physical pain, social reforms and organized struggle are gradually reducing human suffering and producing a more humane and just social order. What, then, is the necessity to explain such improvements in terms of *karmic* rewards and punishments? The simple and straight forward view is that human suffering decreases (except in the theatre of destructive wars) due to the joint impact of science, technology, and an evolving social morality in the course of human life.

The above approach gives due recognition to the role of ethical and spiritual values in the ongoing historical process without postulating reincarnation which is an unverifiable belief, even though it has actually helped billions of people, from times immemorial, to explain why virtuous people suffer in life. This belief does help people to preserve faith that the universe is a cosmos, not a 'chaos' devoid of any meaning or significance. Yet, the fact remains that reincarnation is only one of the ways of resolving the issue of pain and suffering of, prima facie, virtuous persons. It is also a fact that reincarnation tends to promote social passivity rather than social activism.

Consider the suffering of an under-nourished tubercular laborer who has a large family to support. Suppose a believer in *karmic* suffering says that the laborer was, in his previous life, a rich merchant who grossly maltreated his employees and family, and his present sufferings are a recompense as well as an opportunity of spiritual growth through reeducation. Metaphysical issues apart, this type of *karmic* approach to problems of poverty and social suffering puts the focus on sins committed in previous reincarnations rather than on structural and functional social evils here and now. This approach obstructs the fixing of responsibility on human agents and diverts attention from the need to change the system for reducing the said evils. In other words, the concept of *karmic* suffering tends to dilute social activism.

I now turn to animal suffering. They are equally plagued by old age, lack of nutrition, accidents, injuries, premature death, callous exploitation by humans, and so on. Moreover, animals, birds, insects, vegetables, fruits, flowers, mountains, rivers, deserts, stars, etc. show tremendous variety and quality and we accept this fact without invoking reincarnation in their case. Now, if we accept that animals, birds, flowers and plants etc. can be so diverse in structure and grade, without importing the idea of *karma* and reincarnation, we could, very well, do the same with humans.

In the above context special mention must be made of the work of the Society for Psychical Research, founded by Myers, Sedgwick, et al at Cambridge University in the last quarter of the 19th century. Soon afterwards similar societies were established in America and Germany. The main aim of these societies was to make a critical investigation into psychical phenomena, which had attracted popular attention all over the world. The founder members of the Cambridge Society were highly distinguished thinkers and scientists who wanted to study such phenomena as mind reading, telepathy, clairvoyance, fore-knowledge, automatic writing or computation, survival of the dead, communication with spirits, hypnotic trance, reincarnation, etc. in the spirit of disinterested enquiry and with a completely open mind.

These eminent persons were of the view that the first pre-requisite of a truly critical and objective approach to paranormal phenomena was, first, to sort out the genuine from the spurious claims made by mediums, spiritualists, faithhealers, God-men, etc. and, next, to classify the established facts, and, finally, to attempt, an explanation within the conceptual framework of modern thought, as far as this was possible. Where no explanation was possible, but the phenomenon was genuine, rather than imaginary or a conjuring trick the learned Society did not reject the factual evidence, as such, but questioned the adequacy of the basic conceptual framework of modern science, and the hitherto unquestioned assumptions underlying the framework as such.

The approach of the distinguished founders and other members such as William James, Bergson, C.G. Jung, Whitehead, C.D. Broad, Tyrell, *et al*, is thus, entirely free from dogmatism of any sort, be it religious or scientific. Much later on, since the thirties of the 20th century empirical psychologists like, J.B. Rhine, of Duke University, and many others investigated into what came to be called 'extra-sensory perception' (ESP).

While some scientists and thinkers continue to belittle the above investigative work, many eminent persons have come round to accept that paranormal phenomena occasionally do take place, even though they defy explanation within the accepted conceptual framework of modern thought. What is really required is a critical revision of the conceptual framework, as such, to enable us to explain genuine paranormal facts. These eminent thinkers, however, insist that the explanation should satisfy the well-established canons of a valid hypothesis, namely, verifiability, simplicity, consistency, range and predictability.

Several Western investigators have interviewed persons who claimed to remember their previous incarnation. Stevenson and Pasricha examined 300 such cases. But the vast majority of these persons were minor children, under the age of five. In another report listing

1900 cases the majority of the subjects came from Burma, followed by India. Hardly any case has been reported from Islamic or Western countries. The information given by the subject was found to be correct after investigation. However, to my mind, this does not conclusively confirm the truth of the belief in reincarnation.

The puzzling facts relating to genuine ESP phenomena, such as clairvoyance, prophetic dreams, accurate memories of persons, places and incidents in previous births, though hypotheses or possibilities other than rebirth. Freud, Jung, Broad et al have actually shown the way. However, they do not claim to have solved the mystery. Therefore, to my mind, reincarnation too may not make this claim. Here are some additional difficulties in the belief in reincarnation:

1. If the prima facie unmerited sufferings of an individual be regarded as the just consequences of his misdeeds in some previous birth, why should we help a person to escape the natural course of justice? Would it be right to reduce or mitigate the *karmic* punishment of the erring individual?

2. It is a plain fact that contemporary Western affluent societies treat domestic servants far better and more kindly than in Asia. Can it, therefore, be said that all domestic servants in western homes are being rewarded for their good deeds in previous births, while those born in Asia or Africa are being punished for their demerits? This conclusion would land us in a sea of objections.

3. The concept of *karma* seems to imply that malnutrition, dirt and squalor, and a total lack of medical and educational facilities are a punishment to the indigent child for his misdeeds in his previous life or lives, while decent and comfortable surroundings together with ample opportunities for physical, moral, and mental growth are a reward for his good deeds in a previous life. It is quite plain that conditions slowly improved in Western society, as and when, the industrial and agrarian revolutions together with Christian values generated 'space' for humanitarianism in the west from the 18th century onwards.

4. What about the suffering of those persons who become totally insane and lose all their memory or sense of identity? How can they be helped or chastised by suffering when they have lost all their power of judgment?

5. What about the sufferings of animals, which, according to common sense, are neither moral nor immoral but rather amoral? If it be said that a horse or dog who suffers was a guilty human being in his previous birth then how can the suffering of an amoral being be regarded as a punishment to a moral being? How can the sufferings of a dog have an educative function for such a different type of being as man?

Rigorous linguistic analysis of supposed solutions to the enigmas of human life shows that our discourse is riddled with many confusions, latent inner contradictions, misleading analogies, deceptive play of words or sentences that are grammatically quite correct but are shot through with 'cognitive opaqueness'. In the final analysis, we see complex reality through pinholes of varying sizes and we judge momentous issues when we have incomplete or even wrong information. Our vision is, therefore, condemned to be limited and only partly veridical.

Moreover, no perspective on the cosmos can claim to be verifiable in the scientific or logical sense. Any perspective on the cosmos is one among several possible perspectives. It is like one language out of several actual or possible language systems, each of which serves some human need, or the other. No language is true or false, right or wrong, but a particular one may be more developed and useful for a particular purpose, or set of purposes.

A Modern Linguistic-Functional Analysis of the Theory of Reincarnation

The crucial question is as follows: Does belief in reincarnation require one course of action while non-acceptance a different course?

In other words, would a person be required to act in one way if he accepted reincarnation and in a different way if he did not? Let us take a few examples to illustrate this point.

The reincarnation view holds that congenital disease in a child is '*karmic punishment*' for evils actions in a previous incarnation or incarnations. According to the natural scientific view, some defective genes or some pre-natal freak chance caused the defect. However, the crucial issue is not which, view is right or wrong. What is important is to choose between helping the patient with compassion, or holding that there should be no interference in the natural course of justice? If the acceptance or rejection of reincarnation makes no difference to our strategy of proper action, what is the point of the dispute concerning reincarnation?

Likewise, it is not terribly important to decide whether a woman who behaves abnormally, at times, is possessed by an evil spirit or suffers from some brain deformation or functioning, if advocates of different theories prescribe the same therapy. However, if one theory prescribes torturing of the evil spirit through actual torture of the patient, while the other theory prescribes psychoanalysis or counseling a dispute could be understandable. Otherwise the dispute is sterile.

Consider the plight of an untouchable leper in a Calcutta slum. A proponent of the reincarnation view may regard his sufferings as *karmic* punishment for his behavior in a previous incarnation, such as flogging laborers, and raping helpless women. The social scientist, on the other hand, attributes the sufferings of the leper to an uncaring society, inequitable laws, irresponsible population growth, and so on, without importing the idea of reincarnation into his causal analysis of the phenomenon. However, if they both agree to fight poverty or untouchability, the acceptance/rejection of reincarnation will not matter.

The same remarks apply to earthquakes and other natural calamities. Whether an earthquake is a natural phenomenon governed by ascertainable laws, or an earthquake is a Divine visitation could be left unresolved, so long as the disputants readily provide relief and take suitable preventive measures to minimize loss of life and property.

Reflection reveals many spots of 'conceptual opaqueness' when one tries to explain the inexplicable enigmas of human life and the universe. We see complex reality through pinholes of slightly varying sizes. Our vision is condemned to be limited and only partly veridical. Moreover, no perspective on the cosmos can claim to be verifiable in the scientific or logical sense. Like belief in God, life after death, Divine incarnation, revelation, etc. the reincarnation view cannot be proved in the logical or scientific sense. Both the Indian and the semitic perspectives are human responses to the mystery and enigma of the human situation.

The complexities of the human situation and the mystery of the universe never become completely transparent to the autonomous truth seeker. Beliefs, which cannot be scientifically verified or logically proved, depend for their effectiveness, not upon their objective validity, but rather on how 'authentic' the believer really is. This is why numerous Hindus verbally professing *karma* and reincarnation are not at all restrained from doing evil, just as numerous Christians and Muslims verbally professing the Day of Judgment are not restrained either. On the other hand, the sincere and authentic faith in either view does restrain the believer from doing evil and does make him a better human being.

I, therefore, conclude that a well-informed existential response to the mystery of the universe is more desirable than sticking to any theological or philosophical position. If a person is well aware of the facts of life and has no illusions about the human situation, then let him find rest and peace in whatever his or her inner being prompts one to believe. This is the flavor of Shankar's irenic message. He was, by intellectual conviction, a pure monist or absolute idealist, in Western parlance, rather than a monotheist or believer in a personal God. Yet, he did not frown upon popular theism and devoted his entire life to building concord between the way of Knowledge and the way of Devotion. This is also the message of Quranic Islam and Sufism.

Modern spiritual pluralism is also fully comfortable with all hues of monotheism, monism and even atheism, provided the individual responds to the inscrutable mystery of the cosmos with existential awe, humility and a sense of wonder and submission to the mystery of the universe and finds himself or herself driven to the unconditional pursuit of truth, goodness and beauty so long as the gift of consciousness remains with him or her.

# AFTERWORD

Whoever said, 'Let a hundred flowers bloom in the garden' expressed one of the most profound and precious insight humans have slowly won in the course of history. But, perhaps, it is the most difficult to put into practice. I dare say: among all believers today Muslims and right wing Christians find it more difficult than others to accept this message that is clearly found in the Gita, the Quran, as well as in the mystical versions of every religious tradition.

I speak as a Muslim myself when I say that despite the Quran, Sufi traditions, as well as the tradition of numerous Christian saints, both Muslims and Christians in history have been extremely reluctant to practice full religious tolerance. The Christian record, as is well known, began to improve strikingly since the onset of the European enlightenment in the early 18th century. At the very same time, unfortunately, Muslims began to decline in almost every sphere of human activity. This decline reached its nadir with the total extinction of the Ottoman Empire after World War 1.

Lingering memories and group pride in the glorious days of Islamic hegemony over vast areas of Asia and Africa in the pre-modern era have stood in the way of an honest and well informed analysis of the causes of the said decline. The easiest human response (as is well known) is to blame the other for one's own suffering or misfortune. Being human, Muslims fell into this trap long ago and to date remain blissfully unaware of the truth.

Great Muslim reformers, poets, thinkers and statesmen from time to time have come and gone and attempted to awaken fellow Muslims from their dogmatic slumber. However the Muslim caravan has not paid much heed to the lamentations, exhortations and dreams of the wise ones. Even today wild and unverified conspiracy theories continue to grip large sections of even highly educated Muslims in their private discussions on contemporary international relations and world events such as the destruction of the twin towers in America in 2001, and the killing of Bin Laden in Pakistan in 2011.

I find it tragic that a very large number of Muslim believers hardly ever give themselves the self-permission to ask honest and very natural questions about issues connected with their own early sacred history. For example, why and how numerous civil wars and a string of assassinations took place soon after the Prophet passed away: the killing of the third Khalifa; the battle of the Camel fought between the Prophet's beloved wife and the Prophet's beloved cousin and comrade; the Battle of Siffin between close relations and comrades (all Muslim), culminating in the super tragedy of Karbala itself.

Similar instances, as is well known, continually occurred down the centuries in Islamic history. Indeed the present scenario is no different. Yet few Muslim believers have tried to analyze and learn from them. What they have done is to remain content merely with taking sides and defending their own sect or group while maligning the other. This has produced the infamous chasm between the lovers of the house of the Prophet on the one hand, and the supporters of the different Arab tribes and clans of the time, and later, between Mongols, Pathans and others.

In a somewhat similar fashion Muslim believers have hardly tried to ponder over the various issues and aspects of gender justice and have remained supremely satisfied that the Islamic value system leads to perfect social and gender justice, and all that remains to be done in the field of women's welfare and self-realization is the literal implementation of the sharia laws. I respectfully ask my Muslim brothers to rethink these issues in the light of modern sociology and psychology, and the actual experience of the human family, rather than confine themselves to the judgments of stagnant theologians alone. What the Muslims and the world in general need, is the full acceptance of cultural pluralism, empathy for 'they groups', the practice of gender justice and the according of full dignity to all religious traditions, including so called atheists. This approach of full tolerance was actually practiced in ancient Indian and China.

God alone knows the full truth, and we humans should ever beware of possessing exclusive truth and falling into the pit of spiritual conceit and the delusion of self-sufficiency.

We started this work with invoking the name of Allah and we now conclude it with two Quranic verses that stress the virtue of tolerance and two Quranic prayers.

Surah 5, Verse 48

To thee We sent the Scripture in truth, confirming the scripture that came before it, and guarding it in safety: so judge between them by what Allah hath revealed, and follow not their vain desires, diverging from the Truth that hath come to thee. To each among you have we prescribed a law and an open way. If Allah had so willed, He would have made you a single people, but (His plan is) to test you in what He hath given you: so strive as in a race in all virtues. The goal of you all is to Allah. It is He that will show you the truth of the matters in which ye dispute;

Surah 2, Verse 177

It is not righteousness that ye turn your faces Towards east or West; but it is righteousness- to believe in Allah and the Last Day, and the Angels, and the Book, and the Messengers; to spend of your substance, out of love for Him, for your kin, for orphans, for the needy, for the wayfarer, for those who ask, and for the ransom of slaves; to be steadfast in prayer, and practice regular charity; to fulfill the contracts which ye have made; and to be firm and patient, in pain (or suffering) and adversity, and throughout all periods of panic. Such are the people of truth, the Allah fearing.

Surah 113

Say: I seek refuge with the Lord of the Dawn
From the mischief of created things;
From the mischief of Darkness as it overspreads;
From the mischief of those who practice secret arts;
And from the mischief of the envious one as he practices envy.

Surah 114

Say: I seek refuge with the Lord and Cherisher of Mankind,
The King (or Ruler) of Mankind,
The Allah (or judge) of Mankind,
From the mischief of the Whisperer (of Evil), who withdraws (after his whisper),
(The same) who whispers into the hearts of Mankind,
Among Jinns and among men.

Ameen

Appendix 1

APPENDIX 1:
ABOUT THE AUTHOR

Jamal Khwaja was born in Delhi in 1928*. His ancestors had been closely connected with the Islamic reform movement, inaugurated by Sir Syed Ahmad Khan, the founder of the famous *M.A.O. College*, Aligarh in the second half of the 19th century, and the Indian freedom movement under Gandhi's leadership in the first half of the 20th century. After doing his M.A. in Philosophy from the *Aligarh Muslim University*, India, he obtained an Honor's degree from *Christ's College Cambridge*, UK. Later he spent a year studying the German language and European existentialism at *Munster University*, Germany.

At Cambridge he was deeply influenced by the work of C.D. Broad, Wittgenstein and John Wisdom, apart from his college tutor, I.T. Ramsey who later became *Professor of Christian Religion* at Oxford. It was the latter's influence which taught Khwaja to appreciate the inner beauty and power of pure spirituality. Khwaja was thus led to appreciate the value of linguistic analysis as a tool of philosophical inquiry and to combine the quest for clarity with the insights and depth of the existentialist approach to religion and spirituality.

Khwaja was appointed Lecturer in Philosophy at the *Aligarh Muslim University* in 1953. Before he could begin serious academic work in his chosen field, his family tradition of public work pulled him into a brief spell of active politics under the charismatic Jawahar Lal Nehru; the first Prime Minister of India. Nehru was keen to rejuvenate his team of colleagues through inducting fresh blood into the *Indian National*

---

* Jamal Khwaja was born in Delhi on August 12, 1926. However, most official records show 1928 as the year of birth.

Congress. He included young Khwaja, then freshly returned from Cambridge, along with four or five other young persons. Khwaja thus became one of the youngest entrants into the Indian Parliament as a member of the *Lok Sabha* (Lower House) from 1957 to 1962.

While in the corridors of power he learned to distinguish between ideals and illusions, and finally chose to pursue the path of knowledge rather than the path of acquiring authority or power. Returning to his *alma mater* in 1962, he resumed teaching and research in the philosophy of religion. Ever since then Khwaja has lived a quiet life at Aligarh.

He was Dean of the *Faculty of Arts* and was a member of important committees of the *University Grants Commission* and the *Indian Council for Philosophical Research* before retiring as Professor and Chairman of the *Department of Philosophy* in 1988. He was a frequent and active participant in national seminars held at the *Indian Institute of Advanced Study*, Simla.

His works include, *Five Approaches to Philosophy, Quest for Islam, Authenticity and Islamic Liberalism, Essays on Cultural Pluralism,* and numerous articles and scholarly essays. He was invited to deliver the *Khuda Bakhsh Memorial Lecture* at Patna. He was one of the official Indian delegates at the *World Philosophical Congress Brighton*, UK, in 1988, and also at the *International Islamic Conference Kuala Lumpur*, Malaysia, in 1967, and the *Pakistan International Philosophy Congress*, Peshawar, Pakistan, in 1964.

He has visited the USA and several countries in Western Europe. He performed *Hajj* in 2005.

Major Published Works:

Jamal Khwaja has written seven major books. Anyone interested

Appendix 1

in the intersection of Islam and Modernity will find Khwaja to be a reliable guide. His work is magisterial in scope. It is full of passion but remains balanced in perspective. Readers of his work will be in turn informed, inspired, and intellectually liberated.

As complex issues get illumined and perplexities wither away, Muslim readers in particular, will feel emotionally aligned with the Quran and find themselves empowered to live as authentic Muslims in the heart of the multi-cultural global village.

> 1. *Five Approaches To Philosophy: A discerning philosopher philosophizes about the philosophy of philosophy with wisdom and clarity.* (2nd Edition). 158 Pages. ISBN: 978-1-935293-51-4
>
> 2. *Quest For Islam: A philosophers approach to religion in the age of science and cultural pluralism.* (Significantly Enlarged 2nd Edition). 364 Pages. ISBN: 978-1-935293-69-9
>
> 3. *Authenticity And Islamic Liberalism: A mature vision of Islamic Liberalism grounded in the Quran.* (Significantly Enlarged 2nd Edition). 244 Pages. ISBN: 978-1-935293-68-2
>
> 4. *Essays On Cultural Pluralism: A philosophical framework for authentic interfaith dialogue.* 268 Pages. ISBN: 978-1-935293-52-1
>
> 5. *The Call Of Modernity And Islam: A Muslim's journey into the 21st century.* 232 Pages. ISBN: 978-1-935293-94-1
>
> 6. *Living The Quran In Our Times: A vision of how Muslims can revitalize their faith, while being faithful to God and His messenger.* 266 Pages. ISBN: 978-81-321-1046-0
>
> 7. *The Vision Of An Unknown Indian Muslim: My journey to interfaith spirituality.* 326 Pages. ISBN: 978-1-935293-96-5

Khwaja's work is the definitive contemporary discussion regarding the collision of Islam and Modernity. Explore it. You will be profoundly rewarded.

For more information, visit *www.JamalKhwaja.com*

INDEX

A

Adi Granth, *164, 172*
adventures of faith, *130*
agnostic, *59, 100, 130, 154, 194-196, 233*
Akbar, emperor, *140, 145, 164-165, 179-180, 202, 215-216, 219*
Al-Hujwari, *160*
Al-Ghazzali, *80, 211, 217*
Aligarh, *142, 155-156, 182, 237-238*
Amar Das, Sikh Guru, *163*
Amoral, *58, 86, 115, 137*
Amritsar, *164, 174, 177, 185, 220*
analogical,
- affirmation, *40*
- discourse, *35, 40*
Anandpur, *169-171*
Angad, Sikh Guru, *163*
anger, *28, 35, 44, 49, 58, 79, 90, 141*
animal suffering, *38, 130*
Anthropology, *37, 82, 84*
anthropomorphic, *141, 235*
Anthrotheism, *29*
antinomical structure, *139, 142*
antinomies of history, *130*
arbitrary, *97, 131, 147, 230*
Arjan Dev, Sikh Guru, *163-164*
Arjun, *21, 24-32, 39, 47-62, 207*
Armstrong, Karen, *109*
Ashoka, emperor, *180, 200, 208*
ashramadharma, *54-55*
Aspiration, *41, 77, 79-80, 116, 140, 197, 228*
astral,
- determinism, *230*
- configurations, *223-225*
- influence, *230-231*
Astrology, *223-231*
atheism, *100, 115, 196*
atheist, *84-86, 102, 130-131, 193-195, 206, 235*
atman, *21, 26-27, 31-32, 36, 39-41, 45-46, 59, 117, 200, 234*
atomic duty, *55*
Aurangzeb, emperor, *146-147, 166-172, 182, 187, 216*
authentic, *14, 23, 42, 50, 56, 59, 81, 86, 96-99, 103, 109, 111-117, 146, 197, 211*
authentic,
- faith, *14, 116*
- being, *42, 56, 117, 211*
autonomy, *46, 86, 121, 162, 192, 211*
avatara, *29, 32, 39*
awareness, *13, 36-39, 79, 88, 108, 114, 122-123, 131, 134, 141, 147, 192-193, 227*

Index

axiom, *28, 77, 225-226*
Azad, Abul Kalam, *87, 89, 140, 150, 216*

B

Babar, emperor, *147, 186-187, 210, 213*
Babylonia, *142*
Bahadur Shah I, *172*
Banda Bahadur, *172-174*
Beauty, *24, 33, 40-41, 54, 59, 61, 68, 70, 72-75, 77, 81, 99, 116, 131, 191, 194, 237*
Belief, *13-14, 19, 22, 28-29, 37-40, 49, 57, 72-76, 82-84, 91, 95, 98, 100-104, 106, 111-112, 121, 132, 162, 167, 190-191, 194, 196, 199, 211, 226, 235-238, 241-244*
Benares, *142, 181*
Benevolence, *33, 183*
Bhagwan, *22, 31, 96*
Bhakti, *22, 29, 42, 51, 96, 101, 154, 160-161, 204, 220*
Bhim Singh, Raja, *173*
bliss, 32, 39, 70, 233
brahmacharya, 54
Brahman, *21, 24, 26, 28, 31-37, 39-42, 46-47, 54, 59, 96, 100-101, 117, 154, 167, 170, 180, 195, 200, 208-210, 228*
brahmavidya, *22, 29, 42, 49*
British domination, *147*
Buddha, Gautama, *59, 88, 108, 162, 198, 210*
Buddhism, *59, 99, 154, 162-163, 198-200*

C

caste, *13, 47, 55, 100, 149, 151, 155-156, 160, 162, 164, 173, 184, 186, 192, 195, 197-201, 204-205, 209, 233*
cause and effect, *71, 128*
cave of darkness, *139*
chance, *33, 176, 183*
China, *62, 209, 235*
Chishti, Khwaja Moinuddin, *108, 160*
chosen people, *139, 141*
Christianity, *19, 99, 149, 152, 154, 206*
cognitive,
- status, *112*
- therapy, *230*
- vacuity, *35, 40*
compassion, *14, 22, 37, 44, 46, 49, 79, 87, 130, 145, 153*
conceptual,
- innocence, *111*
- permissiveness, *23, 56, 100, 102*
- space, *23, 34, 207*
corruption of the priest, *138*
cosmic,
- Father, *22*
- justice, *37*
- process, *22, 26, 32-33, 37, 39-41, 71, 75, 130, 132*

Index

cosmos, *33-36, 41, 68, 74, 76-78, 98, 100-101, 128*
Covenant of Medina, *110*
criteria of,
- evaluation, *112, 121, 123, 136*
- good history, *121-122*
cultural,
- conditioning, *38-39, 134, 226*
- differentiation, *105*
- imponderables, *120-121*
- inclusiveness, *56*
- stagnation, *126*
cycle of birth and death, *21, 26-27, 31, 58*
cyclical process, *95, 136*

D

dark night of the soul, *113*
Day of Judgment, *125, 162*
death, *33, 37, 45, 58, 67, 71-74, 80, 83, 109, 116, 125-126, 134, 141, 148, 156, 159, 163-167, 173-178, 182, 184, 201, 204, 209-211*
depth responses, *42*
detachment, *44*
determinism, *127, 230*
Dharma, *21, 162-163, 186, 198, 235*
Dharmashastras, *186*
dialectical negation, *40*
dialectics of history, *127*
directive function, *72-73*
Divine,
- decree, *230*

- spark, *71-72*
- wisdom, *131*
Dualism, *22*

E

egoism, *37, 44, 54*
empathy, *122, 192-193, 235*
empirical evidence, *208, 226-227*
epistemological issues, *39*
equality of opportunity, *127, 132, 201*
eschatological future, *125, 131*
ethical,
- action, *42*
- motivator, *73*
- teachings, *21, 204*
- Theism, *22, 32, 154*
ethically fruitful, *36*
evolutionary process, *33*
existential,
- conviction, *112-113*
- interpretation, *68-74, 100, 123, 139, 147*
- perplexity, *34, 192-193*
- response, *41, 76*
- wonder, *97*
Existentialism, *237*

F

fallacy,
- of reductionism, *126*
- of reification, *133*
family planning, *132*

Index

fear, *28, 30, 43-44, 52, 54, 69, 77, 79, 82, 91, 101, 107, 112, 115, 133, 137, 151-152, 186, 194, 204, 211, 214, 217-218, 235*

finite existence, *22, 31, 101*

folklore, *99, 190, 197, 205*

freedom, *43-44, 50, 56, 98, 100, 107, 127, 131-132, 138-142, 151, 167, 184, 190, 192-193, 237*

Fromm, Erich, *146*

fundamentalism, *85-87, 103, 151-152*

G

Gandhi, Mahatma, *63, 89, 120, 140, 150-151, 156*

gender equality, *132*

Ghalib, Mirza, poet, *87, 181-182*

Ghulam Qadir, *178, 184*

Gita, *19-63, 88, 100, 108, 195, 198, 207-209, 233, 247*

Gobind Singh, Guru, *163, 169, 220*

God, *21-22, 28-39, 45, 51, 56-63, 69-84, 89-97, 100-109, 115-116, 125, 128-133, 139, 141-143, 161, 183-185, 194-196, 203-208, 211-213, 217-221, 233, 235, 240, 244, 249*

Golden temple, *164, 185, 220*

grahasta, *54*

greed, *28, 47, 49*

guilt, *37-38, 56, 168, 201, 207, 212*

gunas, *22, 25, 46-47, 199*

gyanayoga, *51*

H

Har Rai, Sikh Guru, *166*

Hargobind, Sikh Guru, *165*

Hari Krishen, Sikh Guru, *166*

Harimandir, *164-165, 174-178*

heaven, *22, 27, 30, 51, 76, 91, 95, 102, 108, 130, 216, 227*

Hindu/Hinduism, *20-22, 28, 54, 56, 59, 63, 87-89, 95-97, 100-103, 109-110, 140, 146-147, 150-157, 159-164, 167, 169, 172-173, 181-188, 196-220, 233-234, 244*

Historical,
- **explanation,** *120-121*
- **intuition,** *138*
- **objectivity,** *121-122*
- **process,** *123-129, 136*
- **role,** *140*

Historiography, *124-125*

horoscope, *226*

human,
- **billiard balls,** *123*
- **body,** *129*
- **condition/situation,** *13, 23, 26, 50, 68-71, 78, 84-86, 113, 116, 121, 137, 139, 141, 146-147, 151, 162, 197*
- **language,** *34*
- **welfare,** *13, 122*

Index

Humanism, *14, 19, 87, 98-102, 107, 110, 116, 148, 202, 205-206, 215, 219*
Humayun, emperor, *187*
humility, *40, 42, 44, 81, 103, 107, 111, 114, 194*

I

Ibn Arabi, *80, 105*
ichha, *28*
identity, *21, 36-41, 90, 105, 147, 167, 200*
idols, *96, 217*
ignorance, *28, 48, 50, 61, 142, 153, 163, 211*
illuminate, *24-25, 32-34, 43, 46*
immortality of hope, *139*
Incarnation, *21-22, 29, 31-32, 39, 57, 76, 109, 233-244*
India, *20, 28, 32, 69, 86-89, 97-102, 108-109, 119-120, 140, 145-156, 159-169, 171, 173-187, 189-220, 223, 225, 230, 235*
inner,
- Satan, *82, 107*
- world, *67, 85, 134*
integrated personality, *97, 229*
Internalized censor, *73*
inter-caste marriage, *205*
inwardness, *77, 82, 107*
Iqbal, Muhammad, *87, 89, 106, 216*
irenic, *23*
isht devata, *100, 150, 196*
Ishwar, *22, 31-32, 39, 100-101*

Islam, *14-15, 19-20, 70, 76, 79-81, 87-90, 97-100, 103-104, 108-110, 124, 146-156, 160-163, 167, 169, 173, 179, 181, 183-189, 201-204, 207, 209-220, 230, 233-234*
I-Thou dialogue, *72*

J

Jai Singh, Raja, *168*
Jainism, *59, 154, 162-163, 198, 200, 204, 208*
Jaspers, Karl, *140, 207*
Jats, *172, 176, 183-184, 187*
Jehangir, emperor, *164-165*
Jews, *98, 110, 140, 185, 209*
Jihad, *156-157*
Jindan, Rani, *180-181*
jiva, *26, 28, 37, 200*
jiva Atma, *27*
jivanmukta, *31*
journey of the spirit, *113*
Jurisprudence, *19, 81*
just recompense, *22, 26, 37*

K

Kabir, Sant, *88, 162-164, 204, 219*
Kabul, *176-179, 185*
Kant, Immanuel, *119, 196, 206*
karma, *14, 22, 26-28, 32, 37-38, 40, 52, 58-59, 88, 108, 162, 200, 233-243*
Kashmir, *179, 181, 184, 208, 212, 214*

Index

Kaurava clan, *21*
Khalsa, Sikh army, *170-171, 174, 179*
Khan, Abdus Samad, *174*
Khusro, prince, *164-165*
knowledge, *13-14, 22, 25, 29, 34, 41-42, 44-52, 56, 69-70, 73, 78, 80, 82-84, 87-88, 104-108, 116, 123, 132, 134, 142, 163, 195, 201, 219, 225, 230, 238*
Krishna, Bhagwan, *21-23, 29, 31-32, 39-40, 56-61, 97*

L

Lahore, *147, 159-165, 174-181, 184, 220*
Lake Shrine Center, *110*
leela, *21*
Lenin, *124*
Liberalism, *85-87, 100, 147, 155, 164-165, 202*
Liebenskind, Claudia, *109*
life-worlds, *111*
Linguistic Analysis, *40, 135, 237*
logical,
- implication, *226*
- Positivism, *35*
- possibility, *124*
lust, *28, 49, 53-54, 58, 137, 146*

M

macro-suffering, *237*
magic, *68, 104, 116*

Mahabharata, *20*
Mahavira, Jain saint, *59, 198*
Mansur, Hallaj, Sufi, *80, 210*
Mantra, *228*
marriage, *195, 199, 202, 204-205, 224, 226, 229*
Marx, Karl, *119, 126, 129*
Marxism, *196*
master races, *141*
Mauryan empire, *140*
metaphysical, *26, 37, 105-106, 111, 125, 131, 134-135, 224, 233, 239*
metaphysical,
- perspectives, *23, 32-34, 37-38*
- reality, *115*
- vision, *23, 32*
Metaphysics,
Mian Mir, Sufi saint, *164-165, 220*
micro-ray of Divine light, *103*
micro-suffering, *237*
milieu, *68, 76, 98, 109, 111, 113*
Mir Mannu, *175-176, 184*
moksh, *95, 234*
Monotheism, *22, 69, 101, 161, 163, 215, 230, 245*
morality, *41, 46, 56, 68, 71, 82, 86-87, 98-101, 107, 113, 115, 197, 231, 238*
Mughal empire, *140, 218*
Muhammad, Prophet, *79-80, 110, 156, 208-209, 213*
mukti, *27, 31, 43*

Index

music, *33, 59, 75, 137, 203, 215-216*
Mussolini, *140*
mystic, *75-78, 80-81, 98-99, 106, 114, 141, 202, 219*
mystical, *29, 31, 38-40, 75-78, 81, 98, 101, 104-106, 109, 113-114, 141, 247*
myth, *99, 112, 116, 161, 164*

N

Nadir Shah, *145, 174-175, 183, 187*
Nakshbandiya, sufi order, *202*
Nalanda, *142*
Namdev, *164*
Nanak, Guru, *160-164, 171, 204*
Nihilism, *58, 100, 196*
nirvana, *95, 234*
Nizam of Hyderabad, *187*
non-being, *26*

O

objective certainty, *34, 41, 112, 132*
ontological, *22, 37, 200*
ontological,
- **dignity,** *133*
- **significance,** *32*
Opaqueness, *39-40, 128, 131, 242, 244*
oppressed minorities, *130*
organic unity, *36, 161, 194*
orthogenetic, *112*

outer reflection, *35*

P

pain, *27, 33, 38, 40, 44-45, 48, 52, 73, 75, 77, 92, 130, 137, 148, 190, 193, 233, 236-239, 250*
panacea, *115, 133*
Pandavas (Aryan clan), *21*
paradox, *68, 99, 127, 155*
paranormal, *78-79, 240*
patience, *44, 79, 131, 151, 201, 229*
peace, *19, 31-33, 39-40, 48, 68, 75-76, 87, 97-98, 101, 103, 113, 152, 156, 165, 170-172, 231, 244*
peak experience, *31*
pearls of wisdom, *20, 46*
perennial relevance, *23*
perplexed, *33, 40, 75, 121, 133, 138*
persecution, *59, 138, 154, 170, 172, 198-199, 206, 208-209*
Philosophy, *20-21, 34, 68, 70, 80-84, 102, 117, 119, 124-129, 133-135, 159, 196, 205-206, 209*
piety, *85, 89, 99, 101, 104, 107, 109, 115, 153, 161, 202, 206, 216-217*
plural interpretations, *56, 105, 154*
Pluralism, *19, 22, 100, 116, 132, 141, 245, 249*

Index

Positivism, *35, 100*
prakriti, 22, 25, 37, 47
predestination, *230*
psychic depth, *133*
Psychoanalysis, *243*
punarjanam, 233
purush, 22, 32

Q

quality of human life, *114, 230*
quest for certainty, *41*
Quran, *19-20, 88, 97-98, 100, 104, 108, 110, 201-203, 20-212, 244, 247, 249*

R

Radhakrishnan, S, *20-21, 43, 200, 208-209*
Rajagopalachari, *89, 155*
Ram Das, Sikh Guru, *163*
Ram Mohan Rai, *163, 181*
Ram Rai, disputed Guru, *166*
Ramanuja, *204*
Ramkrishna Mission, *109*
Ranjit Singh, Maharaja, *147, 159-160, 178-180, 184-185*
Ravi Das, *164*
rebirth, *22, 28, 38, 51, 76, 78, 95, 113, 162, 219, 233-236, 241*
reincarnation, *233-244*
religious faith, *42, 74, 95, 105, 11-112, 183, 193, 203, 236*
religious pluralism, *19*
resting point of faith, *103*
Roman empire, *140*

Rumi, Jalaluddin, *80-81, 87, 90, 92, 96, 102*

S

saatvic, 42, 46-47, 88, 108
Sanga, Rana, *187*
Sankhya, 21-22, 52
sansar, 26-28, 234-235
Sarhindi, Shaikh Ahmad, *212-213, 217-218*
Sarmad, Sufi, *140, 169, 210*
sat (ultimate Reality), *22, 25, 31*
Schimmel, Annemarie, *109*
science, *34, 41, 67-68, 70-71, 73, 81-84, 88, 98-99, 106-108, 114, 116, 120, 129, 134-135, 148, 150, 216-217, 223-226, 231*
scientific, *32, 40-41, 72-74, 82-84, 100, 102, 105-106, 109, 112-113, 116, 120-121, 130, 132, 134-135, 145, 147, 155, 182, 224-226, 230-231, 240, 242-244*
Scientism, *41, 116*
sexual, *28, 68, 71-72*
Shah Ismail, *179*
Shankaracharya, *101*
Shantiniketan, *142*
Sher Shah, Pathan king, *187*
Shibli, Allama, *80, 87, 155*
Shivaji, Maratha ruler, *140, 146, 157, 187, 203, 218-219*
Sikhism, *108, 167, 169, 173, 220, 233*

Index

Singh,
- Dalip, Sikh prince, *181*
- Gulab, Dogra ruler, *180*
- Kharak, Sikh prince, *180*
- Khushwant, *160, 168*
- Lehna, *178*

Somnath temple, *146*
Sorokin, *126*
Spengler, Oswald, *126, 129*
Spirit-centered Humanism, *100, 102, 110*
spiritual, *19-20, 22-23, 28-31, 34, 37, 39-47, 50, 53, 56, 59, 68-75, 78-82, 85, 88, 90, 96, 98-99, 103-110, 113-115, 121, 150, 153, 155, 161-167, 186, 192-194, 198, 200, 204, 211, 218, 234-235, 238-240, 245, 249*
stages of life, *55-56*
stream of consciousness, *117*
striving, *42, 49, 51, 104, 127, 236*
struggle, *29, 33, 67, 77, 115-116, 130, 138, 147, 159, 179, 182, 184, 186-187, 197, 203, 236, 238*
suffering, *22, 27-28, 37-38, 40, 53-54, 73, 75, 77, 80, 92, 98, 116, 130, 140, 148, 185, 190, 233-243, 247, 250*
Suhrawardi, Al-Maqtul, Sufi, *80*
superstition, *84, 161, 163, 230*
Supreme Being, *37, 88, 96, 101, 108*

swadharma, *29, 47, 56*
Syed Ahmad, of Bareilly, *179*
Syed, Sir Syed Ahmad Khan, *87, 89, 150, 155-156, 182, 216, 251*

T

Tagore, Rabindranath, *89, 155, 219*
tamas (dullness), *22, 25, 46-47*
technology, *34, 41, 70, 81, 84, 88, 107-108, 132, 134, 153, 231, 238*
Tegh Bahadur, Guru, *167-169*
telepathy, *239*
telos, *128-129, 133*
temptation, *116, 127*
Theism, *22, 32, 59, 116, 154, 204, 244*
Theology, *19, 56, 78-82, 84, 86-87, 98, 104, 115, 217*
Theopathy, *77, 79-80, 104-105*
Theosophy, *77-80, 104-106*
Theurgy, *77, 79-80, 104, 106*
Tipu Sultan, *187, 202*
tolerant, *154, 161, 165, 192-195*
torture, *130, 164, 243*
Toynbee, Arnold, *126, 129*
transcendence, *55*
transcendental, *40, 55, 136*
Trilok Singh, Dr., *168*
trust in God, *81, 107*
truth-claims, *70, 79, 105-106, 114, 192-196, 224, 226-227*
typology of cultures, *126*

U

Ugliness, *24, 33*
ultimate Reality, *23-24, 31, 58*
uncaring society, *243*
uncontrolled desire, *28, 235*
unexamined assumptions, *116, 227*
unintended consequences, *138*
Universal, *19, 32, 44, 71, 79, 81, 87, 100, 125-126, 134, 140-141, 145, 147, 162, 197-198, 202, 204, 215, 231*
untouchable leper, *243*
Upanishads, *26, 28, 32, 35, 39, 98*

V

Vaishnavite, *21-23, 32, 59*
value judgment, *122-123, 132, 135*
***varna*,** *55-56, 199-204*
Vedanta, *19, 21, 24-25, 28-31, 35-36, 100-101, 109-110, 153, 198, 200, 203*
Vedas, *25, 27, 51, 59, 97, 196-198, 233*
Vishnu, *21, 31-32, 39, 62*
vision of reality, *113*
voluntary poverty, *81, 107*
Vyasa, Rishi, *20-21*

W

Waliullah, Shah, *179*
Waris Ali Shah, Sufi, *108-109*
way of, *33, 58, 76, 111, 115, 119, 131, 133-139, 210, 244, 247*
Wazir, Khan, *172*
Whitehead, A.N., *70, 73, 240*
whole and the part, *117*
wiles of the ego, *82, 107*
wisdom, *20, 44, 46, 50-51, 54, 56, 60, 88, 108, 119, 131, 133-139, 159, 163, 165, 204-207, 210, 220, 225, 227, 230*
work ethic, *82, 107*

Y

Yoga, *22, 27, 40, 49-54, 56-57, 62, 153, 203, 229*
Yogananda, *63, 110*

To learn more about the author - Jamal Khwaja, and his various works visit:

www.JamalKhwaja.com

Download free Digital Books, Lectures, Essays, browse links to related sites and much more...

Publishers website can be found at:
www.AlhamdPublishers.com

www.ingramcontent.com/pod-product-compliance
Lightning Source LLC
Chambersburg PA
CBHW021142080526
44588CB00008B/174